PROFILES
IN
AUDACITY

PROFILES
IN
AUDACITY

GREAT DECISIONS AND
HOW THEY WERE MADE

Alan Axelrod

Sterling Publishing Co., Inc.
New York

Published by Sterling Publishing Co., Inc.
387 Park Avenue South, New York, NY 10016

© 2006 by Alan Axelrod

Distributed in Canada by Sterling Publishing
c /o Canadian Manda Group, 165 Dufferin Street
Toronto, Ontario, Canada M6K 3H6

Distributed in the United Kingdom by GMC Distribution Services
Castle Place, 166 High Street, Lewes, East Sussex, England BN7 1XU

Distributed in Australia by Capricorn Link (Australia) Pty. Ltd.
P.O. Box 704, Windsor, NSW 2756, Australia

ISBN-13: 978-1-4027-3282-9
ISBN-10: 1-4027-3282-1

2 4 6 8 10 9 7 5 3 1

For information about custom editions, special sales, premium and
corporate purchases, please contact Sterling Special Sales
Department at 800-805-5489 or specialsales@sterlingpub.com.

For Anita

Who decided to say yes

My thanks to Michael Fragnito and Barbara Berger,
for having the audacity to publish this book.

Contents

PART THREE:

The Decision of Conscience

PART FOUR:

The Decision to Risk Everything

PART FIVE:

The Decision to Hope

Introduction

THE RUBICON FACTOR

The Rubicon River, near modern Ravenna in northern Italy, is as unimpressive today as it was when Julius Caesar stood on its northern bank in 49 B.C. Small and shallow, it dries up at even the hint of drought. Certainly, it presented no obstacle to the advance of an army. It was just a matter of crossing a little bridge. But as Plutarch, one of Caesar's two early biographers, tells us, the great general "became full of thought" as he approached the river. His "mind wavered," and he "began to go more slowly and then ordered a halt." Julius Caesar stood on the bank of the little river and "for a long time . . . weighed matters up silently in his own mind, irresolute between . . . two alternatives."

The Rubicon divided northern Italy—Cisalpine Gaul, the large province Caesar controlled—from Rome, which was governed by the Senate and dominated by Cnaeus Pompeius Magnus, better known as Pompey. Once Caesar's ally, Pompey was now his archrival, and he had the law on his side. The Lex Cornelia Majestatis solemnly forbade any Roman general from leading an army out of the province to which he was assigned. This meant, quite simply, that if Caesar and the six thousand men with him crossed the Rubicon, they would bring down upon themselves all the vast legions commanded by Pompey and the Senate of Rome.

To cross the Rubicon would mean civil war, maybe impossible to win and certainly tragic for the nation. But if this was a powerful reason not to cross, there was also a compelling reason not to remain on the northern bank. Inaction would perpetuate a peace that had been dictated by a fatally misgoverned Rome. To remain on the far side of the river, in apparent safety, would sooner or later bring calamity. A state misruled cannot long endure.

BORN ABOUT 100 B.C. into a patrician family on the financial skids, Julius
Caesar grew up determined to revive his family's fortunes and to bring
distinction, honor, and wealth upon himself. But he also saw that Rome
was in deep and deepening trouble. Those who governed it were corrupt
and incompetent, in bed with a rapacious class of business tycoons
called the *equites*, or knights, who had grown enormously powerful on
the profits of military and other government contracts. The vast majority
of Roman citizens and subjects, the peasantry who supplied the man-
power of the mighty Roman legions and the labor for everything else,
were oppressed and dispossessed by an economic system that barely
allowed them a living. Rome and its empire were in perpetual turmoil,
convulsed by revolutionary uprisings that alternated with iron-fisted campaigns to quell them. How many more such convulsions could Rome,
barbarians pressing at every frontier, endure?

Through guile, boundless courage, military genius, and an advantageous marriage, Caesar became one of three triumvirs (along with
Pompey and Marcus Licinius Crassus) ruling Rome and its provinces.
His assigned stronghold was Cisalpine Gaul, bounded by the Alps, the
Apennines, and the Adriatic. Here Caesar recruited troops for conquests
beyond the northwest frontier of the republic. By the year 50 B.C., he had
conquered all of Gaul—France up to the left bank of the Rhine—and,
three years later, Crassus was knocked out of the triumvirate when, suffering total defeat at the hands of the Parthians, he lost Syria. This left
Caesar and Pompey to square off against one another.

They did not have to wait long for a showdown. Caesar was due to
resign his provincial governorships and take up a term as consul. Pompey
pointed to a law that obliged Caesar to relinquish his army during the
interval between the expiration of his term as governor and the com-
mencement of his consulship. During this gap, an unarmed Caesar
would be entirely vulnerable to Pompey and other enemies. He therefore
lobbied the Senate either to eliminate the interval between offices or
allow him to retain his army during it. As the date of expiration drew near,
Caesar became impatient and stopped cajoling. He now peremptorily

demanded of the Senate that Pompey be obliged to lay down his arms simultaneously with him. Offended by the consul's insolence, the Senators responded that Caesar was to be treated as a public enemy if he refused to submit on whatever date *they* fixed.

And that was what brought Julius Caesar to the north bank of the Rubicon. To cross it would bring the wrath of Rome thundering down upon him and his men. To cross it would engulf the republic in civil war. But to remain on the northern bank would at best gain nothing and would most likely risk an end to his power. Besides, if it did not destroy Rome, crossing the Rubicon was the best hope of saving it.

According to Plutarch, Caesar stood on the riverbank, discussing "his perplexities with his friends who were there." He "thought of the sufferings which his crossing the river would bring upon mankind." Then, however, he "imagined the fame of the story of it."

Another early biographer, Suetonius, recorded that Caesar remarked to his followers: "We may still draw back; but, once across that little bridge, we shall have to fight it out." Caesar "stood, in two minds," Suetonius relates, then suddenly caught sight of a man, "strikingly noble" and of "graceful aspect," who played upon a shepherd's pipe, played with such captivating beauty that soldiers, including the trumpeters, flocked to him from their posts. The man suddenly seized a trumpet from one of the military musicians, and ran to the river with it. Putting it to his lips, he sounded, with a piercing blast, the Legionnaire's call to advance, then boldly crossed to the other side of the river.

Roused from his thoughts, Caesar called out: "Let us accept this as a sign from the Gods, and follow where they beckon, in vengeance on our double-dealing enemies. *Alea iacta est!*"

The die is cast!

With that exclamation, Julius Caesar crossed the Rubicon, starting a great civil war that would bring him unprecedented power in the Roman world even as it advanced the frontiers of Rome both in extent and through time. Mired in corruption, Rome had been almost surely doomed. By choosing a course that ended this moribund misrule, Caesar gave to the Roman state, and therefore to Greco-Roman civilization, four more centuries of life in the West and six more in the East, bequeathing to the world a heritage that is more than history. It continues to influence and inform cultures and governments, including that of our own nation. Crossing the Rubicon was, by any measure, a great decision.

IN THE NINETEENTH CENTURY, the Scots essayist-philosopher-historian Thomas Carlyle wrote that history was nothing more or less than the "biography of Great Men." The "great man theory of history," as it became known, held sway through the Victorian age of empires, but gave way during the increasingly egalitarian twentieth century to an interpretation of history not so much as that which results from the actions of some key individual, but as the sum total of mass movements and great social forces.

Certainly, it is possible to focus on the social pressures that lay behind Caesar's crossing the Rubicon, the economic and political dispossession of an entire class of people, and to identify those pressures as the "real" cause of the great Roman civil war and, ultimately, of the historical, cultural, and spiritual changes the war made possible. Yet a stubborn fact remains: There was a river, and one man, Julius Caesar, *decided* to cross it. If it is valid to see life-changing, epoch-making history as the product of social forces, it is equally valid to see it as the result of great decisions put into action by the will of an individual.

No question that the will of Caesar was a powerful force. But will is also a universal human faculty, common to us all, the mental faculty by which each of us, every day and every minute of every day, makes choices. It is a faculty each of us shares with Caesar and every other great leader in history. Yet there must be something about or within the will of the Caesars of the world that does set them apart from the rest of us.

Call it the Rubicon Factor.

It is a quality of leadership that enables an individual to define and then to make decisions bearing the highest stakes and then, even more important, to act on the decision that has been made. In short, the Rubicon Factor is the quality that propels some to *break through* and to break through consistently.

What is the nature of this quality? Does everyone have it, or only an exceptional few? Are leaders born with it, or can it be acquired, cultivated, learned? By looking closely at the most courageous decisions of history's greatest leaders and public figures—in the spheres of government, the military, culture, science, civil rights, philanthropy, and business—this book explores these questions and offers answers.

Let us anticipate one of those answers now. Possession of the Rubicon Factor may well be genetic, but it seems clear that it can also be learned, cultivated, applied, and practiced. The stories in this book are fascinating as history, but they are even more compelling as practical cases in point, object lessons for instruction, inspiration, and emulation.

What, for example, can we learn from Caesar's crossing of *his* Rubicon? His two earliest biographers, the Greek Plutarch (A.D. 46–after 119) and the Roman Suetonius (A.D. 69–after 122), offer few clues. Plutarch says Caesar agonized over the decision until "finally, in a sort of passion, as though he were casting calculation aside and abandoning himself to whatever lay in store for him," he exclaimed, "The die is cast"—or perhaps the better translation is "Let the die be cast"; that is, *Roll the dice.*

Suetonius introduced another element into the tale: the appearance of the stranger who plays a shepherd's pipe, seizes a soldier's trumpet, and sounds the call to battle. Was such a man actually present that day? Or perhaps he is a character of fiction, nothing more than Suetonius's attempt to provide an explanation for what neither he (nor Plutarch, apparently) could satisfactorily account for: the process by which Caesar came to his great decision.

The real problem is that neither biographer did much of anything with the clues they themselves provided. Both Suetonius and Plutarch agree that Caesar did not act rashly, that, in fact, he gave a great deal of thought to the consequences of crossing the Rubicon and that he devoted time to consulting with his trusted commanders. Clearly, he understood that taking action would bring the calamity of war. But just as apparent is his understanding that taking no action would also have consequences. In this case, inaction would keep the peace, but it would be peace on Pompey's terms. In other words, surrender.

The price of war is always blood, even in victory. Above and beyond that is the cost of possible defeat. Yet whereas war may bring either victory or defeat, surrender offers nothing other than defeat. Roll the dice, and you may win or you may lose. Hold the dice, and you cannot possibly win.

The Rubicon Factor drives the courage to act even as it creates a fear of failing to act, exposing as an illusion the apparent safety of inaction. With an army of only six thousand men immediately available to Caesar (the rest of his troops lay far beyond the Alps), crossing the Rubicon to provoke Pompey and all the legions of Rome could be seen as an act of arrogance or even madness. Yet, under circumstances Plutarch and Suetonius only hint at, Caesar's decision emerges as highly reasonable.

The reasonable decision is not necessarily the safe decision. In a given situation, the most reasonable course of action may involve grave risks and great dangers. The Rubicon Factor encompasses, in part, the capacity to recognize the reasonableness of risk and, in part, also consists of the courage to act in accordance with reason despite the risks.

A GREAT DECISION ALWAYS has two characteristics. First, it is a choice between or among high-stakes alternatives. Second, it is a decision that *must* be made, that cannot be avoided. As Harry S. Truman once observed, "Presidents have to make decisions if they're going to get anywhere, and those presidents who couldn't make decisions are the ones who caused all the trouble." Truman believed that if a president made a wise decision, that was "good for the country," and if he made an unwise one, "that is too bad"—but it was still much better than failing to make any decision at all.

This book is a journey of exploration among history's great decisions and those who made them. The goal of the journey is to discover, at each stop along the way, the Rubicon Factor, the source of insight and resolve that enabled the decision and that drove the necessary action that followed. The payoff of the journey is knowledge, perhaps even the very knowledge you need to make your own next great decision.

PART ONE

The Decision in Crisis

Cleopatra and the Romans (48–30 B.C.)
THE DECISION TO RESCUE EGYPT

The function of myth and legend is to magnify, to make the subject look greater and of more consequence than he, she, or it probably was. In the case of Cleopatra, however, this function was inverted. Myth and legend have worked to diminish rather than magnify her. They portray her as the most fascinating and (for a time, at least) most successful harlot in all history, the seducer of Caesar and Antony. To be sure, this is quite an achievement. Caesar and Antony, after all, were men of the very greatest consequence. Yet it is not nearly enough. For there was much more to Cleopatra, who made and acted on decisions that nearly set her upon the most powerful throne of the ancient world.

She was the second daughter of King Ptolemy XII and not even an Egyptian. Her father was a Macedonian and a member of the dynasty founded by Ptolemy, a marshal of Alexander the Great, which had ruled Egypt since the death of Alexander in 323 B.C. Yet, of all the Macedonian line, only Cleopatra bothered to learn the Egyptian language, adding it to the eight others she spoke. And with a keen understanding of human nature in general and the Egyptian people in particular, she portrayed herself—perhaps actually regarded herself—as the daughter of Ra, the primary Egyptian sun god.

Ptolemy XII died in 51 B.C., whereupon the throne passed jointly to his fifteen-year-old son, Ptolemy XIII, and to Cleopatra. Under Egyptian law and tradition, she had married her brother when he was twelve, and was therefore the sister-bride of the new king. Law and tradition in Ptolemaic Egypt also decreed that the male should be dominant among co-rulers. Cleopatra, however, did all she could to suppress her brother-husband, seeing to it that his name was dropped from official documents and that his likeness did not appear with hers on coins of the time.

Just how Cleopatra asserted her dominance, contrary to law and tradition, is not known. The fact is that she did it, and civil war broke out between her supporters and those of Ptolemy XIII. More accurately, the civil war did not so much break out as it evolved from the chaotic state in which Cleopatra's father had left Egypt. For some two centuries, the kingdom had been in decline, forced to relinquish more and more control of its destiny and its resources (in the form of exorbitant tribute payments) to its putative ally, Rome. By the time of Ptolemy XII's death, Egypt's imperial holdings—Cyprus, Coele-Syria (the Lebanon valley), and Cyrenaica (northeast Libya)—had been yielded entirely to Rome. In many parts of the kingdom, anarchy reigned and famine was rampant.

Cleopatra made daring decisions. She cut her brother out of the royal loop and ordered mercenaries to kill the sons of the Roman governor of Syria when they came as envoys to ask for her alliance against the invading Parthians. Her boldness alarmed some powerful court officials in Alexandria, the Egyptian capital, and they staged a coup d'état, overthrowing her in favor of Ptolemy XIII—a figure they knew they could easily control. It is believed that Cleopatra fled to Thebaid by 50 B.C., whereupon Ptolemy XIII's new handlers persuaded him to sign a ruthless decree (on October 27, 50 B.C.) banning grain shipments anywhere except to Alexandria. The purpose was to intensify and exploit the ongoing famine by starving Cleopatra and her supporters. (Collateral damage included the starvation of just about everyone else.) But Cleopatra was not one to quietly starve. She recruited an army from among the Arab tribes east of Pelusium, set it against Ptolemy XIII, and, with her sister Arsinoe, set up a base of operations in Syria. Cleopatra then advanced to Ascalon, near Jerusalem, from where she waited and watched.

Rome was also watching. In his own civil war, Caesar defeated Pompey at the Battle of Pharsalus in August of 48 B.C. Pompey, who had been appointed by the Roman senate as guardian of Ptolemy XIII, now fled to find refuge with his ward. But politics was a most unforgiving business in Egypt, and Ptolemy's handlers had no desire to be associated with a loser. As the young pharaoh looked on from a distance, Pompey was murdered as soon as he set foot ashore on September 28. Four days later, Caesar, leading 3,200 Roman infantrymen and eight hundred cavalry, marched into Alexandria. He bore with him the *fasces*, a bundle of rods bound tightly together and surmounted by the head of an axe. The traditional Roman symbol of power and authority, the fasces signified Caesar's intention to take control. Amid riots in Alexandria, Ptolemy XIII fled to Pelusium, and Julius Caesar took up residence in the Ptolemaic palace.

Even from a distance, Cleopatra ensured that she heard and saw all. Cleopatra was a fighter. She had already proven that with Ptolemy. But she knew that Caesar was hardly her weakling brother, and she possessed sufficient military savvy to know that her army of Arabs could not capture Caesar's legions of Rome. She could quit. She could flee. But it was at this moment that she decided to find another means of overcoming Caesar. If her army was incapable of capturing Caesar's army, Cleopatra decided that she would not try to capture his army. Instead, she herself would make Caesar himself her captive.

The portraits Cleopatra had caused to be pressed into coins reveal a face lively and intelligent rather than conventionally beautiful, her chin firm, her forehead broad, her nose delicate but prominent. The Greek biographer Plutarch described her voice as "an instrument of many strings," adding that "Plato admits four sorts of flattery, but she had a thousand." But there was the problem of how to get to Caesar. Although Ptolemy had left Alexandria, his forces still lay outside of the city. Her solution was to have herself rolled up in a carpet, which was carried through enemy lines as an offering to the great Caesar. The gift was unrolled before the conqueror, and, it is believed, the two became lovers that very day. Caesar invited both Cleopatra and Ptolemy to meet with him on the following day. When Ptolemy showed up, the work of his sister-bride was all too apparent to him, and he stormed out of the palace, screaming his betrayal. As Ptolemy attempted to rally the Alexandrian mob, Caesar's guards brought him back to the palace, but he was subsequently released, after which he rejoined his handlers and prepared to wage war on Caesar and Cleopatra.

What, if anything, Cleopatra felt for Caesar—or he for her—cannot be known. All that is certain is that each intended to use the other, and each believed himself or herself to be in control. Yet, even if it was based on politics more than passion, the relationship proved symbiotic rather than exploitative. Caesar needed money to finance his army, and, citing the role Rome had played in restoring Cleopatra's father to the throne in 55 B.C., he asserted his claim that Egypt owed him a debt. Cleopatra, whose pressing need was military power, was quite willing to strike a bargain. Her intention was to use a political-sexual relationship with Caesar to restore the Ptolemies to greatness, beginning with the recovery of southern Syria and Palestine.

But first there was the renewed civil war to win. And that would not be easy. The army that rallied around Ptolemy XIII had swelled to some twenty thousand men and, in November, laid siege to Alexandria. Most of the city's great library, holding the accumulated wisdom of the ancient world, was burned, as were vital warehouses. Outnumbered, Caesar focused on what he deemed the most strategically important feature in the city, the Pharos lighthouse. By holding it, Caesar maintained control over the harbor.

In the meantime, Cleopatra's sister, Arsinoe, slipped out of the palace and into the arms of one of Ptolemy's commanders, Achillas. It was a betrayal for which Cleopatra would never forgive her. The army and the Alexandrian mob proclaimed Arsinoe their queen. In the end, however, Caesar prevailed, winning decisively on March 27, 47 B.C.

While attempting to flee, Ptolemy XIII drowned in the Nile. Following the victory, Caesar restored Cleopatra to the throne, bowing, however, to Ptolemaic law and custom by compelling her to marry her eleven-year-old brother, Ptolemy XIV. Yet it was Caesar and Cleopatra, not Cleopatra and the youngest Ptolemy, who sailed up the Nile in luxuriant triumph together. Some historians record this as an amorous trip of two weeks, others as one of two months. In either case, Cleopatra was spontaneously worshipped as a pharaoh when the couple touched port at Dendara—an honor Caesar knew he would never receive.

By the time of this journey, it was clearly apparent that Cleopatra was pregnant. Although historians have argued whether or not the child was the son of Caesar, Cleopatra herself named him Ptolemy Caesar— or Caesarion—when he was born on June 23, 47 B.C. Caesar was not present at the birth, having left Cleopatra's side to mop up resistance from Pompeian diehards. Among those he captured in this campaign was Arsinoe. Caesar returned to Rome in July of 46 B.C. He sent for Cleopatra and her court, who partook of celebrations in Rome during September and October, during which, among other things, Cleopatra had the satisfaction of seeing Arsinoe in Caesar's ceremonial triumph, trailing behind in chains with the other captives.

Caesar next went to Spain, where, at the Battle of Munda on March 17, 45 B.C., he delivered the final blow to the forces of the conservative republicans who opposed him. Returning again to Rome and Cleopatra, he ordered a golden statue of her placed in the temple of Venus Genetrix, the ancestress of Caesar's own Julian family, and he installed Cleopatra in a villa beyond the Tiber. He also acknowledged Caesarion as his son.

All of this, at the very height of Caesar's popular acclaim, created outrage in much of Rome. Not only did Cleopatra occupy the villa with her husband-brother, but Caesar—who spoke openly of marrying Cleopatra—was, in fact, already married. Thus he proposed to violate not only Roman laws against bigamy, but also the even more important law against marriage to any foreigner.

Judging from the ostentatious luxury with which Cleopatra surrounded herself in Rome, she was little bothered by the public protest against her presence. She had, after all, prevailed in a civil war and maneuvered Ptolemaic Egypt into position to recapture its former glory. Her victory was, of course, short lived. On March 15, 44 B.C., Caesar fell victim to a cabal of assassins.

Following Caesar's murder, Cleopatra seems to have behaved with great discretion, asserting officially that she was in Rome to do nothing more or less than negotiate a new treaty of alliance. But she was well aware that the death of Caesar brought her campaign for power to an abrupt end—at least for now—and she returned to Egypt with the knowledge that, without Caesar, a new Roman political struggle would inevitably begin. She intended to make the most of it—whatever it would become—for herself and for her country.

Cleopatra saw her opportunity in the outcome of the Battle of Philippi, central Macedonia, in 42 B.C. After routing the forces of Caesar's assassins, the victorious Mark Antony seemed poised to inherit Caesar's mantle. Envisioning the conquest of Persia next, Antony sent for Cleopatra, whom he had met in Egypt years ago when she was a girl of fourteen. It is likely that she set out on the journey to Tarsus in Asia Minor with a firm picture of Mark Antony in mind. Caesar had been a man of lofty intelligence and great wit—an opponent, an ally, and a lover who in every way was a worthy match for her. Antony, she understood, was made of very different stuff. Handsome, bold, and dashing, he was a notorious womanizer, and he was by no means celebrated for his brains. Commanding great power, he was nevertheless a weak man, as Cleopatra saw it, and she intended to use him. It would be far easier than it had been with Caesar. With his death, one door had slammed shut; with the arrival of Mark Antony, another swung wide open.

Cleopatra loaded her barges with gifts to flatter Antony, but she also delayed her departure to pique his expectation. And when she approached Tarsus, she entered via the River Cydnus in a barge of singularly rich beauty. It was pure theater. With Egypt on the verge of complete economic collapse, her oarsmen pulled the barge with silver oars, assisted by a wind that filled purple sails. Handmaidens arrayed as Erotes and Nereids attended to Cleopatra, who was dressed as the goddess of love herself, Aphrodite. If it all seems heavy-handed and vulgar in the retrospect of history, so it probably seemed to many who actually beheld it—except for Mark Antony, a man, Cleopatra correctly surmised, of most vulgar and heavy-handed sensibilities.

Cleopatra also understood that her greatest asset, beyond her charms—enhanced by the theatrical barge—was her status as queen of Egypt, descended from the venerable Ptolemaic line. Mark Antony loved women, but he loved royal women most of all, and his own wife, Fulvia, was nothing more than the daughter of middle-class parents.

Cleopatra read her man perfectly. Soon after her arrival, he set aside his plans for the Persian invasion, and he set aside as well all thought of the faithful Fulvia, who labored back in Rome, doing all she could to prevent the youthful Octavian—rival heir to Caesar's authority—from gaining the ascendancy. Shamelessly, Antony focused on the present pleasures of Cleopatra, whom he followed back to Alexandria, enthralled.

With Caesar there had been a trade-off. He had granted Cleopatra his protection, which meant that she was never a truly independent monarch. Antony, thoroughly smitten and unable to think strategically, willingly acknowledged Cleopatra sovereign of Egypt. What she saw in Mark Antony was a new opportunity to use a Roman as the means of attacking Rome or, at least, holding it at bay. Not only did Antony offer her a second chance to restore Egypt—the first chance having been robbed by the death of Caesar—he seemed to offer an even better chance. Apparently equal to Caesar in the authority he wielded, Antony was simple-minded by comparison and utterly pliant. Whereas Caesar never entirely succumbed to Cleopatra's wiles, Antony was utterly consumed by them.

It was not until 40 B.C. that Antony left Alexandria to return to Italy in order to hammer out an agreement with Octavian. This entailed marrying Octavian's sister Octavia, Fulvia having died. For three years, the restless Antony fruitlessly negotiated with Octavian and tolerated marriage to Octavia, even as he pined for Cleopatra. At last, he left for Egypt again, reasoning that, like Caesar before him, he would use her wealth to finance the Persian campaign he had earlier put off. As usual, Cleopatra's mere presence deprived Antony of all will and self-control. *Use* her? He *married* her.

It was an act of foolish arrogance, and Cleopatra should have tried to prevent it. She saw marriage as the means of bringing Antony entirely under her control, but failed to anticipate that it would also unite all of Rome against him and, by extension, against her as well. Had she herself succumbed to passion? Possibly. More likely, however, in this high-stakes game of global politics, it was her first short-sighted move, a fatal strategic lapse. Having risen to a level of brilliance that very nearly made her the precarious queen of a bankrupt country, empress of the world, Cleopatra began an accelerating downward spiral.

While Antony had been in Rome, Cleopatra turned her attention to Herod of Judaea, the most powerful of Rome's client kings and a friend of Antony's. Herod rebuffed her seduction, however, and on Antony's return, Cleopatra not only persuaded Antony to give her large portions of Syria and Lebanon she also asked for the balsam groves of Jericho, which were part of Herod's kingdom. When Antony found the gumption to refuse this, Cleopatra turned her wrath on Herod with attempts to sow discontent among the women of his household.

In the meantime, Antony pursued the costly and unsuccessful Persian campaign. Even after the campaign failed, he returned to Alexandria in 34 B.C. to celebrate a fictional triumph. With Cleopatra, Antony paraded through the city, the couple seated on golden thrones among their own three children and Caesarion, whom Antony proclaimed to be Caesar's son—a move intended to cast Octavian, merely adopted by Caesar, in the role of bastard. Cleopatra seemed to get all that she had desired. She was publicly hailed the queen of kings, and Caesarion the king of kings. Alexander Helios, one of her sons with Antony, was given Armenia (which Antony had conquered—though only temporarily, as it turned out) and territory beyond the Euphrates. Ptolemy, his brother, was awarded the lands west of the Euphrates, while Cleopatra Selene, the boys' sister, was made ruler of Cyrene.

But the glory, all of it, was illusory. Back in Rome, Octavian did not sit still. He seized Antony's will (a document historians judge to be of dubious authenticity) from the temple of the vestal virgins, to whom Antony had purportedly entrusted the document, and published to the people of Rome the terrible facts: Antony had given Roman lands to a foreign woman and intended ultimately to transfer the capital of the empire from Rome to Alexandria, where he meant to found a new dynasty.

While Antony and Cleopatra dissipated during the winter of 32–31 B.C. in Greece, the Senate of Rome stripped Antony of his prospective consulate for the following year. Responding to Antony's letter declaring his divorce from Octavia, Octavian moved the Senate to declare war not against Antony, but Cleopatra. The Egyptian queen's alienation of Herod deprived her and Antony alike of a much-needed ally.

Now they stood alone against Rome.

On September 2, 31 B.C., Octavian engaged the combined fleets of Antony and Cleopatra at the naval Battle of Actium. Suddenly losing heart in the midst of the fight, Cleopatra took her ships to Egypt, leaving Antony's ships to their fate. Antony withdrew from the scene of battle with a few ships, followed Cleopatra and her fleet, and boarded the queen's flagship. For the next three days, despite their being on the same vessel, he refused to see her. Suddenly, however, he decided to reconcile.

But the situation by then was hopeless. Returning to Alexandria, Cleopatra apparently decided that her only option was to die—or, rather, not simply to die, but to die with renown. Her final manipulation of Antony, she decided, would be to induce him to kill himself for love of her. Retiring to her mausoleum, she sent messengers to Antony to tell him she was dead. The news, combined with the defeat at Actium, had the desired effect. Antony fell on his sword and, dying, was carried to Cleopatra's mausoleum. When he discovered that she was still alive, he did nothing more before he passed than bid her to make peace with Octavian.

CLEOPATRA HEEDED ANTONY'S ADVICE—after a fashion. Octavian visited her, and she did all she could to seduce the man. When this failed, she understood that she would suffer the same fate as her sister Arsinoe under Caesar's captivity: she and her children would be led in chains in Octavian's triumph ceremony. This realization prompted her to choose death over disgrace. She committed suicide, quite possibly by exposing herself to the bites of several asps. Not only was this snake a symbol of divine royalty, but Egyptian religion taught that death by snakebite guaranteed immortality. Cleopatra's life had been a series of extraordinary, sexually charged but intensely political decisions in what was very nearly a successful effort to rescue her birthright—the kingdom of Egypt—and elevate herself to the greatest throne of the ancient world. Even in suicide, however, Cleopatra declined to relinquish choice, making what she must have believed was a decision for immortality.

Queen Boudicca and the Invaders (ca. A.D. 60)
THE DECISION TO RESIST

Today, the British call her Boudicca. In Roman annals, she was Boadicea. To her people, a Celtic tribe known as the Iceni who occupied East Anglia (southeastern Britain near present-day Norfolk) in the first century, she was Boudiga. It was the name they gave her, after the Celtic goddess of victory. No one knows what name she was born with. And no one knows much more than that she was born into the Celtic aristocracy about the year A.D. 30, then married Prasutagus, king of the Iceni, in 48 or 49.

The Celts in general—and the Iceni in particular—were a proud and warlike people who gave the conquering Romans a great deal of trouble. In A.D. 43, however, Prasutagus submitted to Roman authority, allowing the Iceni to become a client kingdom of the Roman empire in exchange for the right to continue to rule his people and lands. The benefits to the Iceni were considerable: protection, improved education, and more employment, as well as imperial funding and loans. But the costs were also substantial: a significant degree of slavery and often-burdensome taxes. Nevertheless, Prasutagus and Boudicca prospered under Roman rule, and the Celtic queen bore her husband two daughters, their names unknown to history.

Then, in 60 or 61, Prasutagus died, leaving Boudicca regent of the Iceni and guardian of their daughters' inheritance, which consisted of money and heirlooms left over after he had rendered to Nero most of his lands and other possessions—as required of a client king deemed to be in debt to Rome. The Celtic king's mistake was trusting Nero's sense of justice, which, quite simply, the Roman emperor did not possess.

Within days of Prasutagus's death, soldiers of the chief Roman administrator of Britain, Catus Decianus, called on Boudicca and brutally seized everything her husband had left to her and her daughters. Then the troops fanned out and plundered and destroyed the homes of Iceni nobles, seizing family members and selling them into slavery. Returning to Boudicca, they demanded immediate repayment of Roman loans made to maintain the Iceni court. When Boudicca protested her inability to pay, she was taken prisoner and publicly whipped, while her daughters were turned over to the Roman legionnaires for their pleasure.

After Boudicca was turned loose and reunited with her daughters, she had a decision to make. She could continue to lead her people in submission to Rome, or she could lead them in rebellion against the most powerful empire the world had ever known.

She chose rebellion.

Many historians dismiss Boudicca's rebellion as the desperate act of a woman who had suffered a terrible personal assault. While little is known for certain about how she organized the rebellion, the few facts available argue against mere desperation. Boudicca was well aware that various tribes were already in scattered rebellion against Rome, and she rallied not just her own people, but appealed to the leaders of other tribes as well. By the time she finally launched her rebellion, she had gathered an army some 100,000 strong. This was not the product of an emotional outburst, nor was it an act of desperation, but a skillfully plotted, carefully organized revolution with a very real chance of success. Boudicca decided to transform her own pain and outrage into the fuel that drove a major military movement.

The war she made was indeed horrific. She began by attacking Camulodunum Colonia, modern Colchester, which was a colony of retired Roman officers and their families. She coordinated this attack with spies inside the town, and ravaged Colchester for some days. A messenger managed to escape to Londinium (London), but he must not have painted a very vivid picture of what was happening at Colchester, for the procurator (Roman governor) dispatched just two hundred legionnaires, who were rapidly consumed by Boudicca's vast army.

After finishing off the town and killing everyone in it, Boudicca moved on. The Boudiccan army encountered the five thousand troops of Petilius Cerialis's IX Legion Hispana, ambushed them, and killed every last foot soldier. Only Petilius himself, together with his cavalry, managed to retreat, leaving Boudicca to advance against London. This market city, spread over some 330 acres at the time, was quickly deserted by the Roman garrison charged with its defense. Boudicca razed London and killed everyone she encountered there. It is said that the fires she ignited were so hot that they reduced the city to a layer of hard red clay, ten inches thick, which, in places, still lies below the streets of the modern British capital.

From London, Boudicca turned to the northwest and attacked Verulamium (St. Albans), whose population consisted entirely of Britons who supported Roman rule. By this time, her army had swelled to perhaps two hundred thousand, against which the Roman governor of Britain, Suetonius Paullinus, could muster a mere ten thousand legionnaires. Intent on the destruction of St. Albans, Boudicca overlooked her opportunity to crush the legion sent against her. It was a fatal error. Suetonius positioned his troops on the top of a sloping hill within what the Roman historian Tacitus described as a "defile," a kind of gorge. At the rear of the Roman troops was a forest. This meant that attackers would have to approach uphill and from a single direction only. Boudicca must have observed this, but she believed that the overwhelming numbers she commanded would nevertheless prevail.

Tacitus described the appearance of the Celtic queen during this battle as "almost terrifying." Doubtless, this was an understatement. Like her warriors, she may have painted herself blue, a color intended to inspire special terror. Certainly, the sheer numbers alone must have been awe-inspiring. Yet the Romans were highly trained, and they had great confidence in Suetonius. He ordered his forces to array themselves in a tight phalanx formation, their shields together forming one great continuous shield, against which the Celtic spears, hurled uphill, were ineffective. Then, rapidly consolidating his men into a wedge, Suetonius ordered a hail of Roman javelins. They decimated Boudicca's hordes, who panicked and broke just as Suetonius followed up his javelin assault with a combined infantry and cavalry charge from the front and the flanks—a devastating double envelopment that left some eighty thousand Celts dead and quickly ended the rebellion.

AFTER GREAT INITIAL SUCCESS, Boudicca had been outgeneraled in the final battle. According to legend, she made her way home and poisoned herself. Although some historians point to the paucity of Anglo-Roman archaeological artifacts in Norfolk as evidence of the severity with which the Roman administration raked the rebel countryside—dead people don't make artifacts to leave behind—others point out that, following Boudicca's rebellion, the Roman administration of Britain was generally kinder, gentler, and more enlightened. If this was the case, Boudicca did succeed in bringing a measure of relief to her people. But perhaps this is less important than how her stand against injustice and tyranny survives in British history and legend as an inspiring example of a decision to refuse slavery and to lead the fight against tyranny, no matter how apparently overwhelming. Little wonder that Prime Minister Winston Churchill cited the precedent of the Iceni queen when he led his people in resistance against the legions of another empire nearly two thousand years after Boudicca.

Elizabeth I and the Spanish Armada (1588)

THE DECISION TO SAVE THE NATION

Elizabeth Tudor was born, at Greenwich Palace on September 7, 1533, a disappointment. King Henry VIII and Anne Boleyn, her father and mother, wanted a son and heir in a royal world where, really, only boys much mattered. A boy could become a king. A girl could become a queen, but, in the early sixteenth century, queens generally counted for very little. As one flabbergasted Londoner was heard to exclaim when she first laid eyes on Queen Elizabeth shortly after her coronation, "Oh Lord! The Queen is a woman!"

If Elizabeth came into the world as a disappointment, her early life in that world brought even worse. After Elizabeth was born, Anne Boleyn tried hard to have a son, but suffered a miscarriage in 1534, and, in January 1536, gave birth to a stillborn boy. On May 2, 1536, Henry had her arrested and tried on trumped-up charges of serial adultery and even incest with her brother. She was sent to the block on May 19. Eleven days later Henry married Jane Seymour and had with her a son, Edward. Sickly from birth, the boy was not expected to live, but, when he did, Henry paved the way to his inheritance of the throne by coaxing Parliament into declaring Elizabeth a bastard. She was banished from court and raised on an estate called Hatfield.

The death of Henry VIII in 1547 did not improve the lot of young Elizabeth. The king's last wife and widow, Catherine Parr, married Thomas Seymour, England's lord high admiral, who immediately began scheming against his brother, Edward Seymour, regent to the ten-year-old Edward VI. Edward Seymour put a stop to Thomas's plans by ordering his execution, but he also accused Elizabeth of having had an affair with his brother and of having conspired in his treasonous plot. Bad as this was, the situation grew even worse after poor Edward VI succumbed to his many ills in 1553 at age sixteen. Now Elizabeth's half-sister, the Catholic Mary I, became queen of England and accused Protestant Elizabeth of continually plotting against *her*.

In January 1554, one Thomas Wyatt led a Protestant rebellion in Kent. Mary accused her half-sister of complicity in the rebellion and had her arrested and imprisoned in the Tower of London, the very place in which Anne Boleyn had been held prior to execution. After two months here, in the shadow of the ax, Elizabeth was transferred to house arrest at an estate called Woodstock. Physically freed after about a year, she spent the entire reign of Mary I under the anxiety of impending rearrest and was truly liberated only after Mary I died childless on November 17, 1558.

Elizabeth I was queen at last. But the country to whose throne she ascended was a poor and troubled place. Bloody Mary, as her sister was called, had violently persecuted Protestants in her effort to reverse the Protestant Reformation of her father, Henry VIII, and return the nation to Catholicism. Married to King Philip II of Spain, she had led England into a disastrous war on behalf of Spain, which had brought the country to the verge of economic ruin and civil war. The England Elizabeth inherited was described by one traveler of the time as "the arse of the world." Yet through a combination of force of personality, economic savvy, and political will, Elizabeth I began the rapid transformation of England from an insular European backwater to the island nexus of what would eventually become the greatest empire since Rome. However, in May 1588, when Mary's widowed husband, Philip II, assembled in the port of Lisbon an invasion fleet consisting of 122 ships carrying 19,000 men—the Spanish Armada—England was still very far from enjoying the glory it would later attain.

At the end of the sixteenth century, Spain was Europe's greatest military power and its richest kingdom. England at the time had a growing, but still diminutive navy and an army that was both puny and inconsiderable by Continental standards. The kingdom's coastal defenses, built by Henry VIII, were obsolete and hopelessly vulnerable to modern naval artillery fire. Philip II had no wish to rule England as part of the Spanish Empire, but he burned with zeal to return the country to the "true church," to restore Catholic lands and property usurped by Henry VIII, to reopen the monasteries, to restore Catholic worship, and, most of all, to put a Catholic on the English throne. Agreeing to support an invasion, the Pope excommunicated Elizabeth I (even though she was Protestant), absolving her subjects of any duty to obey her. Philip prepared his Armada, charging it with the mission of holding the narrow sea between England and Flanders, where the Duke of Parma, a brilliant general, commanded Spain's Army of Flanders. The Armada would secure safe passage for Parma's forces and would also carry additional troops as well as massive amounts of supplies and siege artillery.

England's prospects for successfully repelling the invasion did not look bright, and there was no shortage of courtiers and advisers in Elizabeth's court who advised the monarch—a mere woman, after all—to salvage England and herself by coming to some accommodation with Philip. As Elizabeth saw it, however, to "save" the country in this manner would be to lose it. She decided to fight.

In making this decision, she did not forget the many lessons of her imperiled childhood and young womanhood. In the ways of the world, Elizabeth was a hard realist. She knew that it was one thing to declare that she would fight, but quite another to succeed in resisting so powerful an enemy as Spain. She decided, therefore, not to fret over England's weaknesses, but to exploit its strength, which she found in its people and herself. She turned to Sir Francis Drake, her kingdom's most skillful seafarer and its boldest privateer (a mariner who practiced state-sanctioned piracy). Back in 1572, Elizabeth had presented Drake with an official privateering commission and sent him off to plunder Spanish

New World ports. In 1577, she sent him privateering again, and with just five ships manned by no more than two hundred men total, Drake plundered Spanish towns and vessels throughout South America. He even claimed California for his queen, christening it New Albion. In 1585, as Anglo-Spanish relations rapidly deteriorated, Elizabeth defied the advice of such highborn seafarers as Sir Richard Grenville and Sir Martin Frobisher, as well as her own secretary of state, Lord Burghley, and once again sent Drake, now in command of a fleet of twenty-five ships, against the overseas empire of Spain. Drake captured Santiago in the Cape Verde Islands, Cartagena in Colombia, St. Augustine in Florida, and Santo Domingo in Hispaniola. The effect of these triumphs led by a single man with a small fleet was devastating to Spain. The nation's credit all but collapsed as the Bank of Spain went broke, the Bank of Venice (which had made immense loans to Philip II) nearly followed suit, and the important Bank of Augsburg refused to extend any more credit. When Philip began making threatening noises about mounting an invasion, Elizabeth, in 1587, commissioned Drake to "impeach the provisions of Spain" and fitted him out with thirty ships. Drake led these in an attack on the Spanish harbor of Cádiz, destroying in the space of thirty-six hours thousands upon thousands of tons of shipping as well as supplies—the very core of the great Armada Philip planned to hurl against England.

Drake's action delayed but did not stop the advance of the Armada. And that is when Elizabeth turned to herself. In 1588, while dispatching a large defensive naval force to meet the Armada, she set out personally to rally the ground troops whose mission it would be to repel an amphibious landing. For few in England believed that the English fleet, composed of a core of navy warships and a large auxiliary flotilla of armed merchant vessels, could stop the mighty Armada.

To a man, Elizabeth's advisers pleaded with her not to venture into Tilbury Camp, where the English army had assembled to meet the invaders. Given what they believed was the great instability of England on the verge of invasion, many close to Elizabeth feared that Catholic sympathizers would aid the Spanish by attempting to assassinate the queen. To walk among so many armed men, they warned her, was the height of folly.

Elizabeth surely understood that the danger was real, but she believed that the far greater danger lay in seeming—now, of all times—to neglect her duty by failing to make personal contact with the defenders of her realm. She wanted them to see her willingness to share their dangers and, by so doing, she was confident that she could inspire victory. Thus, at Tilbury Camp, on the eve of the anticipated invasion, the queen, arrayed in the body armor of a cavalry officer, spoke to her troops. She did not trumpet her personal courage or honor, but conveyed to her men her absolute trust: "My loving people," she began, "we have been persuaded by some that are careful of our safety to take heed how we commit ourselves to armed multitudes for fear of treachery, but I assure you, I do not desire to live to distrust my faithful and loving people." And then she continued:

> Let tyrants fear, I have always so behaved myself that under God I have placed my chiefest strength and safeguard in the loyal hearts and good will of my subjects. And therefore I am come amongst you as you see at this time not for my recreation and disport, but being resolved in the midst and heat of the battle to live or die amongst you all. To lay down for God and for my kingdom and for my people my honour and my blood even in the dust.

Powerfully, unmistakably, she told them of her intention to share *their* fate. Yet she also made it clear that, under her leadership, she and her loyal followers would become masters, not victims, of that shared fate, and that, in the victory to come, all would be rewarded:

> I know I have the body of a weak and feeble woman but I have the heart and stomach of a king, and of a King of England too, and think foul scorn that Parma or Spain or any prince of Europe should dare invade the borders of my realm to which rather than

any dishonour shall grow by me, I myself will take up arms, I myself will be your general, judge, and rewarder of every one of your virtues in the field. I know already for your forwardness you have deserved rewards and crowns [coins; that is, money] and we do assure you in the word of a prince, they shall be duly paid you.

FOR ELIZABETH I, THE DECISION TO SAVE THE COUNTRY was no matter of appeal to abstract concepts of patriotism. It consisted, rather, in laying her life on the line and in offering tangible, real rewards to those who followed her. In an immediate, physical, and spiritual sense, Elizabeth assumed personal command, presenting herself as the army's general. Yet, ever the realist, she also nominated a "Lieutenant-General," a commander with the practical military experience she knew she did not possess, a lieutenant to "be in my stead." She assured her troops that "never prince commanded a more noble or worthy subject" than their military leader, and she further proclaimed her complete confidence that, "by your obedience to my General, by your concord in the camp and your valour in the field we shall shortly have a famous victory over those enemies of God, my kingdom and of my people."

They were great words, eloquent words, and, backed by Elizabeth's personal presence combined with her good sense, they proved far more than empty words. By deciding to order resistance, then deciding openly to share with the lowliest soldier the dangers of that resistance, Queen Elizabeth descended from her throne to embrace her people—yet, in doing so, she retained her regal presence. Inspiration spread like a sweet contagion.

As it turned out, the troops at Tilbury Camp were never called upon to repel invaders, because none were able to land. The English fleet had made two attempts to intercept the Armada in Iberian waters during June and July, but the English vessels were blown back by storms. Worse, when the Armada appeared in English waters, the defensive fleet was caught by surprise, in the process of reprovisioning at Plymouth. As best they could, the English captains pursued the Armada up the English Channel, but managed to sink only two of the enemy ships. Then, unexpectedly, the Spanish admiral, the duke of Medina Sidonia, suddenly decided to anchor off Calais on August 6. This gave the English a magnificent opportunity, which they were quick to seize. Fire ships—flaming English hulks—were sent against the anchored Spanish fleet, resulting in the destruction of four Spanish vessels and, more importantly, forcing the entire Armada to flee to the north, sailing around Scotland and Ireland in order to maneuver back toward home. In these brutally storm-tossed waters, thirty-four or more Spanish ships were lost, the Spanish Armada decisively defeated, and England saved from invasion.

Beethoven and Deafness (1802)

THE DECISION TO OVERCOME

One of the most pervasive popular myths about Ludwig van Beethoven (1770–1827), regarded by generations of musicologists and music lovers alike as the greatest composer who ever lived, is that he was universally misunderstood, unrecognized, and unrewarded during his own lifetime, that only after his death was his greatness appreciated. In fact, Beethoven was widely regarded, even early in his career, as a composer of extraordinary merit and a very fine pianist. He not only made a good living, but was the artist whose achievements probably did the most to change the way composers were rewarded for their work. Traditionally, throughout the seventeenth and eighteenth centuries, composers had to rely on the patronage of wealthy nobles, in whose employ they were regarded as little more than specialized household servants. Beethoven likewise commanded some noble patronage, but he made his living mostly from public performances and sales of his compositions.

By the summer of 1801, during the height of his early success, Beethoven found his prosperous and promising career under grave threat. He wrote to his friend Karl Ameda on July 1, 1801, that he was "having a miserable life, at odds with nature and its Creator, abusing the latter for leaving his creatures vulnerable to the slightest accident . . . My greatest faculty, my hearing, is greatly deteriorated." Beethoven had been aware of a developing problem for perhaps as long as three years before he wrote of it to Ameda, but it was about this time that Beethoven's friends began noticing that he was becoming withdrawn, avoiding company and conversation. As he explained to another friend, Franz Wegeler, later in 1801, "How can I, a musician, say to people 'I am deaf!'" Yet he also swore to "defy this fate . . . if I can." Some five months later, he wrote again to Wegeler: "I will seize Fate by the throat. It will not wholly conquer me! Oh, how beautiful it is to live—and live a thousand times over!" It is clear that he was conflicted—despairing on the one hand, yet determined to win through on the other.

In 1802, one of the many physicians from whom Beethoven sought a cure sent him to Heiligenstadt, a bucolic village outside Vienna. Time spent in the peace and quiet of the country, the doctor hoped, might allow his hearing to rest and recover. Doubtless, Heiligenstadt did little or nothing for Beethoven's ears, but the new surroundings did temporarily lift the composer's spirits, and it was here that he composed the sunny Second Symphony, which betrays no signs of his inner despair. Despite what he had earlier written about seizing fate by the throat and drinking deeply of the joy of life, it must have become obvious to him that his hearing was not getting better. As spring and summer gave way to a somber autumn, Beethoven, thirty-two years old, wrote a will, a letter his biographers call the "Heiligenstadt Testament," which was addressed to his brothers, Carl and Johann, on October 6, 1802. The document provides rare insight into the master's state of mind in this, the most terrible crisis for one who (as he once declared) "lives wholly in music."

"Oh you men who think or say that I am malevolent, stubborn, or misanthropic, how greatly do you wrong me," Beethoven wrote. "You do not know the secret cause which makes me seem that way to you. From childhood on, my heart and soul have been full of the tender feeling of goodwill, and I was even inclined to accomplish great things. But, think that for six years now I have been hopelessly afflicted, made worse by senseless physicians, from year to year deceived with hopes of improvement, finally compelled to face the prospect of a lasting malady (whose cure will take years or, perhaps, be impossible)." He explained that, although his natural inclination was to be sociable, he was now "compelled to isolate myself, to live life alone. If at times I tried to forget all this, oh, how harshly was I flung back by the doubly sad experience of my bad hearing. Yet it was impossible for me to say to people, 'Speak louder, shout, for I am deaf.' Oh, how could I possibly admit an infirmity in the one sense which ought to be more perfect in me than others, a sense which I once possessed in the highest perfection, a perfection such as few in my profession enjoy or ever have enjoyed.—Oh I cannot do it; therefore forgive me when you see me draw back when I would have gladly mingled with you."

Beethoven's despair was not entirely artistic or vocational. It was human: "I am bound to be misunderstood; for me there can be no relaxation with my fellow men, no refined conversations, no mutual exchange of ideas. I must live almost alone, like one who has been banished. . . . If I approach near to people a hot terror seizes upon me, and I fear being exposed to the danger that my condition might be noticed." He described his feeling of "humiliation . . . when someone standing next to me heard a flute in the distance and I heard nothing, or someone standing next to me heard a shepherd singing and again I heard nothing." He continued: "Such incidents drove me almost to despair; a little more of that and I would have ended my life." Only "my art," he explained, stopped him from committing suicide. Yet the way he ended this letter to his brothers made it unmistakably clear that he was indeed writing his last will and testament, for he entreated his brothers, "as soon as I am dead," to ask his physician "to describe my malady . . . so that so far as it is possible at least the world may become reconciled to me after my death"—that is, understand and forgive his reclusive, apparently misanthropic behavior.

Beethoven asked his brothers to divide his "small fortune (if so it can be called)" fairly between them, and he closed the testament by asking for their forgiveness. He went on to advise his brothers to "recommend virtue to your children; it alone, not money, can make them happy. I speak from experience; this was what upheld me in time of misery. Thanks for it and to my art, I did not end my life by suicide—Farewell and love each other."

As with his earlier letters to Ameda and Wegeler, the Heiligenstadt Testament was less a statement or declaration than it was a dialogue with himself, a discussion of how he might overcome or become reconciled to his fate. It is a window into his decision-making process. He seemed to admit to himself that the one aspect of his fate that he must yield to was ending his career as a virtuoso pianist. This was a hard blow, both spiritually and financially. Not only did Beethoven love to perform; the monetary rewards of performance were substantially greater and more reliable than what he could expect as a full-time composer. Yet despite Beethoven's realization that this aspect of his career was now over, his decision nevertheless to continue to live "for his art" was an acknowledgment that, deaf or not, he would be able to continue composing. He seemed to have accepted that, because his growing deafness banned him from the salon and the stage, he would actually be compelled to dedicate himself all the more fiercely to composition. Perhaps he further intuited that this, in turn, would lead him to create music more profound than any he had yet written. If his deafness shut him off from the everyday noise of the world, delightful though that noise was, it would also usher him more deeply into the musical space of his own imagination.

IF NOTHING HAD GONE WRONG WITH HIS HEARING, could Beethoven have written the late piano sonatas, the late string quartets, or the Ninth Symphony? We cannot know. But we do know that Beethoven decided not to be defeated, even by what was for him the worst catastrophe imaginable. And we know, too, that his decision to live beyond his deafness, to refuse to accept it as the ultimate and terminal tragedy, allowed the creation of the great works that, among so much more, prompt us to ask wonderfully unanswerable questions.

Tecumseh and an Indian Nation (1806)
THE DECISION TO UNITE IN STRUGGLE

The America into which Tecumseh was born was a world coming to an end. Son of a Shawnee war chief, his mother of Creek and Cherokee ancestry, Tecumseh was probably born in Piqua, near modern Springfield, Ohio, in about 1768. In 1774, his father, Puckeshinwa, was killed at the Battle of Point Pleasant during a pre-Revolutionary conflict called Lord Dunmore's War. During the American Revolution itself, his older brother, who raised him after Puckeshinwa had been slain, died, and in Little Turtle's War (1790–95), which followed the Revolution—and in which Tecumseh himself fought—another brother fell.

Although much of his family had perished in battle, Tecumseh discovered that he had a genius for war, and he came to command the admiration of tribes throughout the Old Northwest (as the territory encompassing modern Ohio, Indiana, Michigan, Wisconsin, and Illinois was then called). Tecumseh also earned the respect of the whites who fought him, because, although fierce, he was also just and compassionate, persuading his fellow warriors to treat prisoners with respect and without torture.

General "Mad Anthony" Wayne ended Little Turtle's War with his victory at the Battle of Fallen Timbers—in which Tecumseh fought valiantly—and dictated the terms of the Treaty of Fort Greenville, which secured from the defeated tribes vast tracts of the Old Northwest. Tecumseh refused to sign the treaty, not out of defiance or anger, but from a conviction that no single Indian or even entire tribe had the right to give up land. The land, he declared, belonged to all Indians and to all tribes. To allow the separation of the Indians from their land would bring about the end of all Indian people, consummating the very Armageddon into which he had been born.

Tecumseh's decision not to sign the Treaty of Greenville was motivated by a profound understanding of the treaty's consequences. It was not a simple rejection of a white demand. In fact, what was unique about Tecumseh was the way in which his dedication to rescuing the world of the Indians did not compel him to turn his back on the world of the whites. On the contrary, he embraced that world and learned all he could from and about it. He was literate, and, with the aid of a frontier schoolteacher, Rebecca Galloway, he studied history, literature, and the Bible. He wanted to understand the white people so that he could more effectively defend his own people.

The decision not to sign the Treaty of Greenville left Tecumseh with a seemingly insurmountable dilemma: he had to find a way to make his people strong enough to avoid nothing less than the final and absolute end of the world.

But how?

For now, Tecumseh did no more than to move west, into the present area of Indiana. Here he gathered a following of local Indians, but, as always, also commanded the respect and even admiration of many white settlers. In the meantime, President Thomas Jefferson, eager to promote further national expansion into Ohio and Indiana, took a new tack with regard to the Indians. Instead of waging war against them, he would *change* them. The Indians of the southern frontier, the Choctaw, Chickasaw, and Creek, were agricultural people and therefore sedentary, willing to live on legally defined plots of land. In the Old Northwest, however, the tribes were hunters, who ranged with their game and therefore required vast hunting grounds. They resisted confinement. Jefferson proposed to convert these hunters into farmers and teach them to cultivate parcels of land belonging to them individually. And what belonged to them individually they could also sell. Any Indian who wished to sell his land to a white settler could then be "removed" westward, to the newly acquired Louisiana Territory.

Jefferson directed the man he appointed governor of the Indiana Territory, William Henry Harrison, to obtain "legal" title to as much Indian land as he could purchase. Jefferson reasoned that as white communities peacefully developed within or adjacent to Indian-owned lands, the Indians would become dependent on trade with the whites, running up debts so large that they would be forced to sell their land. In this way, peacefully, the white population would continue to push the Indians to the west. Tecumseh looked on with growing alarm as, between 1803 and 1806, Harrison acquired some seventy million acres west of the boundary between white and Indian settlements that had been established by the Treaty of Greenville. Tecumseh now saw that the Indian people could survive neither prolonged warfare with the whites nor prolonged peace among them.

By dint of countless years of cultural tradition, the Indians of the Old Northwest (and throughout most of the United States) had become committed to tribal society. Within a given tribe, this created great cohesion, but there was an apparently intractable resistance among tribes to unite with one another. Tecumseh came to understand that the Indians were a great people, but their tribal fragmentation made them weak in comparison to the whites, who were truly united. (And he understood from what he saw in the present, as well as from all that he had taught himself of white history, that unity, in the white world, always trumped disunity.) He further recognized that, whether or not his Indian brothers realized it, the Indian people were already united in the collective cataclysm wrought by white "civilization." Despite their efforts to further divide the Indians by breaking up the land and making treaties with this or that tribe, the whites had actually united the Indians in a common victimization.

Now he knew how to make his people strong. Tecumseh made a second, momentous decision to convert this negative union, a union of common disaster, into the basis of something entirely new in Indian culture: a positive, aggressive, effective union of all the Indians in the country. Tecumseh, who was known as a powerful orator—and who probably built his persuasive skills through a combination of Indian oratorical tradition and his reading of the Bible and other books of the white man— began traveling from one village to another in the early 1800s, spreading his message of Indian union. In this, he acted on the meaning of his very name: *Tecumseh*, "goes through one place to another." During this period there also occurred the religious transformation of his brother, Tenskwatawa, soon to be known as the Shawnee Prophet. Tenskwatawa began preaching a return to traditional ways and the elimination of white customs, including the practice of Christianity and the drinking of liquor.

Tecumseh decided that wedding his brother's native religious message to his own political message would create the most powerfully persuasive case for Indian unity. However, he saw that time was on the side of the white man, who continued to divide Indians one from another and to separate Indians from their land, to impoverish them, to make them dependent on white trade, white religion, and white customs. When Indian despair and rage erupted into war, it was invariably war fought by a handful of Indians against a greater number of whites, war that ensured defeat and the further wasting of the Indian people. To buy more time, Tecumseh threatened the whites with the prospect of much bigger wars. In the western frontier region, as yet thinly settled by whites, this would retard settlement long enough for him and his brother to continue traveling with their unification message. Tecumseh proposed that the Indians needed to sever all ties with the white man and forge a union stretching from the Great Lakes to the Gulf of Mexico. Yet even as he preached among the far-flung Indian villages, Tecumseh also addressed white audiences, preparing them for the Indian union by arguing that Governor Harrison was acting both illegally—in violation of the boundaries created by the Treaty of Greenville—and immorally, acquiring land from minor chiefs and tribal minorities who had no authority to sell anything.

Governor Harrison grew increasingly alarmed by the power of the combined preaching of Tecumseh and Tenskwatawa. When the pair spoke among the Delawares, the governor himself appeared and urged the tribe, who had many ties to the white settlements around them, to drive the "Shawnee Prophet" and his brother from their midst. Harrison called Tenskwatawa a false prophet and challenged him to prove his holiness. In this challenge, the governor had made the fatal mistake of underestimating Tecumseh, who, a few days later, announced that, on June 16, 1806, Tenskwatawa would give the proof desired by causing the sun to stand still and go dark. Harrison had not counted on the fact that Tecumseh could read an almanac. An eclipse that day, as promised, crystallized the Prophet's reputation not only among the Delaware, but among all, far and wide, who soon heard of the wonder he had performed.

Now Tecumseh and Tenskwatawa moved provocatively east, where white settlement was thicker, and they established a headquarters village at the site of the abandoned Fort Greenville itself. By 1807, Shawnee, Pottawatomie, Ottawa, Winnebago, Ojibwa (Chippewa), and Wyandot leaders and their warriors were assembling there. Even as the dream of Indian unity was apparently coming to pass—Indians coming to Tecumseh rather than he going to them—Tecumseh saw that the world of the whites was again beginning to divide. With each passing month, a new war between the Americans and the British seemed more and more likely.

In April 1808, Tecumseh, Tenskwatawa, and their many followers left Fort Greenville to move west again, back to Indiana, where, at the confluence of the Wabash River and Tippecanoe Creek they established Prophet's Town. A month later, Francis Gore, Britain's royal administrator in Ontario, invited Tecumseh and some 1,500 prominent chiefs to a great conference at Amherstburg on the Canadian side of Lake Erie. Tecumseh, who had been preaching total separation from whites, accepted the invitation. As the white man had long used Indian disunity against the Indians, so Tecumseh decided to use white disunity against whites. Cautiously, he forged a British-Indian alliance. Via Canada, the British would supply Tecumseh and his union of tribes with ordnance, ammunition, and military aid.

Governor Harrison and other white American leaders regarded Tecumseh as a brave and skilled warrior, but they underestimated his political sophistication and savvy. Even as Tecumseh was negotiating with the British, Tenskwatawa was talking with Harrison, assuring him that he and his brother wanted peace—and, from the governor, provisions promised by treaty.

Reassured, Harrison left the Shawnee Prophet alone and returned to the business of acquiring yet more Indian land. In the fall of 1809, Harrison concluded the Treaty of Fort Wayne, by which he purchased three million acres in the Wabash Valley. As Tecumseh knew it would, this outraged the tribes and the chiefs who were not party to the treaty, and it sent the Sac and Fox tribe—hitherto hesitant to associate with Tecumseh—into his brotherhood, along with about half of the Miami tribe and most of the Wyandots. In July 1810, Harrison told President James Madison that a general Indian uprising was in the making. In August, he met at Vincennes, Indiana, with Tecumseh, who demanded a repudiation of the hated Treaty of Fort Wayne. Harrison at first indignantly refused—but then agreed to report Tecumseh's objections to the president.

"I hope," Tecumseh replied, "the Great Spirit will put sense enough into his head to induce him to give up this land: it is true, he is so far off he will not be injured by the war; he may sit still in his town and drink his wine, whilst you and I will have to fight it out."

That autumn, yet more tribes joined Tecumseh's confederacy, and the united warriors began raiding the frontier. Meeting with Harrison again late in July 1811, Tecumseh laid out his plan for Indian unity and told the governor that he did not want war, but warned that, this time, the Indians would not be divided and conquered. For now, Tecumseh had at his command thousands of warriors—a number greater than any army Harrison could throw against them.

—

WHAT TECUMSEH HAD ACHIEVED WAS TRULY REMARKABLE, a degree of intertribal unity unprecedented in American history. Encouraged, he tried to do even more, undertaking, late in the summer of 1811, a recruiting expedition into the South, among the Chickasaw, Choctaw, and Creek, whose numbers offered the potential of perhaps 50,000 more warriors. But, except for a militant Creek faction known as the Red Sticks, these tribes rebuffed his overtures. Worse, Governor Harrison took advantage of Tecumseh's absence to attack Prophet's Town. On November 6, 1811, Harrison took up a position two miles from the Indian settlement. That night, Tenskwatawa assured the assembled warriors that they would go into battle under the protection of a magical fog. Therefore, on the morning of November 7, the Indians attacked—and, at the Battle of Tippecanoe (which would help propel Harrison to the White House), they were defeated. Although uninjured, Tenskwatawa was the greatest casualty of the battle. Tecumseh's followers lost faith in the Shawnee Prophet, and they deserted the union in large numbers.

For his part, Tecumseh now turned to an alliance with the British as the War of 1812 finally erupted. He accepted a commission as a brigadier general in the British army and proved a fierce and valuable ally, bringing many Indians to the British side. However, he never fully trusted his British allies, nor they him, and when Harrison defeated the combined British and Indian forces at the Battle of the Thames on October 5, 1813, Tecumseh lived just long enough to see his dream of unity crumble before he, too, fell on that day.

Truman and the A-Bomb (1945)

THE DECISION TO END A WAR

When Harry Truman took the oath of office at 7:09 P.M. on April 12, 1945, two hours and twenty-four minutes after the death of Franklin Roosevelt, he knew nothing of an "atomic bomb." During his eighty-two days as FDR's vice president, he had never been briefed by Roosevelt on the bomb or, for that matter, on much of anything else. After the swearing-in ceremony, which lasted no longer than a minute, Truman spoke to the Cabinet. When that meeting ended, Secretary of War Henry L. Stimson mentioned privately to the new president that he had to talk with him about a "new explosive of incredible power." It was not until April 25 that Stimson made a full presentation to the president, although James F. Byrnes, soon to become secretary of state, had already told Truman that the new weapon might be so powerful that it could wipe out entire cities, "killing people on an unprecedented scale." Stimson's presentation went into all the details, but whereas Byrnes had stressed that the bomb would probably end the war and put the United States in a position to dictate whatever terms it wished, Stimson expressed great concern over how the weapon would shape the future of humankind itself.

Between them, Byrnes and Stimson defined the reward and the risk of one of the most consequential decisions ever made by a world leader. It was a decision to end a war of unprecedented devastation with a weapon of unprecedented devastation, a weapon that put into humanity's hands the means of its own total annihilation. The stakes do not get higher than that.

After the war, and for years, Truman was repeatedly questioned about the decision. That is understandable. People wanted to know what could possibly drive the choice for Armageddon. Just how does one endure the agony of such a decision-making process and come through, at the end of it, with a decision?

The former president's questioners waited for the answer, the strings of their anticipation tuned to their tightest. But always the questioners were met with the same disappointing answer. What he said during a Q-and-A at an April 1959 Columbia University lecture is typical. Asked, as usual, what his most difficult decision had been, Truman answered that it was going to war in Korea.

That was harder than deciding to drop the atomic bomb? a somewhat incredulous student asked.

Truman replied, as he always did, that the "atom bomb was no 'great decision.'. . . It was merely another powerful weapon in the arsenal of righteousness. The dropping of the bombs stopped the war, saved millions of lives. It was a purely military decision."

This attitude did not reflect the bravado of afterthought. Naval Intelligence officer George Elsey was Truman's aide during the war. He recalled: "Truman made no decision because there was no decision to be made. He could no more have stopped it [the bomb] than a train moving down a track." Winston Churchill likewise recalled that the "decision whether or not to use the atomic bomb to compel the surrender of Japan was never an issue. There was unanimous, automatic, unquestioned agreement around our table."

No decision? Automatic? Anyone who had any experience with Truman knew that, in fact, he never failed to make a decision, and there was never anything "automatic" about the decisions he made. But he was so incisive and absolute a decision maker that it often appeared as if he breezed through the process. He was not a man who agonized, at least not visibly. The president's job, Truman believed, was to make decisions, and he was very good at his job. Instead of a nameplate on his desk, he had his famous sign proclaiming, "The Buck Stops Here." He explained in 1952: "The papers may circulate around the government for a while but they finally reach this desk. And then, there's no place else for them to go. The president—whoever he is—has to decide. He can't pass the buck to anybody. No one else can do the deciding for him. That's his job."

The idea, of course, was always to make the *right* decision. But this was less important than making *some* decision. In a collection of manuscripts he left to his daughter, Margaret, Truman wrote, "Presidents have to make decisions if they're going to get anywhere, and those presidents who couldn't make decisions are the ones who caused all the trouble." Of course, the *right* decision was the best decision, but the worst possible outcome did not result from a *wrong* decision. It resulted from the failure to decide.

The atomic bomb was successfully tested at 5:29 A.M. on July 16, 1945, in a remote stretch of the Alamogordo Army Air Base now called Trinity Site, in the New Mexico desert. At that moment, Truman was attending the Potsdam Conference with Churchill and Stalin just outside of war-ravaged Berlin. Receiving the news, what Truman felt most was a sense of relief that the "gadget" (as the scientists called it), which had consumed two billion 1940s' dollars, had worked. On July 20, he discussed with Generals Dwight Eisenhower and Omar Bradley the possible role of the bomb in the Pacific war. Eisenhower voiced his opposition to using it, arguing that the United States should not be the first nation to deploy such a horrific device.

The Supreme Allied Commander of the European theater was not alone in this opinion. In the weeks leading up to the Trinity test, a chorus of protest rose from the very scientific community that had worked on the top secret project. On June 11, 1945, Professor James Franck issued the confidential report of a committee of seven distinguished scientists who pleaded that the bomb not be used in an unannounced attack against Japan, but instead "first revealed to the world by a demonstration in an appropriately selected uninhabited area." Among the seven was no less a figure than Leo Szilard, who might justly be deemed the father of the massive effort to create the bomb—the Manhattan Project—since he was the man who had persuaded Albert Einstein, back in 1939, to write to President Roosevelt, urging him to authorize a crash program of atomic weapons research with the goal of beating the Nazis to the bomb.

Another panel of top atomic scientists, including Manhattan Project scientific director J. Robert Oppenheimer and Enrico Fermi, leader of the team that had created the world's first sustained nuclear chain reaction, issued a report on June 16 finding "no acceptable alternative to military use" of the bomb. But on June 27, Undersecretary of the Navy Ralph A. Bard wrote a memorandum expressing his opinion that dropping the bomb without warning would undermine "the position of the United States as a great humanitarian nation," especially now that Japan seemed so close to surrender. On July 3, Szilard himself circulated a petition calling atomic bombs "a means for the ruthless annihilation of cities" and appealing to the president to forbid their use. Fifty-nine Manhattan Project scientists signed the petition, but Szilard withheld it and circulated a second petition on July 17, which garnered sixty-nine signatures. In addition, on July 13, eighteen scientists at the Oak Ridge, Tennessee, laboratory signed a petition similar to Szilard's. A few days later, sixty-seven more Oak Ridge scientists signed yet another petition calling for the destructive power of the bomb to be "adequately described and demonstrated" before it was used against Japan. Nevertheless, of 150 Manhattan Project scientists polled at the University of Chicago, 131 voted for the immediate military use of the atomic bomb.

It is unlikely that the petitions, pleas, and protests ever actually reached Truman, but he was well aware of them as he listened to his advisers propose various alternatives to the bomb.

Before the bomb became a reality, two Pacific war endgame options were on the president's desk. One was to continue the conventional bombing of Japan, along with a naval blockade. The bombing campaign had already destroyed most major cities; the fire bombing of Tokyo alone had killed some 120,000 people. The objective of coupling the bombing with a naval blockade was to simultaneously pummel and strangle Japan into surrendering. The toll would be very heavy against Japanese civilians, and the war would drag on for probably well over another year. Worse, many American strategists believed that the combination of bombing and blockade would never produce unconditional surrender.

The Japanese would allow all of their cities to be destroyed and themselves to be starved, all the while taking a toll of Allied lives. So far,
combat experience supported this bleak prediction. Throughout the
entire war, no Japanese military unit had ever surrendered. The taking of
each Japanese-held Pacific island had been incredibly bloody, battles
ending only after virtually every Japanese defender had been killed. Iwo
Jima was a prime example. A speck of volcanic land, it was defended by
21,000 Japanese soldiers and sailors. Thirty thousand U.S. Marines
landed on February 19, 1945, after heavy naval and B-24 bombardment,
yet the island was not declared conquered until March 16. Even then,
Japanese resistance—utterly hopeless though it was—continued through
April and May. By this time, more than 20,000 of the 21,000 Japanese
defenders had been killed, and the Americans captured a mere 212
combat troops. Casualties among the American forces were 24,733 killed
or wounded. If this rock had been defended so fiercely, how dearly would
the Japanese mainland be bought? Those who agreed that bombing and
blockade alone would not end the war advocated an immediate, massive,
all-out invasion of the Japanese homeland. This would almost certainly
bring a quicker end to the war than bombing and blockade, but strategists believed the war would still not end before June 1946, and it would
cost (according to the most optimistic estimates) a minimum of 250,000
Allied lives, mostly American. Total Allied invasion casualties, killed and
wounded, were expected by most to approach a half million. General
Douglas MacArthur put the number at a million.

For Truman, such figures outweighed the moral objections of the
scientists and even made imperiling the future of civilization itself seem
like a reasonable risk. And there was another element that had to be fac-
tored into the equation. At the Potsdam Conference (July 17–August 2,
1945), Truman and Churchill lobbied vigorously to get Stalin to commit
the Soviet Union to a declaration of war against Japan. At this point, the
single pressing objective was to defeat Japan, but both Truman and
Churchill understood that a Russian presence in that country might well
mean that Japan, or at least the northern part of it, would become a

Soviet satellite after the war. By ending the war before the Soviets could begin to invade, the atomic bomb would preempt Stalin's claim on the country.

Some continued to insist that Japan was so near surrender that there was simply no need to use the bomb. Eisenhower cited intelligence reports indicating that Japan was indeed finished, notwithstanding that it kept on fighting. What Eisenhower and others at the time did not know is that the Japanese themselves had conducted studies in January 1944 and had already concluded that the war was lost. But that didn't matter. The Japanese militarists might no longer have the means to resist defeat, but they could continue to choose not to surrender. During the three months between April 12, when Truman took office, and the successful test of the atomic bomb on July 16, a *defeated* Japan inflicted American battle casualties amounting to almost half the total from three full years of the Pacific war.

Truman concluded that military defeat alone would not bring Japan's surrender. However, some of the president's close advisers said that this all depended on what definition of surrender the Allies were willing to accept. Some close to Truman theorized that the Japanese refusal to surrender was not so much an act of will as it was the result of inability. In all its long history, Japan had never been successfully invaded and had never surrendered. In a collective, cultural sense, the Japanese did not *know* how to surrender. It was not in the people's cultural vocabulary. In view of this, some advisers argued that the war would not end until the Allies redefined *surrender* by modifying their demand for unconditional surrender. A negotiated peace, they believed, was possible. Secretary of War Stimson suggested making the end of resistance, not unconditional surrender, the definition of Allied victory. (Other advisers countered that unconditional surrender had been the Allied objective from the very beginning and that it was what the Nazis had already been forced to accept. Anything less would be appeasement and would make a mockery of all that had been sacrificed in the Pacific war. Besides, the American people would never stand for it.)

The final argument against using the atomic bomb was both moral *and* apocalyptic. It held that no matter how terrible the current war was, atomic weapons were worse. Morally, their use constituted a war crime on an unparalleled scale. In apocalyptic terms, the use of the bomb would usher into warfare a force so powerfully evil that the survival of civilization itself—perhaps all life on earth—would be threatened.

There can be no mistake that Truman grasped both the moral and apocalyptic dimensions of the atomic bomb. He noted in his diary on July 25, 1945, that "We have discovered the most terrible bomb in the history of the world. It may be the fire of destruction prophesied in the Euphrates Valley Era, after Noah and his fabulous Ark." But Truman recognized that his vision of an apocalypse was ultimately hypothetical, whereas the reality of war was here and now. It was a reality that relentlessly killed and maimed American and Allied (as well as Japanese) troops. To his wife, Bess, Truman wrote that he believed the bomb would "end the war a year sooner . . . and think of the kids who won't be killed! That's the important thing."

"As president," Truman remarked in a 1956 memoir, "I always insisted on as complete a picture as possible before making a decision, and I did not want fuzzy statements that concealed differences of opinion." He read voraciously, both history and biography, as well as exhaustive reports prepared by his staff. "You get all the facts and you make up your mind" was Truman's capsule summary of the decision-making process.

It was the process by which the atomic bomb decision was made. Truman consulted with his advisers. He thoroughly immersed himself in the available plans for bringing the Pacific war to an end: blockade and conventional bombing, invasion, or the atomic bomb. He studied the casualty estimates associated with all of the alternatives. He consulted with authorities on Japanese culture and character. He did all he could to make himself an expert on the technical aspects of the bomb. (In later life, he advised any young person with aspirations to politics to get an education in history *and physics*.) If the decision, when it came, seemed to be "no decision" or an "automatic" decision, it was because, like all truly great decisions, it had been prepared for so thoroughly that it appeared, at last, inevitable.

The bombs, of course, were dropped. The first was used against Hiroshima on August 6, 1945. Eighty thousand were killed by the blast, and another fifty to sixty thousand died of injuries or radiation poisoning over the next several months. The dropping of the second bomb, on Nagasaki, August 9, did not require a separate presidential decision. Pursuant to a July 25 military directive authorized by Truman, additional bombs were to be "delivered on [specified] targets as soon as made ready by the [Manhattan] project staff." Therefore, when the second bomb was ready, it was used. A total of seventy thousand died at Nagasaki. In a radio speech that evening, President Truman explained: "I realize the tragic significance of the atomic bomb. . . . But we knew that our enemies were on the search for it. . . . We won the race of discovery against the Germans. . . . We have used it against those who attacked us without warning at Pearl Harbor, against those who have starved and beaten and executed American prisoners of war, against those who have abandoned all pretense of obeying international laws of warfare. We have used it to shorten the agony of war, in order to save the lives of thousands and thousands of young Americans. . . . We shall continue to use it until we completely destroy Japan's power to make war. Only a Japanese surrender will stop us."

On August 10, Truman received a message from the Japanese government, declaring that it would accept unconditional surrender as stated in the Allies' Potsdam Declaration, but with the understanding that the emperor would remain on the throne. This, therefore, was "unconditional surrender" on one condition, and it forced on Truman the need for a second momentous decision.

Some advisers argued for flat rejection of the surrender. There was a third atomic bomb ready now, and it could be used to pressure the Japanese further. Truman responded by ordering that no more atomic bombs were to be dropped without his explicit directive. To Secretary of

Commerce Henry A. Wallace he said that he could not stand the thought of killing "all those kids," by which he meant, this time, *Japanese* kids.

Truman returned to the Potsdam Declaration, reread it, then made his decision. He recorded in his diary on August 10: "[The Japanese] wanted to make a condition precedent to the surrender. Our terms are 'unconditional.' They wanted to keep the Emperor. We told 'em we'd tell 'em how to keep him, but we'd make the terms." After securing the agreement of the other Allies, the official reply to the Japanese surrender was transmitted and included the statement that the emperor would remain but that he would be "subject to the Supreme Commander of the Allied Powers." And while he waited for the Japanese reply, Truman ordered conventional air raids against Japan to recommence on August 13. Japanese acceptance came on August 14.

—

DECISIONS INVOLVING THE HIGHEST POSSIBLE STAKES must always be elevated on a fulcrum of fact. That Truman's decision to use atomic weapons against Japan was based on fact does not mean it was cold and devoid of emotion. The collection and assessment of fact does not require abandonment of feeling. Truman, clearly, was moved by a strongly emotional desire to end the war and, ultimately, to save lives. This emotion overshadowed his powerful sympathy for the Japanese women and children he knew would perish in an atomic attack. What the collection and assessment of facts does both require and enable is the abandonment of taboos and sacred cows. It requires opening the mind. It puts all options on the table. Once the alternatives are clearly arrayed before the decision maker, the act of deciding can appear virtually inevitable, regardless of the stakes involved.

With sufficient preparation, the most momentous decisions become remarkably simple—even those on which the future existence of humanity itself depends. This is a curiously disturbing thought. Certainly, it disturbed the many people who, in later years, asked Truman to talk about his "most difficult" decision, only to be told that the decision to use atomic weapons had not been difficult at all. Most of us need to believe that high-stakes decisions, turning-point decisions, *must* be agonizing, the degree of pain somehow indicating the degree of rightness of the decision. This belief makes it especially hard for many of us to face making high-stakes decisions. After all, who wants to inflict pain on oneself? Truman's genius as a decision maker was his ability to see that self-torment was not a necessary adjunct even to decisions with the very highest of stakes and the greatest of consequences. To be sure, the hard work of preparation, study, and analysis was called for, but he believed that anguish was neither essential nor helpful.

John F. Kennedy and the Cuban Missile Crisis (1962)

THE DECISION THAT SAVED THE WORLD

Many, perhaps most, Americans view the thousand days of the Kennedy presidency as a time of courage and idealism, a time when greatness was not an abstraction but a matter of national policy. Yet the fact is that Kennedy entered the White House by one of the narrowest electoral margins in American history, he faced a hostile Congress, and he began his administration with the tragic humiliation of a bungled attempt to invade Cuba at the Bay of Pigs on April 17, 1961. This unmitigated military and diplomatic disaster was greeted by Soviet Premier Nikita Khrushchev as a sign of the new administration's weakness, and he rushed in to exploit this perceived flaw by covertly sending nuclear-armed missiles to Cuba along with the technical and military personnel to install and operate them.

On October 14, 1962, a U.S. U-2 spy plane photographed Soviet SS-4 missiles being readied on the island, along with missile bases under construction. At breakfast on the sixteenth, President Kennedy was presented with the photographs, and he immediately convened his closest advisers, the Executive Committee (or ExComm), to consider the nation's options, faced as it was with nuclear weapons parked some ninety miles off the Florida coast. Kennedy directed ExComm to evaluate the situation and formulate advice as quickly as possible, but he was determined not to make the U-2 intelligence public until he had decided on a definitive course of action. As a leader who had already badly stumbled in Cuba, he could not afford to be seen as anything other than absolutely confident and decisive. Accordingly, despite the increasing level of anxiety of those around him, JFK followed his planned schedule of routine trips and meetings.

On the evening of October 18, he met with ExComm and other advisers. Dean Acheson, former secretary of state under President Truman, strongly advised an air strike to knock out the missiles before they became operational. To delay, he argued, would be to invite the possibility of a nuclear launch against the United States. This would, of course, trigger a nuclear response by the United States, which, in turn, would provoke a full-scale nuclear response from the Soviet Union. The result? World War III and, quite probably, the annihilation of civilization itself.

Another adviser, former secretary of defense Robert Lovett, suggested a naval blockade to intercept and turn back Cuba-bound Soviet ships carrying missiles and any other offensive materiel. JFK's national security adviser, McGeorge Bundy, counseled a wait-and-see attitude. If an air strike might provoke (or prevent) World War III, a blockade might prompt the Soviets to make a move against West Berlin—that democratic, Western-allied enclave surrounded by Soviet-controlled East Germany. Bundy advised waiting to see if the installation of the Cuban missiles was part of a general Soviet aggression, which would include action against West Berlin.

By the conclusion of the October 18 meeting, Kennedy tentatively announced his intention to set up a limited naval blockade, and, on the 19th, he met with Secretary of Defense Robert McNamara and members of the Joint Chiefs of Staff. General Maxwell Taylor, chairman of the

Joint Chiefs, reported that, initially, the chiefs concluded that air strikes combined with a blockade constituted the only effective response. But, on further discussion, they decided that they could not guarantee that air strikes would knock out all the missiles and they believed that the strikes would almost certainly provoke the Soviets to launch whatever missiles survived them. Furthermore, Taylor explained, air strikes might have an adverse effect on America's military alliances. Kennedy agreed, pointing out that an air strike would give the Soviets "a clear line" to take Berlin and that U.S. allies would see the United States as a pack of "trigger-happy Americans" who lost Berlin because they could not endure the situation in Cuba. Daring to think beyond the immediate threat of missiles off the American coast, Kennedy argued that Cuba was some six thousand miles from Europe and, therefore, America's European allies "don't give a damn about it." Worse—he reasoned—if the Soviets, provoked by an air strike on Cuba, moved against Berlin, the United States would be left with "only one alternative, which is to fire nuclear weapons—which is a hell of an alternative—to begin a nuclear exchange." Whatever else a crisis does, it tends to cause acute nearsightedness. Everyone focuses on what is closest at hand, while more distant threats and consequences become a soft blur. Kennedy, however, remained remarkably sharp-eyed.

At this juncture, President Kennedy's brother, Attorney General Robert F. Kennedy, had the extraordinary courage to make a terrible observation: "I don't think we have any satisfactory alternatives." If the problem were confined to Cuba, the decision to act aggressively would be relatively easy. But the problem was Cuba *and* Berlin. However, RFK continued, "if we do nothing, we will have problems in Berlin anyway. So, we have to do something."

General Curtis LeMay—the U.S. Air Force chief of staff who, as commanding general of the 20th Air Force in World War II had been responsible for dropping atomic bombs on Hiroshima and Nagasaki— seized on the younger Kennedy's observation. He argued that a blockade and political talks in the absence of air strikes and a ground invasion of Cuba would not avert World War III, but, on the contrary, would provoke it. Failure to act with maximum aggression in Cuba would invite the Soviets to take West Berlin, an act, as the president had just declared, that would touch off a nuclear war. Then LeMay invoked the historical precedent that, in one way or another, was on the minds of everyone present. A blockade without an air strike and invasion, he said, was "almost as bad as the appeasement at Munich." By this, LeMay was recalling the decision of British Prime Minister Neville Chamberlain in 1938 to "appease" Adolf Hitler with the Munich Pact, by which Britain and France effectively gave Nazi Germany a part of Czechoslovakia in return for Hitler's word that he would seek no further territory. Not only did the appeasement policy fail to prevent World War II; by encouraging Hitler's aggression, it actually served to make the war inevitable. Even more immediately to the point, everyone listening to LeMay knew that Kennedy's father, Joseph P. Kennedy Sr., was the U.S. ambassador to Britain in 1938 and had been an enthusiastic supporter of appeasement. "I just don't see any other solution," LeMay concluded, "except direct military intervention right now." Other members of the Joint Chiefs of Staff joined LeMay in his insistence on a full-scale air strike and invasion, arguing that to do less would bring nuclear blackmail.

No set of decisions in history were of greater consequence than those John F. Kennedy was about to make. The stakes were nothing less than the survival of America, of democracy, and of human civilization. The alternatives, as Robert Kennedy had observed, were limited at best and, quite possibly, all bad. The world had seen situations like this before, most recently in the summer of 1914, when all Europe mindlessly allowed events unfolding from the assassination of an Austrian archduke in the obscure Balkan city of Sarajevo to pull the entire continent and much of the rest of the planet into World War I. President Kennedy, who at this time had just finished reading Pulitzer Prize–winning historian Barbara Tuchman's great history of the beginning of that war, *The Guns of August*, was determined not to make the mistakes of 1914, not to surrender to the rushing tide of events his intelligence, judgment, will, and authority. Despite the pressures of the recent past—the fiasco of the

Bay of Pigs and his own father's involvement in the fatal pre–World War II policy of appeasement—despite the urging of military advisers and Senate leaders, despite a keen awareness that each passing minute increased the danger from the Cuban missiles poised against America, President Kennedy made his first and most important decision of the Cuban Missile Crisis: He would not allow fear to usurp judgment and to close what few doors remained open. Instead, he would continue to make the decisions that enabled other decisions and, in this way, ensure that the problems, grave as they were, would remain capable of some human solution. He knew this: It is a bad thing to make the wrong decision, but it is far worse to decide on a course that gives up to unfolding events the power of decision itself. The most consequential decision JFK made during those bleak October days was to act in ways that made it possible to keep making decisions. With the ability to continue maneuvering came the hope of a successful resolution to the ultimate crisis of life and death.

Still following his public schedule, President Kennedy made a trip to Chicago on October 20, but cut it short (pleading a cold) to return to Washington after his brother told him that more missiles had been discovered. In an ExComm meeting on Sunday, October 21, JFK decided that the air strike option simply risked too much, especially because it would kill or injure anywhere from ten to twenty thousand Soviets and Cubans. That would alienate U.S. allies and almost certainly bring a massive retaliation, which, in turn, would require a massive U.S. response. On October 22, however, when Kennedy took the Cuban situation to a meeting of Senate leaders, their nearly unanimous response was to mount an air strike. It was at this point that President Kennedy decided to take the case to the American people in a dramatic television broadcast carried on all the networks.

Looking straight into the camera, the president greeted his "fellow citizens" on the evening of the twenty-second. "This Government, as promised, has maintained the closest surveillance of the Soviet military buildup on the island of Cuba. Within the past week, unmistakable evidence has established the fact that a series of offensive missile sites is now in preparation on that imprisoned island. The purpose of these bases can be none other than to provide a nuclear strike capability against the Western Hemisphere." He went on to explain that he was creating a naval "quarantine"—the word had been carefully chosen, since a "blockade," under international law, is an act of war: "All ships of any kind bound for Cuba from whatever nation or port will, if found to contain cargoes of offensive weapons, be turned back. This quarantine will be extended, if needed, to other types of cargo and carriers. We are not at this time, however, denying the necessities of life as the Soviets attempted to do in their Berlin blockade of 1948." President Kennedy also announced that he had called a meeting of the Organization of American States, so that the actions of the United States would have the support of the entire hemisphere. At the OAS meeting the following day, every member of the organization voted support for the quarantine. In the meantime, President Kennedy set U.S. military alert status to DEFCON 3, two levels above normal status and two levels below war. In Cuba, Fidel Castro mobilized all of his military forces.

While the naval quarantine was a step far short of air strikes and invasion, it was hardly passive or benign. On Tuesday, October 23, when all the warships of the quarantine were in place, new aerial reconnaissance photography revealed that some Soviet missiles were now poised for launch. In this hair-trigger situation, what would happen when the first Soviet ship reached the quarantine line? Would it stop? Would it permit inspection? Would there be an armed exchange? Would the sinking of a Soviet ship trigger a missile launch in Cuba? Or a move against Berlin?

Beginning on the twenty-third, the pace of events accelerated dizzyingly. To Secretary of Defense McNamara, Kennedy stated his opinion that Moscow would order ships carrying offensive weapons to turn around before they reached the quarantine line. He did not think, he said, that Khrushchev wanted a showdown. Nevertheless, Kennedy now approved a plan to destroy any Cuban surface-to-air missile (SAM) site that shot down a U.S. reconnaissance flight. (But when a U-2 aircraft was shot down on October 27, he declined to issue the order for an attack.)

As for the first quarantine line confrontation, that seemed to be imminent on Wednesday, October 24, when several Soviet freighters approached at high speed. As U.S. captains and crews anxiously watched, however, the Soviet ships stopped, having received orders from Moscow to hold their positions. In the meantime, throughout the United States, civil-defense authorities began conducting air-raid drills. In many schools across the nation, children practiced responding to alerts by "ducking and covering" under their desks. Within ExComm, the president and his advisers started to discuss plans for invading Cuba, Kennedy concluding that an invasion would surely trigger at least some missile launches.

On October 25, Thursday, Adlai Stevenson, U.S. ambassador to the United Nations, publicly confronted the Soviets with the evidence of the missiles. The Soviet U.N. ambassador seemed stunned at the extent and depth of U.S. intelligence, and it even appeared possible that his own government had been keeping him largely in the dark. In any case, he declined to respond to the evidence, and, at this point, with the whole world watching, President Kennedy ordered the alert level raised to DEFCON 2—a state of readiness just short of war, with missiles locked on Soviet targets. It was the highest level of alert in post–World War II American history.

At last, on Friday, October 26, the White House received a long telex from Khrushchev offering to remove the missiles if President Kennedy would make a public pledge not to invade Cuba. Simultane-ously, however, U.S. surveillance revealed that the pace of construction at the missile sites was increasing. And, even as Robert Kennedy met secretly with Soviet ambassador to the United States Anatoly Dobrynin to discuss the removal of U.S. missiles in Turkey, near the Soviet Union, Fidel Castro urged the Soviets to commit to a nuclear first strike against the United States if U.S. forces invaded his island. To make matters worse, on this day—which had begun so hopefully with the Khrushchev telex—the United States conducted a high-altitude nuclear test detonation in the Pacific, as previously scheduled. No one had thought to cancel the test, and Kennedy feared that the Soviets would take it as a blatant provocation.

On the twenty-seventh, the crisis was compounded by an inadvertent U-2 encroachment into Soviet air space and by the shoot-down of a U-2 over Cuba. Worse yet, a *second* bomb test, this one of a thermonuclear device, was conducted in the Pacific. ExComm then received a second letter from the Soviet premier, which was far less conciliatory than the first. Kennedy cut through ExComm's tortured discussion of the new letter by deciding simply to ignore it and to respond only to the first telex. He agreed to make a pledge to refrain from invading Cuba, and, through a private and unofficial diplomatic back channel, agreed to remove the missiles stationed in Turkey.

———

ON OCTOBER 28, KHRUSHCHEV RESPONDED by making a Radio Moscow broadcast in which he announced that the Soviet missiles in Cuba were being dismantled. The Cuban Missile Crisis was at an end, although U.S. Navy ships remained on station until November 21, when negotiations were finally concluded for the withdrawal of Soviet bombers from Cuba.

PART TWO

The Decision
to Venture

Columbus and the New World (1492)

THE DECISION TO JOURNEY
TO THE EDGE AND BEYOND

Not long ago, Christopher Columbus was universally celebrated in classrooms across the United States as the heroic discoverer of America. By the 1960s and the height of the Native American civil rights movement, Columbus was also increasingly condemned as an advocate of slavery for Native Americans and the initiator of some four hundred years of almost continual warfare between whites and Indians in the New World. The first white-Indian war broke out in 1493 between the Taino Indians, of the island Columbus called Hispaniola, and the garrison he left there when he returned to Spain. To add insult to injury, so far as Columbus's reputation was concerned, it became increasingly clear to scholars that Columbus was by no means the first European to have sailed to the New World. The Viking captain Leif Ericson discovered a place he called Vinland, part of Newfoundland, about A.D. 1000, years after another Norseman, Bjarni Herjólfsson, sighted—but did not land on—Newfoundland in 986. In 1007, Ericson's brother Thorfinn Karlsefni settled on Vinland and fathered with his wife, Gudrid, the very first Euro-American child, a son named Snorro.

So why remember, let alone celebrate, Columbus?

Those who still venerate him often complain that his reputation was tarnished by politically correct "revisionist" historians. In fact, Columbus's recommendation that Spain enslave the people he mis-named Indians (because he thought he had sailed to Japan, which he believed was a part of India) shocked even his patrons, Queen Isabella and King Ferdinand of Spain, who rejected the idea. A contemporary of Columbus, the Franciscan friar Bartolomé de Las Casas, was so appalled by the cruelty of Columbus and other early Spanish explorers that he wrote eyewitness books to protest it.

There is no denying that Columbus saw himself as a conqueror and behaved in ways that even some prominent people of his own time found unacceptable. There is also no denying that he was not the first Euro-pean who saw and even trod the earth of the New World. But it also cannot be denied that, however flawed the character of Columbus may have been, his decision to embark on a voyage into the unknown was per-sonally extraordinary and, historically, of the greatest significance. True, he was not the first to go, but his voyage was the first that mattered. Whereas nothing came of the Viking explorations, which had no impact on Europe and little impact on the New World, Columbus's four voyages initiated an age of exploration and settlement, creating—for better or worse—a new civilization in the Western Hemisphere.

All of this began with the decision of one man to weigh anchor in a familiar port and sail from it into the unknown.

To Isabella and Ferdinand of Spain, he was Cristóbal Colón, and to history, he became Christopher Columbus, but he was born Cristoforo Colombo in Genoa, in 1451, the son of a weaver. Young Colombo did not learn to read and write until he reached adulthood. As a youth, probably to escape apprenticeship in his father's trade, he took to the sea rather than to books and later claimed to have sailed as far as Iceland. If this is true, he may well have heard there the stories of Leif the Lucky and a place called Vinland, so that the seeds of 1492 may well have been planted in so unlikely a place as Iceland sometime before 1479 (the year he returned to Genoa). From Genoa, Columbus sailed to Portugal, where he married Felipa Perestrello e Moniz, the daughter of a Portuguese nobleman. The following year, his young wife died while giving birth to their son, Diego, but by this time Columbus had already sailed far from his family—at least in a voyage of his own imagination. He had, by this time, taught himself to read, and he sought out shadowy manuscripts recording westward sea voyages. Schoolbook mythology talks about how Columbus decided that the world was round and set out to prove that by his first voyage. The fact is that by the end of the fifteenth century only the most benighted of people still thought the world was flat. The notion of a spherical world had been around for at least seventeen hundred years, certainly since the Greek mathematician Eratosthenes of Cyrene (ca. 276–195 B.C.) actually calculated the earth's circumference with surprising accuracy. But Columbus probably knew nothing of Eratosthenes and instead relied on his reading of Marco Polo and the work of the Greek astronomer Ptolemy (ca. 100–170) to estimate global distances. Marco Polo wrote that Japan was fifteen hundred miles east of China, and Ptolemy grossly underestimated the circumference of the earth even as he overestimated the size of the Eurasian land mass. Columbus was confirmed in these errors by reading the miscalculations of the Florentine cosmographer Paolo dal Pozzo Toscanelli, and he also underscored in his copy of Pierre d'Ailly's *Imago Mundi* this extraordinary statement: "Between the end of Spain and the beginning of India is no great width" and the sea joining them "is navigable in few days with a fair wind."

Now, the conviction that something can be done is not necessarily sufficient reason to decide to do the thing. There were other, positive pressures on Columbus. Among the misinformation disseminated to generations of American schoolchildren concerning Columbus, there is one indisputable truth. His principal objective in contemplating a global voyage was not to find a New World, but to pioneer a shorter route to Asia—a continent rich in gold and, even more valuable during an age without refrigeration or vacuum packaging, spices, essential to preserving foods and making even spoiled foods palatable. If the world was a globe, then it was possible to sail west to get to the East. Why do such a thing? Because in Columbus's day, getting to Asia required an epic overland caravan, and the sea offered a much easier, cheaper, and faster route. The nation that controlled this route would become richer than any other nation. And the man who gave that nation this route would just as surely become richer than any other man.

That was a powerful incentive to decision. But there was even more. Medieval Europe was suffering from exhaustion. In a predominantly feudal world, economic opportunity was severely limited. Even among the privileged classes, primogeniture held sway, meaning that all of a father's possessions—riches, lands, and titles—went to his firstborn son, leaving everyone else in the lurch. With Europe effectively used up, there was a compelling cultural and economic imperative to set sail. Columbus's idea was to get the gold and corner the spice trade in Asia, but also to lay claim to whatever hitherto undiscovered realms he might find along the way. If he could find Europe a New World while en route to another part of the Old, so much the better.

If medieval society was constrained and limited, so was the medieval mind—at least from the perspective of how most of us think these days. Columbus's conviction that his sources had correctly calculated the distances between Europe and Asia was, doubtless, partly the result of his own intellectual willfulness. He *wanted* them to be correct. But his conviction was also a product of medieval habits of reasoning. Medieval logic was resolutely deductive. One did not reason from what one observed, but, rather, observed whatever one had already reasoned. Most of the accepted authorities had concluded that Asia did not lie very far from Europe; therefore, sailing to Asia could only provide empirical proof of what deduction had already revealed as true.

Thus it was in 1484 that Columbus confidently approached King John II of Portugal with a proposal that he fund a voyage to Japan. John turned Columbus down, not because he wasn't interested in a shortcut to Japan, but because he was actually a more original thinker than

Columbus. He refused to accept the calculations even of the venerable Ptolemy, believing them to be incorrect by at least a factor of two—and that, John concluded, represented a distance beyond the range of the ships of the day. (Besides, John was already financing the efforts of his own seafarers to navigate a more conventional eastward route to Asia by rounding the coast of Africa.)

Having made his decision to sail, Columbus refused to surrender. He next approached Don Enrique de Guzmán, Duke of Medina Sidonia, only to be rebuffed again. After this disappointment, he appealed to the Spanish noble Don Luis de la Cerda, Count of Medina Celi, sufficiently intriguing him that he arranged for Columbus an audience, on or about May 1, 1486, with Queen Isabella I of Castile.

Columbus well understood that realizing his decision meant moving the Spanish monarchs to a decision of their own. He believed he had a compelling case, but, at some point, he must have added to it one more element, which he hoped would tip the balance in his favor. Spain was locked in a struggle for the very soul of the kingdom. Isabella and Ferdinand were prosecuting a long religious war against the Moors, the Muslims who had long held most of Spain, and they were about to declare another kind of religious war against another people who shared the Iberian peninsula with Catholic Spaniards: the Jews. Columbus must have discussed with Isabella how Spain's reaching out to Asia and whatever other places lay along the way would be an opportunity to extend the influence of the Holy Roman Catholic Church as well.

Thus to the cultural and material motives for sailing, Columbus added a spiritual motive. Was it a coincidence that the final authorization for the first voyage of Columbus was issued on April 29, 1492, the very day a royal Edict of Expulsion—the mass deportation of Spain's unconverted Jews—was publicly announced in most of the larger Spanish cities? And was it another coincidence that the scheduled date of Columbus's departure, August 2, 1492, was also the deadline Ferdinand and Isabella had set for the sailing of all of Spain's unconverted Jews? (Indeed, on August 2, so many Jews sailed—three hundred thousand—

that Columbus had to set sail from the dusty obscurity of little Palos de la Frontera, a maritime inlet of the Gulf of Cadiz, rather than from a larger port, and, even at that, he was compelled to delay his departure until 8:00 A.M. on August 3.) And was it a final coincidence that the voyage had been financed in part by anticipated revenues from the property the exiled Jews were forced to forfeit?

But the sailing was a long way off from Columbus's first meeting with the Spanish queen. For a half-dozen years, with his son Diego in tow, the mariner was obliged to haunt the Spanish court while the monarchs pondered and vacillated. He did not idle during this time, but worked diligently to make a host of influential friends, including a prominent and prosperous courtier named Luis de Santangel. After Isabella and Ferdinand finally rejected Columbus's proposition early in 1492, Luis intervened, put up some of his own money, and succeeded in persuading the royal couple to sponsor the voyage after all.

THE DECISION TO JOURNEY TO THE EDGE AND BEYOND, by definition a decision to take the most extreme action imaginable, was made on the basis of elements so compelling as to seem, in retrospect, to have made the decision virtually inevitable. There was Columbus's medieval confidence in venerated geographical authorities; there was, quite possibly, the way his imagination had been fired by tales heard in Iceland; there was the prospect of unparalleled personal wealth and power; there was the pressure of life in a spent society; and there was the appeal to a sense of religious mission and obligation. But retrospect is of no value at the time a decision is being made. Compelling as the known elements driving the decision were, Columbus also possessed a seasoned mariner's knowledge of the dangers that faced him and, doubtless, he could imagine even more dangers unknown. Perhaps the final element in his decision is one that cannot be enumerated or described. It is whatever has always driven certain people at certain times to dare.

Galileo and the Universe (1633)

THE DECISION TO RETHINK REALITY

The basic story is familiar even to people with only the most casual interest in science. Galileo Galilei published a book supporting the revolutionary idea proposed by the Polish astronomer Copernicus that the Sun, not the Earth, was the center of the planetary system—the known universe—and that the Earth orbited the stationary Sun. This view ran contrary to the Bible and to the teachings of the Roman Catholic Church. Galileo therefore ran afoul of the Inquisition and, under threat of imprisonment, torture, or even worse, recanted his support for Copernicus and "confessed" that the Earth was in fact stationary and at the center of all creation. The familiar story concludes with the ostensibly penitent Galileo rising from his knees and muttering under his breath, "Eppur si muove"—*But still it moves.*

There is some truth in this popular tale. Galileo did publish a *Dialogue* in which he advanced the theory of the heliocentric (Sun-centered) "universe" as opposed to the geocentric (Earth-centered) one accepted by the Church. For this, he was summoned to Rome for a trial by the Inquisition. While he was not threatened with any specific punishment, Galileo was well aware that in 1600 Giordano Bruno had been burned at the stake for insisting (among other heresies) that the Earth moved around the Sun. However, Galileo was also a devout Catholic—his passion for science never displaced his religious faith—and his recantation may have grown as much from his sincere faith as from fear of the Inquisition. As to his supposed recantation of his recantation—*But still it moves*—it is highly unlikely that Galileo, advanced in years at age seventy and chronically ailing, would have risked affronting the Inquisition in this most insolent manner.

Even with these additions and explanations, the story is still very incomplete. Galileo's decision to champion a radical view of reality was both more compelling and more complex, involving as much spiritual and theological struggle as it did intellectual processing. The decision may have been rooted in a legacy from his father. Vincenzio Galilei was a musician, who wrote a book so revolutionary that his own former music teacher succeeded in blocking its publication for three years. Finally published in 1581, *Dialogue of Ancient and Modern Music* argued against tuning instruments in accordance with the strict mathematical principles held at the time as well-nigh sacred, and instead advocated achieving the greatest beauty of sound by tuning a given instrument to suit its own physical nature.

Vincenzio was more interested in the actual sound than he was in mathematics, but, beyond aesthetics, the significance of his proposition must have had a profound effect on Galileo. Whereas tuning in accordance with mathematically determined intervals required nothing more than obedience to received authority, tuning to achieve the greatest degree of actual beauty rejected authority in favor of experiment. As Vincenzio wrote, "It appears to me that they who in proof of any assertion rely simply on the weight of authority, without adducing any argument in support of it, act very absurdly. I, on the contrary, wish to be allowed freely to question and freely to answer you without any sort of adulation, as well becomes those who are in search of truth."

Ask most people what Galileo was, and they will answer that he was an astronomer. But those more familiar with the history of science will point out that his greatest contribution to science was not his body of astronomical observations, epochal as these were, but, rather, the foundational procedure of science itself: the experimental method. Like his father before him, Galileo refused to rely on the precedent of authority in the determination of truth. Whereas the typical medieval thinker learned all he could from the accepted canon of great books, then attempted to apply these teachings to the world, Galileo regarded the world, not books, as his chief text. Rather than apply set truths *to* that world, he sought ways to extract truths *from* the world. His method was inductive—experiential and experimental—rather than deductive. In this, he was among the first of the great thinkers of the Renaissance, a product of the spirit of an age that was leaving behind as outmoded a host of medieval patterns of thought.

Galileo was driven by a positive passion for experimentation, a need to reevaluate and revise the perception and interpretation of reality based on what he himself saw and he himself thought. Precise observation was paramount. Around 1585, he invented a hydrostatic balance for weighing very small quantities with unheard of accuracy. He also questioned the most basic of assumptions. Aristotle stated that the velocity with which an object fell was proportional to its mass. That is, a ten-pound object would fall ten times faster than a one-pound object. Even if Aristotle had not been the one ancient philosopher medieval thinkers revered above all others, accepting his body of thought as absolute truth and beyond any questioning, the proposition had the powerful appeal of common sense.

But Galileo thought it absurd.

He invited anyone to imagine dropping a one-pound and a ten-pound ball simultaneously from a tower: "Try, if you can, to picture in your mind the large ball striking the ground while the small one is less than a yard from the top of the tower." And if that picture weren't sufficiently absurd, he suggested imagining "them joining together while falling. Why should they double their speed as Aristotle claimed?" Not content with a mere thought experiment, however, Galileo, around 1589, climbed to the top of Pisa's famed eight-story leaning tower, dropped two cannonballs, and observed that they hit the ground almost simultaneously—interfered with only by air resistance.

Nothing escaped his challenge. Take ice. Aristotle—and everyone else—held that ice was obviously heavier than water, but nevertheless floated because the flat-bottomed shape of ice could not pierce the fluid surface of liquid water. Galileo pointed out that if you submerged a piece of ice then let it go, it bobbed up to the surface—and had no trouble piercing the fluid surface from the underside of that surface. Galileo argued that ice floated because it was less dense than water and therefore not heavier, but lighter. This insight prompted him to write an entire book, *Discourse on Bodies That Stay Atop Water or Move Within It.*

The same passion for experiment, the conviction that observation and experience were superior to any authority when it came to determining the truth, drove Galileo to enthusiastically embrace the latest invention from Holland, the telescope, and to make improvements on it that allowed him to study the heavens. He saw that the Moon resembled the Earth, with mountains, valleys, craters, and myriad imperfections. To Aristotelians as well as theologians, who regarded the heavenly bodies as perfect, these observations were shocking and ultimately unacceptable. Even worse were Galileo's observations of sunspots—for the Sun was universally regarded as an even more perfect body than the Moon.

The sunspots were especially intriguing to Galileo, because, as close observation revealed to him, they moved. Galileo drew two conclusions from what he saw. First, he decided that the individual sunspots were not moving at all. Rather, they moved not independently, but with the surface of the Sun, a conclusion that led him to further conclude that the Sun rotated. This ran contrary to Aristotle as well as the Church. Second, noting that the sunspots appeared over time to rise and fall with respect to the Sun's equator, he came to an even more important conclusion: The course of the sunspots was actually steady, but only appeared to move up and down because of the annual revolution of the Earth around the Sun. Since both the Earth and the Sun were tilted on their axes, Galileo argued, the sunspots, from our perspective, *appear* to rise and fall.

Now, Galileo was not the first to conclude that the Earth was not the center of the known universe, and he was not the first to suggest that the Earth orbited the Sun. The ancient Greeks Pythagoras, Plato, Aristarchus, and Archimedes all believed this, and, in the century before Galileo, Copernicus had proposed a complex mathematical proof of the heliocentric system. Even before he noted the sunspot phenomena, Galileo was being won over to the Copernican point of view because it accounted for the motion of the planets more simply and more comprehensively than the geocentric concept worked out by the second-century Greek astronomer Ptolemy. As Galileo saw it, Copernicus did a more adequate job than Ptolemy of explaining what one actually observed in tracking the motions of the planets. Galileo's own sunspot observations lent further experimental, observational support to Copernicus, as did another seemingly unrelated observation. Galileo decided (incorrectly, as it turns out) that the rhythmic motion of the tides was the flux and reflux of the sea that resulted from the Earth's two motions—that around its own axis and that around the Sun.

Galileo was by no means a lonely maverick genius. He was a prominent professor, an internationally renowned "natural philosopher" and mathematician, a sought-after tutor for the sons of the wealthy, and a prosperous maker of telescopes and navigational instruments. He was not wealthy, but he was solidly well off. Moreover, he was a sincere Catholic, among whose friends were highly placed clergymen, including Maffeo Cardinal Barberini, who became Pope Urban VIII. Certainly, Galileo had no whimsical desire to espouse a cosmic view that ran counter to the teachings of the Church, but he found it impossible, over the years, to resist the mounting weight of evidence that converted him to the Copernican view. Mathematics, planetary observation, the phenomena of sunspots, the very tides of the ocean—all spoke to him of an Earth in orbit around the Sun.

The decision, then, was not between Aristotle/Ptolemy on the one hand and Copernicus on the other, but between publishing his evidence in support of Copernicus—and risking death—or keeping silent. It was a long and tortured decision, which can be traced from a private letter of 1613 to his decision in 1632 to publish his findings to the world.

In 1613, Galileo wrote to one of his students, Benedetto Castelli, addressing the problem of reconciling Copernican theory with the Bible. Enemies of Galileo got hold of the letter, hastily transcribed it, and sent faulty copies to officials of the Inquisition. Galileo defended himself and, in the process, composed an expanded version of the Castelli document in a letter addressed to the Grand Duchess Christina, arguing that it was possible for scientists to make scientific observations and hypotheses without invading the territory of theologians. In other words, faced with a profound crisis of intellectual revelation versus spiritual revelation,

Galileo was trying to figure out a way by which his work could coexist with the teachings of the Church. It was a forlorn hope, because the Church was in the first throes of the Counter-Reformation and was in no mood to accept any unorthodoxy. In 1616, the Inquisition issued an edict condemning Copernican astronomy as "false and contrary to Holy Scripture." At about this same time, Church officials admonished Galileo to refrain from holding, teaching, or defending Copernican theory.

A good Catholic, a sincere believer, Galileo tried to do just this. But, beginning in 1618, his participation in a controversy about the nature of comets evolved into a book titled *Il saggiatore* (The Assayer), published in 1623. An exposition of the scientific method, it called the universe a "grand book . . . which stands continually open to our gaze," but it was a book intelligible only to those willing to learn the language of mathematics. *Il saggiatore* greatly impressed Maffeo Cardinal Barberini, who, virtually at the moment of its publication, was named Pope Urban VIII. Papal approval of the book elevated Galileo to a new height of prestige and emboldened him to share with Urban his theory of the tides as proof of the motions of the Earth. Surprisingly, Urban gave Galileo permission to write a new and more comprehensive book about theories of the universe, including the Copernican theory, provided that he treat it exclusively as a hypothesis.

At last, it seemed, Galileo had been given a way out of the dilemma posed by his own faith on the one hand and what his intellect made of the weight of observational and mathematical evidence on the other. He decided that it was time to go public with his theories. Accordingly, he labored slowly, even fitfully, on a work he called *Dialogo sopra i due massimi sistemi del mondo, Tolemaico e Copernicano* (*Dialogue Concerning the Two Chief World Systems, Ptolemaic and Copernican*). At last completing it in 1630, Galileo took conscientious care to send it to the censor of the Inquisition; however, a severe outbreak of plague disrupted communications between Florence and Rome, and Galileo requested that the censoring be done in Florence. This was agreed to, and the Roman censor forwarded his criticisms and reservations to Florence. In the meantime, Galileo wrote a preface to the book, which emphasized the hypothetical nature of what he had written. This was sufficient to slip the volume past the Florentine censors. The *Dialogo* was, accordingly, published in Florence in 1632, with the permission of the Inquisition.

It was a witty book, written not in learned Latin, but in colloquial Italian and, therefore, accessible to the masses—or at least to the literate portion thereof. The form of the work is a three-way dialogue among Salviati (a thinly disguised Galileo), Sagredo (an open-minded layman), and Simplicio (a committed Aristotelian). Its substance is a summoning of all the arguments for the Copernican theory versus those in favor of the Aristotelian geocentric cosmology. Not surprisingly, and despite Galileo's claim that everything presented was merely hypothetical, the Copernican view wins hands down, and Simplicio is made to appear, in a word, simple. Worst of all, Galileo gives the final word to Simplicio, who declares that the omnipotent God could have fashioned the universe in any way he wanted, regardless of physical laws, and still make it appear to us as it does. This was the very position articulated by Urban VIII, and when he read it, he felt that Galileo had taken advantage of his leniency and liberality to mock and betray him. For that reason, he authorized the Inquisition to examine the book and summon Galileo to a trial in Rome. The outcome of this was Galileo's famous recantation.

OF COURSE, THE GENIE WAS ALREADY OUT OF THE BOTTLE. The book had been published and was widely distributed. The evidence, which had moved Galileo to proceed with apparent caution yet, undeniably and inevitably, in headlong opposition to both Aristotle and the Church, remained no less compelling. Because of Galileo, and despite his recantation, the Earth could not and would not remain motionless at the center of the universe.

As for Galileo himself, he was sentenced by the Inquisition to a benign and comfortable house arrest, which was quite agreeable to an old and increasingly infirm man. He settled ultimately in a pleasant villa near Arceti, in the Florentine hills, where he completed *Discorsi e dimostrazioni matematiche intorno a due nuove scienze attenenti alla meccanica* (*Dialogues Concerning Two New Sciences*), which he had begun earlier and which presented in full his work on motion, including the law of falling bodies. Galileo died on January 8, 1642, at the age of seventy-eight.

Meriwether Lewis, Thomas Jefferson, and the American Wilderness (1803)

THE DECISION TO EXPLORE

Two million square miles of the unknown—the expanse between the Mississippi River and the Pacific Ocean. What to do with it? Thomas Jefferson and Meriwether Lewis decided to explore it.

The great expedition that set off from St. Louis, Missouri, on May 14, 1804, and returned on September 23, 1806, is known to history as the Lewis and Clark Expedition, but the most significant partners in the decision behind the endeavor were the nation's third president and his private secretary, Meriwether Lewis. How they reached this decision is, in part, a mystery, or, at least, beyond analysis. Asked why he decided to attempt to climb Mount Everest, mountaineer George Mallory replied famously, "Because it is there." To a significant degree, this could have been Jefferson and Lewis's answer with regard to their decision to explore the great West. In the sublime closing paragraphs of F. Scott Fitzgerald's *The Great Gatsby*, the novel's narrator Nick Carraway contemplates the dead Gatsby's empty Long Island mansion and the American dream it once embodied. Carraway has a vision of the "new world," a land that "had once pandered in whispers to the last and greatest of all human dreams; for a transitory enchanted moment man must have held his breath in the presence of this continent, compelled into an aesthetic contemplation he neither understood nor desired, face to face for the last time in history with something commensurate to his capacity for wonder." To Jefferson and Lewis, the vast unknown West must likewise have seemed commensurate to *their* capacity for wonder. The decision to venture into it—physically—was very nearly inevitable, a decision to act on the dictates of wondrous imagination. Jefferson and Lewis were kindred spirits, and their decision was mutual.

Anyone who has read much of anything about Thomas Jefferson knows him as a man of limitless curiosity, whose intellect and imagination ranged across law, politics, philosophy, music, literature, science, and nature. As a seven-year-old boy he listened, rapt, to Thomas Walker's account of his travels beyond the Cumberland Gap, to unknown lands in which Jefferson's father, as a member of the Loyal Land Company, had a speculative interest.

Almost immediately after the American Revolution, Jefferson tried to instigate several far-western explorations. In 1783, he interested George Rogers Clark, hero of the frontier theater of the Revolutionary War, in a project to explore the country from the Mississippi River to California. Jefferson hoped to preempt the British, who, he had heard, were contemplating just such an expedition. Clark was game, but the project came to nothing. In 1785, while Jefferson was serving in Paris as U.S. minister to France, he learned that Louis XVI was backing a far western expedition. Jefferson tried to raise an alarm in the United States, suggesting that the country's revolutionary ally was not above attempting to reestablish itself in America at the expense of the new nation. Again, nothing happened. The next year, Jefferson had a stimulating meeting with John Ledyard, a fellow American who had sailed with Britain's celebrated Captain Cook and, with him, had briefly explored America's Pacific Northwest. To Jefferson, Ledyard proposed traveling overland from Moscow through Siberia and thence across the Bering Strait. Disembarking in Alaska, he would walk across the American continent and, eventually, through the doors of the Capitol, where he would deliver his personal report on the great West. Jefferson, credulous and entranced, voiced his enthusiastic support, and Ledyard actually started out, venturing into Siberia only to be arrested by agents of Catherine the Great and deported to Poland.

Doubtless, Jefferson was genuinely concerned that England or France would explore and lay claim to the West before an American could get to it, but his enthusiasm for exploration seemed to have a deeper source. He wanted to explore the West to *discover* the West. He wanted to explore it because it was there.

In the meantime, however, George Washington's secretary of war, Henry Knox, motivated by the more concrete objectives of international politics, decided to send a secret military expedition to the far West in 1790, mainly to get a jump on explorers from other countries. He commissioned Lieutenant John Armstrong to lead a party, but Armstrong and his men never even made it across the Mississippi. Two years after this abortive sortie, Jefferson returned to the project, proposing that the American Philosophical Society, of which he was an esteemed member, underwrite a full-dress scientific expedition, and he secured the endorsement and financial backing of such luminaries as Robert Morris, Alexander Hamilton, and George Washington himself.

Among those who heard of the project was eighteen-year-old Meriwether Lewis. Like Jefferson, he had grown up near the frontier, in Albemarle County, Virginia—although he had also spent time in the even more remote Georgia frontier country. Neither Jefferson nor Lewis were products of the American wilderness, but their proximity to the frontier put them between the settled, civilized, learned world of the East and the truly new, unknown world of the West. Quite literally, their *place* between worlds impelled them to be explorers. They had the knowledge and other benefits of civilization on the one hand, and the lure of the wild unknown on the other. Jefferson knew the Lewises well and had been a friend of Meriwether's father. He admired the boy, who seemed to him both curious and courageous, always full of questions about the herbs, plants, and animals around him. In particular, Jefferson recognized in young Meriwether Lewis a need (as Jefferson put it) to "ramble." He loved more than anything to wander. And that fact struck Jefferson about Meriwether Lewis from the very beginning.

Hearing of the project of exploration, Lewis called on Jefferson and "warmly solicited me to obtain for him the execution of that object." Jefferson warned him that "the person engaged" to make this trek across the entire continent "should be attended by a single companion only, to avoid exciting alarm among the Indians." This prospect, however, "did not deter him."

In the end—he did not say why, but, doubtless, the teenager's youth counted most against him—Jefferson awarded the commission not to Meriwether Lewis but to the well-established French botanist André Michaux. Michaux got as far as Kentucky when Jefferson learned that the naturalist had an agenda of his own, a secret French mission to recruit an army of American volunteers to attack Spanish possessions west of the Mississippi. Jefferson compelled the French government to recall Michaux, and this expedition, too, came to nothing.

But Jefferson forgot neither the notion of exploration nor Meriwether Lewis. The young man volunteered for militia service to help quell the Whiskey Rebellion in 1794, and, discovering that he had a taste for the military life, joined the U.S. Army the next year, securing a commission as ensign. It was very much in character for Lewis, since the army at that time was a tiny band of fewer than thirty-five hundred officers and men, widely dispersed throughout the frontier as a kind of police force. Life on military outposts perched at the edge of the wilderness was solitary—each garrison consisting of well under a hundred men—and there was plenty of opportunity to "ramble," especially after Lewis became regimental paymaster, charged with delivering pay to outposts throughout the Ohio country: the frontier West. Yet there was also discipline in the army and an opportunity to acquire and practice the art of leadership. Lewis thrived, earning promotion to captain on December 5, 1800.

On February 23, 1801, a few days before his March 4 inauguration, Thomas Jefferson wrote to Meriwether Lewis, inviting him to become his personal secretary. His letter made it clear that he was to be no ordinary secretary. While there would be certain household duties, Lewis would also be expected to "contribute to the mass of information which it is interesting for the administration to acquire. Your knolege [sic] of the Western country . . . has rendered it desirable . . . that you should be engaged in that office." Lewis accepted enthusiastically, and the two began a remarkably close partnership.

Historians and biographers have pointed out that, at this point in his life, Jefferson was a widower with two grown and married daughters. Meriwether Lewis, whose father had died when he was a child, became something of a surrogate son to Jefferson, dining with the president and often talking late into the night with him. Given the range of Jefferson's mind and the breadth of his interests, these conversations must have been both fascinating and a magnificent education for Lewis. Almost certainly, they focused increasingly on geography, natural science, and Indian affairs, and it is likely that Jefferson even took self-conscious pains to impart to Lewis his own profound knowledge of such subjects as topography, biology, and botany. We cannot know for certain that Jefferson had appointed Lewis with the idea of the expedition firmly in mind. Perhaps that idea was in the back of his mind, and perhaps he was only barely conscious of it. But, despite the disappointment of one abortive attempt after another, Jefferson clearly never abandoned the idea.

His decision to proceed, when it finally came, seems to have come suddenly, though it was also the fruit of seeds planted during his own Albemarle County childhood. In 1801, *Voyages from Montreal, on the River St. Laurence, through the Continent of North America, to the Frozen and Pacific Ocean*, by Scots explorer Alexander Mackenzie, was published in London. Jefferson ordered the book as soon as he heard of it, but it did not arrive at Monticello, where the president and his secretary were spending the summer, until 1802. *Voyages* both alarmed and electrified the pair. Although Mackenzie had been unable to find a commercially viable passage to the Pacific, he, a foreigner, *had* reached the Pacific. And that was bad. But, of course, it was also good—because it meant that such a trip was possible.

Spurred by the Mackenzie volume, Jefferson decided to act.

Generations of American schoolchildren have been taught that Jefferson sent Lewis and Clark on their expedition after he had purchased the vast Louisiana Territory from France. Having purchased more than eight hundred thousand square miles of land, it seemed only logical that he find out what was on it. The truth is that the Louisiana Purchase played no role at all in the decision to explore the West. In fact, at the time of his decision, Jefferson had no idea that the Louisiana Territory might even be for sale. He had decided to negotiate with Emperor Napoleon I for nothing more than the purchase of New Orleans, so that this key Mississippi River port town, vital to the trade of the young nation, would be in American hands. Only later, well after plans for the Lewis and Clark Expedition had been finalized, did Napoleon's wily minister Talleyrand offer Jefferson not only New Orleans, but all of France's territory on the North American continent.

Either before the summer was over or at the very beginning of fall—there is no precise record of the event—Thomas Jefferson offered Meriwether Lewis command of an expedition to the Pacific. That no detailed record of this decision exists is in itself revealing. It suggests that Jefferson made the decision on his own, that he discussed it with no one (other than Lewis), that he sought no one's advice, and, most of all, that he spent no time looking for other candidates or volunteers. He knew Lewis was the man he wanted, and he knew that, if he asked him, Lewis would go. Only later did he explain his feeling that it "was impossible to find a character who to a compleat science in botany, natural history, mineralogy & astronomy, joined the firmness of constitution & character, prudence, habits adapted to the woods, & a familiarity with the Indian manners & character, requisite for this undertaking. All the latter qualifications Capt. Lewis has."

It was a most peremptory and presumptuous statement: *Impossible* that *anyone* else could be found who possessed all of these requisites? Jefferson hadn't even looked.

But, of course, he felt no need to look. He had made of Meriwether Lewis a son. Indeed, thirty-one years his junior, Lewis was a kind of alternative version of Thomas Jefferson. Both men had been raised near the frontier, the verge dividing the known from the unknown. Both men had an insatiable need to "ramble"—Jefferson through the thickets of politics and the fields of philosophy, Lewis through the lush mysteries of the American wilderness. What better emissary than this young doppelgänger could Jefferson send into the unknown heart of the continent? It was a sudden decision that also represented the work of a lifetime.

And so it was for Meriwether Lewis. A rambler since childhood, a disciplined rambler since joining the army, an eager student curious about all things in nature, he too had lived a life that all along pointed to the moment in which he said to his president, *Yes, I will go.*

As for the danger, well, that was part of it, part of the risk and part of what made the venture all the more inviting. The risk, both Jefferson and Lewis had every reason to believe, was manageable. Both men were on intimate terms with the frontier, especially Lewis, who, as a peripatetic regimental paymaster, had spent much time wandering through some of its remotest reaches. The appeal of the danger may have meant something different to each man. Jefferson had little love for the military, but he was eager to introduce into the young nation's life a new kind of heroism, not founded on martial exploits, but on the exploits of an enlightened mind, imagination, and spirit of exploration. The proposed expedition represented a field in which this new kind of American heroism could be amply and gloriously realized.

Those familiar with the later life of Meriwether Lewis may see something darker in his attraction to the project. Lewis, always a hard drinker and long prone to depression (what contemporaries, including Jefferson, described variously as "melancholy" or "hypochondria"), took increasingly to the bottle and suffered increasingly from depression in the years following the expedition. After Lewis resigned from the army, President Jefferson named him governor of the Louisiana Territory in 1807. In October of 1809, while he was en route to Washington, Meriwether Lewis began drinking very heavily at an inn on the Natchez Trace near Nashville, Tennessee. On the eleventh, he shot himself in the head. Discovering that the ball had merely grazed his skull, he shot himself again, this time in the chest. He died a short time later.

WAS HIS EAGERNESS TO EMBARK, years before, on an expedition into the unknown a symptom of a latent death wish? Perhaps. But that hardly matters, since he did not die on that most hazardous of adventures and, indeed, he was such an effective leader that only one of thirty-one members of the expedition died (from a burst appendix, which would have doubtless killed the man even had he dwelled in the heart of any great city of the time). As for the achievement of the expedition, Lewis and his handpicked co-captain, William Clark, charted the course of the wide Missouri, made contact with more than fifty Indian tribes, cataloged a fantastic array of hitherto unknown plants and animals, and even unearthed the bones of a forty-five-foot dinosaur. In their eight-thousand-mile journey, they had hoped to discover the fabled American "Northwest Passage" to the Pacific, but concluded (correctly) that a commercially viable route did not exist. Nevertheless, the Lewis and Clark Expedition opened up the West, raising the curtain on a century of migration to this expanse. If it was some dark demon that played a role in sending Meriwether Lewis to risk death in this great exploration, that decision was nevertheless an affirmation rather than a negation of life. The defining decision in the life of Meriwether Lewis, it was also a defining decision in the destiny of the American nation.

Charlie Goodnight
and the First Cattle Drive (1866)

THE DECISION THAT CREATED THE COWBOY

Against the will of Governor Sam Houston himself, Texas left the Union at the outbreak of the Civil War, and the men and boys of the state went off to fight. When they came back, defeated, most of what they had left was gone or in ruins. Houses were fallen down, property foreclosed, investments turned to dust. About the only thing left in Texas was cattle.

Before the war, Texas had a longhorn population of several hundred thousand. Most things, when you abandon them, diminish and die, but the longhorn herds—left during the Civil War years to graze and breed on their own throughout the Texas grasslands—grew. Ex-Confederates came back to a Texas rife with poverty and longhorns. The hundreds of thousands had grown to millions. They were strays, belonging to no one—or, rather, belonging to no one until someone roped, gathered, and branded them. Put your brand on an unbranded longhorn, and he was yours. The wealth of impoverished Texas was on the hoof.

Building a herd—riding out, rounding up, and branding the cattle—was hard and dangerous work, but even when that was done, there was still the task of converting the animals into cash. With millions of cattle roaming the Texas range, you couldn't get much money selling a cow to your neighbor. You had to figure out a way to get the cattle to places where people were hungry and didn't already have "beeves" of their own. That's where Charlie Goodnight came in.

He was born in 1836, on the family farm in Macoupin County, Illinois. His father died of pneumonia in 1841 when Charlie was just five, and, soon after, his mother married Hiram Daugherty, a neighboring farmer. Charlie got all the formal schooling he would ever get—about six months' worth—before his mother and stepfather took him in 1845 on an eight-hundred-mile journey south and west, to Milam County, Texas, near Nashville-on-the-Brazos. The little boy rode all the way, bareback, on a white-faced mare named Blaze.

The trek toughened up young Charlie, who, settled with his family in the Brazos bottoms, learned to hunt and track from an old Indian named Caddo Jake. When he was eleven, he hired out to neighboring ranches and, by fifteen, found work as a jockey for a Port Sullivan racing outfit. Putting on a show never much appealed to Charlie, however, so he returned to his mother—who had become a widow for the second time—and younger brothers and sisters. He did all kinds of plantation and ranch work before 1853, when his mother married the Reverend Adam Sheek, a Methodist preacher. Three years after this, Charlie partnered with his stepbrother, John Wesley "Wes" Sheek, to start a cattle business of their own. In 1857, the partners trailed their herd of about four hundred longhorns up the Brazos River to the Keechi Valley in Palo Pinto County. Here, at a place called Black Springs, they built a fine log cabin for their parents.

Wes Sheek soon married, settled down, and assumed the main responsibility for tending to the herd while Charlie ran freight as well as trailed the cattle to market. During this time, he learned the harsh lessons of survival on the trail, and he also met Oliver Loving, a former Kentuckian, who, like him, ran cattle.

In the decade of the 1850s, as Texas became more thickly settled, clashes with local Indians became increasingly frequent and ugly. Like many of his neighbors, Goodnight joined the Texas Rangers, serving mainly as a scout in fights against the Comanche. When the Civil War broke out, Goodnight's ranger outfit was attached to the Frontier Regiment. Unlike many other young Texans, he did not go east to fight in the big battles, but spent most of the war in pursuit of hostile Indians and white "border ruffians." Riding the range from the Canadian River to the headwaters of the Colorado and the Brazos, Goodnight burned into his memory the intimate details of the rolling prairies and the Llano Estacado.

When his enlistment ended in 1864, Goodnight returned to Palo Pinto County, where he found that the herd he shared with Wes Sheek had grown from a few hundred to five thousand head. Like other returning Texans, the partners grew this number even more by rounding up and branding strays. Yet who was there to buy them?

Some other ranchmen, discouraged by the poor Texas market, had started driving their herds to Kansas railheads for shipment to Eastern markets. The profits in that direction were slim and made slimmer by the huge cut the railroads demanded. Just because cattle moved in herds, Charlie Goodnight decided, didn't mean *he* had to. Everybody knew that there was a market for beef in the East, but that, Charlie decided, was precisely the problem: Everybody knew it, and everybody was already supplying that market, the plenitude driving prices down.

Charlie's family had brought him to Texas from Illinois because, like others of enterprising spirit, they saw new opportunities in the West. Why, Charlie Goodnight asked himself, turn back east now? If the West had been a land of opportunity in the 1840s, it offered even more in the 1860s. He knew that gold and silver mining were big in Colorado, and he also knew that the Indian Wars were heating up out there and in New Mexico. Both mining and soldiering meant a concentration of men, and men had to be fed. While every other cattleman was shipping cattle to the populous East—a sure thing—Goodnight would send his to the thinly settled but booming West, where the demand for beef, he was willing to gamble, would be tremendous and where he would have very little competition in satisfying it, at least until the others caught on.

Trouble was, of course, that driving cattle across well-traveled trails to well-established railheads was getting to be routine, whereas no one had ever sent a large herd west. Having ridden it as a Texas Ranger, Goodnight knew the country well, well enough to know that he needed a partner—and not a stay-at-home like Wes Sheek. He remembered Oliver Loving, who had more trail cattle experience than just about anyone else.

He struck an agreement with the older man, and in 1866, the two built up a trail herd of two thousand longhorns, hired eighteen riders, and set out along the Southern Overland Mail Route to the head of the

Concho River. There they paused to let the cattle drink their fill of water for what both men knew would be a long, dry trek across the desert.

Charlie Goodnight and Oliver Loving started from Belknap, Texas, aiming to reach Fort Sumner, New Mexico. Of their 2,000 head, they lost some 400 on the trail—300 from thirst, another 100 trampled to death when they finally reached the watering hole. At the end of the journey, however, the army quartermasters at Fort Sumner paid the spectacular sum of eight cents a pound for the partners' stringy longhorns, netting a profit of $12,000—which Goodnight and Loving took right back to Texas to buy up another herd for the drive up the Pecos River. The trail they blazed through the unforgiving land was dubbed the Goodnight-Loving Trail and, in a short time, became one of the most heavily trafficked routes in the Southwest.

Not that it was easy for a handful of men to control hundreds, even thousands of powerful, hungry, thirsty animals. Stampede was a constant danger, injuries of all kinds were common, and the Indians were rarely friendly. Oliver Loving was fatally wounded by Indian warriors in 1867, on the partners' third trip along the trail. Mostly, there was the continual labor of driving, feeding, and watering the stock. That was the work of the cowboys. Keeping those cowboys from starving was Goodnight's responsibility, and that took a bit of inventing. Goodnight bought an army-surplus Studebaker wagon and modified it by installing what he called a "chuck box," replete with shelves and drawers. He fitted the chuck box to the back of the Studebaker so that the trail cook could store his implements in good order. The box had a hinged lid. Close it, and the storage space was converted into a large table big enough to fix meals on. Goodnight attached a water barrel to the wagon, sufficient to hold two days' supply, and he put alongside this a row of hooks, boxes, brackets, and the all-important coffee grinder. Almost as scarce as water on the plains were trees, so Charlie slung canvas, hammock-style, under the wagon to hold firewood and kindling. Finally, he installed another wagon box to carry the men's bedrolls, personal items, and food supplies. The chuck wagon, heart of any trail drive, was born.

And so was the vocation of those who made use of the chuck wagon, who rounded up the cattle, who branded the cattle, who assembled the herd, and who drove the herd hundreds of miles and more to wherever a demand for beef made profit a reasonable prospect. Before Charlie Goodnight, Texas had many ranchers, and the ranchers employed many ranch hands—common agricultural laborers. What Goodnight did was transform the ranch hand into the cowboy, surely the most beloved and celebrated worker in American history. Looked at in cold, hard socioeconomic terms, cowboys were typically the poorest of the poor. Goodnight hired Confederate veterans who had been dispossessed of family, friends, and what little they may once have owned. Despite stereotypes engendered by generations of dime novels, movies, and television programs, most cowboys bore little resemblance to Tom Mix or John Wayne. They were men who took the job because they could get no other. Mexicans, Indians, and African Americans shared the bottom rung of the socioeconomic ladder with poor whites, and they did a lot of the cowpunching during the twenty years or so that constituted the heyday of the trail cattle industry—the era before the proliferation of railway lines made the long overland drives a thing of the past. Downtrodden and exploited as individuals, the cowboys nevertheless came to be regarded as American knights errant—noble, brave, pure, and beholden to no one, in a country free of the petty traps set by urban oligarchs, politicians, and police.

THE INDUSTRY CHARLIE GOODNIGHT CREATED in turn created a great mythic figure, whose character, compounded of reality and imagination, has profoundly shaped much of American life, even at the most sophisticated levels of big business and politics. Goodnight did not intend this, of course, when he made his decision in 1866 to take the path less traveled, which offered as much danger as opportunity. But that was, after all, a typically American decision, and so, in the hindsight of history, it is not surprising that it should have spawned an archetype of American legend.

As for Charlie Goodnight himself, the decision to rebuild his life after the Civil War by turning away from the crowd paid off. Over the years, he made and lost more than a few fortunes, but, in the end, he became a very wealthy man. He founded Goodnight College, which operated from 1898 to 1917 in the Panhandle town of Goodnight, giving local ranch kids the education Charlie himself had missed. He became a leading researcher in the field of animal husbandry, and the buffalo he raised on his properties helped the wild herds to recover from almost certain extinction. His experiments with wheat and other crop hybrids led some to dub him the "Burbank of the Range," and his advocacy on behalf of the Pueblo tribes of New Mexico was influential on sorely needed Indian-policy reform in Washington. Goodnight spent his last years investing in Mexican mines, and even produced a movie of his vision of the West. He long outlived the trail-drive industry he had begun, dying in 1929, at ninety-three, in his winter home in Phoenix, Arizona.

Edison and Electric Light (1878–79)

THE DECISION TO SUBDIVIDE THE SUN

Since 1879 and the appearance of Thomas Edison's most famous invention, the incandescent electric lamp, generations have waxed poetic about how the "Wizard of Menlo Park" vanquished the darkness and mastered a hitherto ineluctable fact of creation, the separation of day from night. Edison himself did nothing to discourage those who painted him as a wizard. After all, that image was good for business, and it attracted much-needed investment capital. However, Edison never made the mistake of believing his own press. He understood quite well that his incandescent electric lamp was neither a poem written against the darkness nor a miracle of biblical proportions. In fact, as he saw it, this invention was no quantum leap of inspirational genius, but merely a step, the *right* step, in solving a problem he had carefully defined.

The truth is that Thomas Edison did not invent electric lighting. In 1806, fully four decades before Edison was even born, the distinguished British scientist Sir Humphry Davy exhibited to the British Royal Society a literally dazzling demonstration of electric light. He had cobbled together a device consisting of two charcoal rods wired to banks of sulfuric acid batteries. When the rods were drawn close to one another, a spark bridged the gap between them, creating a sizzling, hissing, and brilliant arc. Yet Davy's electric arc light did not illuminate the world. Indeed, it was of no practical, commercial value. The batteries were unwieldy, hazardous, and quickly exhausted, and the charcoal rods rapidly burned away.

Over the years, others pursued Davy's invention, and when workable electric generators began to appear in the 1860s and 1870s, a number of inventors patented arc lamps. Even so, these were at best marginally commercial. Although used throughout the late 1870s and early 1880s, arc lights were blindingly brilliant, making the devices only useful in such applications as searchlights, streetlights, and (occasionally) for lighting large interior spaces like factories, department stores, and train stations. In the home and in smaller interior spaces, where light was needed most, they were quite useless. There was no way to regulate, dim, or control the arc light, and while hard-compacted carbon rods were a substantial improvement over Davy's soft charcoal, they were still quite speedily consumed, making the maintenance of arc lamps both labor-intensive and costly. Yet it seemed obvious to many inventors that electric lighting had a future. In this, Thomas Edison was just one of the crowd. For he did not work in the splendid isolation that is part of the romanticized image of the creative genius. Instead, he kept his eyes open and took a profound interest in how others did things and addressed problems.

One day in 1878, he visited the Connecticut workshop of William Wallace. A brass and copper founder by trade, Wallace was an inventor by avocation and had been working on an electric arc-lamp system with the help of a full-time electrical inventor named Moses Farmer. Edison knew that Wallace and Farmer did not have a revolutionary approach to the arc lamp, but what did intrigue him, more than their lamp, was the generator system they had built to power the lamps—eight of them, in a row, all at once. Now *that*, Edison concluded, was worth looking at. No one before had developed a generator sufficiently powerful and efficient to do this.

Impressed, Edison was moved to action. As he explained to a reporter for the *New York Sun* just one month after his visit to the Wallace workshop: "I saw for the first time everything in practical operation. It was all before me. I saw the thing had not gone so far but that I had a chance. I saw that what had been done had never been made practically useful. The intense light had not been subdivided so that it could be brought into private houses."

In five sentences spoken to a reporter, Edison related the moment that inspired the creation of what is surely one of humankind's seminal technologies. It is the moment Thomas Edison decided to subdivide light. Let's take it apart.

"I saw for the first time everything in practical operation. It was all before me," Edison said. Just what was "before" him? Eight arc lamps powered by a single generator.

And that meant—what, exactly? It did *not* mean that Edison had found the solution to the problem of electric light. We know that much because of the next two sentences: "I saw the thing had not gone so far but that I had a chance. I saw that what had been done had never been made practically useful." These two sentences somewhat contradict the first sentence: "I saw for the first time everything in practical operation." If this first sentence were left standing on its own, it would mean that Wallace and Farmer had solved the problem, had invented a practical electric light. But, Edison recognized, they had done no such thing.

Even as he saw everything in practical operation, Edison also realized that "the thing" had not gone all the way, and, therefore, he still "had a chance." Wallace and Farmer had in operation a practical solution to producing electricity, a generator capable of energizing eight arc lamps, but that was just the point. They were still *arc lamps*, with all the short-comings and inadequacies of the existing technology. "I saw that what had been done had never been made practically useful," Edison said. "The intense light had not been subdivided so that it could be brought into private houses." Here is no flash of sudden genius, no bolt of inspiration from the blue, but an almost building-block-like identification and analysis of a problem that had been only partially solved:

1. A generator can power multiple lamps; this is a practical breakthrough.

2. The lamps so powered are still *arc* lamps; therefore, I still have a chance to innovate profitably.

3. The light has "not been subdivided so that it could be brought into private houses."

The partial solution, the new generator, energized Edison's thinking, enabling him to move beyond what Wallace and Farmer had accomplished to what they had failed to achieve. It was in this failure that Edison saw sufficient space for an invention of his own.

But look again at the language of that final sentence. We are drawn immediately to a word at once pedestrian in its businesslike connotation yet almost lyrical in its application to the subject at hand. *Subdivided* reads like a term out of a legal contract. Applied to light, however, it seems suddenly magical. For who other than a genius could speak of "subdividing" so insubstantial an essence as light?

Who other than a genius? A truly creative businessman.

IN LOOKING AT EIGHT ARC LAMPS illuminated by a single generator, Edison understood that what he really saw was electricity, a form of energy, being retailed like any other commodity. But if Wallace and Farmer had figured out a way to "subdivide" electric energy, they had not devised a similar subdivision of the *form* of electric energy that made electricity useful and profitable as a commodity: light. To exploit electricity as a retail commodity, Edison decided that he had to learn how to exploit light itself the same way—to subdivide *light* so that it could be retailed to the consumer. And having defined his task, he returned to his Menlo Park workshop to begin the long and tedious task of subdividing light, the process of "inventing the light bulb."

Theodore Roosevelt and the Panama Canal (1901–3)

THE DECISION THAT REVISED GLOBAL GEOPOLITICS

"During the nearly four hundred years . . . since Balboa crossed the Isthmus [of Panama], there had been a good deal of talk about building an Isthmus canal," President Theodore Roosevelt wrote of the situation as it existed in 1902. "So far it had all resulted merely in conversation." And after four centuries of such "conversation," the president determined that "the time had come when unless somebody was prepared to act with decision we would have to resign ourselves to at least half a century of further conversation."

The time had come. These four words are the essence of any great decision. There was and there remains a great deal of controversy surrounding President Roosevelt's decision to step into Central and South American politics in order to take control of the land through which American interests would dig a canal joining the Atlantic to the Pacific. Whether one calls this enlightened internationalism or blatant imperialism, there is no arguing that the decision behind it—Theodore Roosevelt's decision—was bold on what must be described as a planetary scale. TR's detractors said (and some still say) that the decision was the product of egomania combined with hypernationalism, while his admirers believed (and continue to believe) that the decision was the selfless product of truly global thinking. What the president himself thought was that the decision was neither more nor less than what history—time itself—demanded.

The time had come. Great decision makers—and whatever else Theodore Roosevelt was, he was a great decision maker—possess a fine sense of the ripeness of things. They know *when the time has come*, and it is this knowledge that drives the decisions they make.

TR came to the Panama Canal decision with an understanding that the project of joining the Atlantic to the Pacific had been four centuries in the making. In 1901, the president approved the Hay-Pauncefote Treaty with Great Britain, which, along with negotiations with the French Panama Company, gave the United States possession of a permanently neutral canal zone through which the U.S. government had the right to dig a canal.

The next decision to be made was where, exactly, the canal should be dug. The best place (according to the engineers Roosevelt favored) was across the narrow Isthmus of Panama; in 1903 Roosevelt authorized his secretary of state, John Hay, to sign the Hay-Herrán Treaty with the government of Colombia, which at the time held Panama. But the government of Colombia was, Roosevelt observed, "in a constant state of flux," and Panama had for the past fifty years agitated—often violently— for independence from that country. "The experience of over half a century," Roosevelt wrote, "had shown Colombia to be utterly incapable of keeping order on the Isthmus."

When, after a coup d'état, the Colombian Senate rejected the Hay-Herrán Treaty in 1903, President Roosevelt concluded that "we were dealing with the government of an irresponsible alien dictator, and with a condition of affairs on the Isthmus itself which was marked by one uninterrupted series of outbreaks and revolutions." Moreover, he believed that "when we submitted to Colombia the Hay-Herrán Treaty, it had been settled that the time for delay, the time for permitting any government of anti-social character, or of imperfect development, to bar the work, had passed."

In short, it was time to begin the canal, and Panama was ripe for its independence. President Roosevelt turned to Philippe Jean Bunau-Varilla, a French engineer who had worked for the French Panama Canal Company (which had tried and failed to build a canal in the 1880s). Bunau-Varilla had been instrumental in negotiating the doomed Hay-Herrán Treaty on behalf of the United States; now the Roosevelt government supported him in his effort to foment the bloodless coup that brought about Panamanian independence. The provisional government of the new nation named Bunau-Varilla minister plenipotentiary and, in that role, he quickly concluded the Hay–Bunau-Varilla Treaty, giving the United States the right to build a canal through a canal zone it controlled.

For his actions in Panama, Theodore Roosevelt was criticized by many as an imperialist of the most blatant kind. He answered these criticisms in his *Autobiography* of 1913 simply by declaring that "The time for hesitation on our part had passed." The canal, its neutrality guaranteed by the United States, was "imperative," Roosevelt wrote, "not only for civil but for military reasons." There was an "immediate" need for "easy and speedy communication by sea between the Atlantic and the Pacific." The need was such that it would "not admit of indefinite delay. The action of Colombia had shown not only that the delay would be indefinite, but that she intended to confiscate the property and rights of the French Panama Canal Company. . . . If we had sat supine, this would doubtless have meant that France would have interfered to protect the company, and we should then have had on the Isthmus, not the company, but France; and the gravest international complications might have ensued."

For Roosevelt, mere charges of imperialism paled beside the imperative need to make a decision demanded by the very flow of events. The time was ripe *now* and "to have acted otherwise than I did would have been on my part betrayal of the interests of the United States, indifference to the interests of Panama [whose people wanted independence from a Colombian dictatorship] and recreancy to the interests of the world at large," which would benefit from a transoceanic canal whose neutrality was guaranteed by a great nation.

It is a revelation to read Theodore Roosevelt's own account of the Panama Canal decision. The narrative occupies just seventeen pages of his *Autobiography*. Of those pages, only the last one and two-thirds discuss the actual physical feat of digging a canal through some forty miles of dense and disease-plagued jungle. Roosevelt barely alludes to Ferdinand de Lesseps, who, having built the great Suez Canal in Egypt during 1859–69, failed after a decade of heartbreaking work to build one in Panama. Indeed, most of those one and two-thirds pages are devoted to the process of making yet another decision: whether to dig a sea-level canal or a lock canal. TR convened a board of engineers to address the question. A majority, consisting of all the non-American engineers, advocated a sea-level canal, while a minority, consisting of all the American engineers, favored a lock canal. "Studying these conclusions, I came to the belief that the minority was right." While a "sea-level canal would be slightly less exposed to damage in the event of war," and while its "running expenses would be lower," a lock canal would "cost only about half as much to build and would be built in half the time, with much less risk." A lock canal would also allow for the quicker passage of large ships. "Accordingly I recommended to Congress . . . that a lock canal should be built, and my recommendation was adopted."

———

BASED ON ROOSEVELT'S ALLOCATION OF INK—about 95 percent to the story of the Panama Canal decision and a mere 5 percent to how it was built—we can conclude that, for him, the decision was almost everything; that once a decision had been made, once ripeness had been recognized and acted upon, the execution of the decision was practically inevitable. Problems, no matter how formidable, would be solved for the simple reason that, the decision having been made, they *had* to be solved. When Congress "insisted upon having [the canal] built by a commission of several men," Roosevelt wrote, he "tried faithfully to get good work out of the commission." Finding it "quite impossible," however, he issued an executive order putting one man, Colonel George Washington Goethals, in charge of construction and engineering while another, Dr. William C. Gorgas, solved the yellow fever problem that had ended the hopes of de Lesseps years earlier. Make the decision, the right decision, the necessary decision, Roosevelt implied, and the men will be found who are capable of transforming that decision into successful action, even if their assignment is to do no less than reshape the planet and the politics that go with it. As Shakespeare's Edgar put it in *King Lear*, "Ripeness is all."

The Wright Brothers and the Airplane (1903)

THE DECISION TO FLY

At about 10:35 on the morning of December 17, 1903, Orville Wright made the first sustained powered flight in an aircraft heavier than air. The decision that took him aloft was the end product of a process that had begun twenty-five years earlier, when Orville was seven years old and his brother, Wilbur, eleven. In 1878, the boys' father, Milton Wright, a bishop in the United Brethren Church who held strong beliefs—including a belief in the value of educational toys—gave Wilbur and Orville a present. It was a toy helicopter designed by an early French aeronautical experimenter named Alphonse Pénaud. In 1912, during testimony in one of many patent suits he and his brother became involved in, Orville described the toy as "actuated by a rubber spring which would [drive a four-bladed rotor and] lift itself into the air." Orville explained that "Our interest [in flight] began when we were children," when "Father brought home to us [this] small toy." It so fascinated him and Wilbur that "We built a number of copies of this toy, which flew successfully." In fact, "we undertook to build the toy on a much larger scale," but "it failed to work so well."

The boys had hoped to build one sufficiently large and powerful to enable them to fly, but they never did it, and, when they grew up, they went into a different line of work altogether, opening up a bicycle shop in their hometown of Dayton, Ohio. At the end of the nineteenth century, bicycles were at the cutting edge of transportation technology, and riding a bicycle, which involved speed and balance, was perhaps the closest one could get to flying without actually leaving the ground. At any rate, the boys never forgot their dream of flight, and, beginning in 1890, they regularly followed news reports about the exploits of Otto Lilienthal, a German experimenter with gliders. In 1896, they read that he had been killed in a glider crash.

Wilbur later recalled in an essay titled "Some Aeronautical Experiments," that "the brief notice of his death aroused a passive interest which had existed from my childhood," and from this point on, Wilbur and Orville Wright started thinking seriously about manned flight.

The subject was like a lens, focusing the time and attention of the young men whenever they weren't busy in the bicycle shop. In the spring of 1899, they read a book on ornithology, which included (according to its subtitle) a "Dissertation on Aeronautics." Orville later explained that he and his brother concluded that there was nothing "about a bird that could not be built on a larger scale and used by man. If the bird's wings would sustain it in the air without the use of any muscular effort, we did not see why man could not be sustained by the same means." In June, Wilbur wrote to the Smithsonian Institution—at the time, the center of what little aeronautical research was being carried out—requesting copies of "such papers as the Smithsonian Institution has published" on aeronautics and a list of other works "in print in the English language." His object, Wilbur explained, was to learn "all that is already known" about flight. When the material arrived, the young men read avidly. In studying the failures of aeronautical experimenters, Wilbur wrote, "we found many points of interest to us."

In fact, in a remarkably brief period of time, the Wrights—mostly Wilbur at first—combed through virtually all of the existing literature on aeronautics. Wilbur cut through the texts like a razor. As he explained in a 1901 lecture delivered to a meeting of engineers in Chicago, he readily reduced the problem of manned flight to three requirements: wings to provide lift, a power plant that would move the aircraft forward with enough velocity to create sufficient air flow over the wings to generate lift, and, finally, a means of controlling the aircraft. Astoundingly, Wilbur Wright was the first experimenter to draw up this simple, straightforward list. Even more astoundingly, he was the first to realize that the problems relating to the first two requirements had already been largely solved. His reading had revealed equations and data that would enable him and his brother to design wings and to calculate just how powerful an engine would be required for flight. But it was also clear to Wilbur that the final requirement, a means of control, had hardly begun to be addressed. A means of control was essential to achieving equilibrium, and, Wilbur wrote in 1899, "the problem of equilibrium constituted the problem of flight itself." Lack of a means of control was what had killed Otto Lilienthal.

The problems of wings and power, the Wright brothers judged, were well on their way to solutions. Perhaps the single most important decision they made was a determination to solve the one problem that remained unsolved: control.

Control would be their focus, the area in which the greatest innovation and invention were required. Wilbur came to this conclusion—and Orville readily concurred with it—not intellectually or theoretically, but intuitively. They recognized it as the problem every bicyclist had to solve, and it was solved, they knew, not by theory or calculation or even by observation, but by experience. To "ride a bicycle" was to *control* the bicycle, to achieve equilibrium on the bicycle (which, in effect, constituted the problem of bicycling itself), and the only effective way to master control and achieve equilibrium was to ride. By analogy, Wilbur and Orville decided that the only way to learn to control a flying machine was to fly. That, obviously, was a dangerous proposition, but, as Wilbur explained to the Chicago engineers in 1901, "if you are looking for perfect safety, you will do well to sit on the fence and watch the birds; but if you really wish to learn, you must mount a machine and become acquainted with its tricks by actual trial." And so the Wright brothers came to the point of a decision that involved the highest stakes of all: life or death. Flight without a means of control was highly dangerous, yet you needed to fly in order to create a means of control.

They would fly. But they would not commit suicide.

The death of Otto Lilienthal had made a powerful and lasting impression on the Wrights. The German experimenter had flown a kind of hang glider, in which the only means of control was shifting the weight of the pilot's body. Wilbur concluded that "Lilienthal's apparatus" for achieving equilibrium in flight was "inadequate." He based this conclusion not only on "the fact that it failed," but on his own observations, which "convince me that birds use more positive and energetic methods of regaining equilibrium than that of shifting the center of gravity." Wilbur Wright concluded that a bird achieved control and maintained equilibrium not by merely shifting its body weight, but by turning the leading edge of one wing tip up and the other down.

It was a brilliant insight, but how could this be imitated in an artificial wing?

The solution came to Wilbur Wright when he was working in the bicycle shop one July day in 1899. He looked at the rectangular box in which an inner tube had been packed. The end tabs had been ripped off. He picked up the empty box and twisted it in his hands. That's when it hit him: create a wing that could be twisted in a controlled fashion.

Still unwilling to risk life and limb, Wilbur and Orville built a small model wing out of bamboo, paper, and strings. Proving the principle sound, they built a biplane kite with a five-foot wingspan, the warp of the wings controllable by means of strings attached to sticks held in the kite flier's hand. In August 1899, the brothers successfully flew and controlled the kite. Now they felt ready to build a "man-carrying machine."

As the brothers planned it, this would not yet be a full-fledged glider, let alone a powered aircraft. Instead, this next step was designed as a manned kite. Wilbur planned to build a tower about 150 feet high. "A rope passing over a pulley at the top will serve as a sort of kite string," he wrote. The idea was to make a sustained tethered flight that would allow for practice and experimentation without all the risks associated with free flight. In this way, Wilbur explained, he and his brother could "escape accident long enough to acquire skill sufficient to prevent accident."

The first snag they hit was wind. They needed to find a place where there was enough of it—a sustained breeze of about fifteen miles per hour, which, according to the brothers' calculations, was what was required to lift the kite. Wilbur contacted the United States Weather Bureau and, after reviewing a statistical list the bureau sent him, concluded that Kitty Hawk, North Carolina, offered sufficient wind, as well as isolation. Moreover, a crash landing in relatively soft beach sand or even in the ocean seemed preferable to an impact on the kinds of surfaces available in Ohio. Also, the dunes at Kitty Hawk gave sufficient elevation to take the place of a specially constructed tower for the tethered flight experiments.

In the fall of 1900, the Wrights built a craft with a biplane wingspan of seventeen feet five inches. The pilot would lie on his belly across the middle of the lower wing, his feet resting on a T-bar that controlled the warp of the wings. A hand control operated the elevator, which was on a horizontal stabilizer mounted in front of the wings instead of behind them, as on a modern airplane. Over several days in September and October, the brothers flew the giant kite without a pilot. Probably on October 3, Wilbur climbed aboard, attained an altitude of perhaps fifteen feet, then frantically shouted for the men holding the tether ropes to "Let me down!" The kite clearly needed more testing—unmanned. But when they returned to manned flights, it became clear that tethering the aircraft prevented the pilot from truly resolving the mysteries of controlled flight. On October 18, 1900, they began making untethered glides from the top of a dune. Telling themselves that the sand would minimize the damage and injury caused by a crash, they made flight after flight and were delighted by what they learned. The brothers—and the world— were on their way to sustained and controlled flight.

But when the Wrights returned to Kitty Hawk in 1901 with a brand-new machine—this one designed from the ground up as a glider, not a kite—they were met with deep disappointment. The machine flew, but not as their calculations told them it should. The wings provided just one-third of the lift the numbers predicted. This was devastating, because the Wrights had been operating on the assumption that the problem of lift had been solved by those who had gone before them. After the Wrights left Kitty Hawk on August 22, 1901, Wilbur, recalled, "we doubted that we would ever resume our experiments." On the train back to Ohio, Wilbur turned to his brother: "Not within a thousand years would man ever fly!"

Wilbur and Orville returned to the business of making and selling bicycles, and perhaps they really would have given up their aeronautical experiments had it not been for an invitation from another aeronautical pioneer, Octave Chanute, for Wilbur to deliver an address to the Western Society of Engineers in Chicago. Wilbur accepted, and the labor of composing his speech required him to go over, in detail, the successes and failures of the past two years of experiments. In the course of doing this, a possible source of the enormous disconnect between theory and reality, numbers and actual performance, became clear. There was nothing wrong with the principles of aeronautics or the equations that underlay them. The problem was the data. The Wrights had simply accepted a figure for the all-important coefficient of air pressure that they had not confirmed by actual experiment. To determine this figure accurately, they hit on the idea of constructing a wind tunnel. Next to the airplane itself, the wind tunnel was the Wright Brothers' most important contribution to the development of aviation.

The wind tunnel allowed the Wrights to test many dozens of wing shapes on a small scale and accurately measure the lift produced by each. Strangely, this research, conducted indoors during November and December 1901, was more exhilarating for the brothers than flying at

Kitty Hawk. Exciting as that work was, it had been, up to this point, a matter of trial and error—as it turned out, with error predominating. Now, however, in the quiet of their bicycle shop, they had the first-hand, original data to enable them to create the most efficient wing. And, in this, they had liberated themselves from the past, from the work of others.

The new glider for 1902 was based on the wind tunnel tests and was larger than the earlier machines, its wingspan ten feet longer, yet its wings sleeker, their chord (the straight-line distance from the leading edge to the trailing edge) two feet shorter than the previous model. Controls and control surfaces had also been improved, and when the brothers tested the glider at Kitty Hawk in the fall of 1902, they made flights of greater and longer durations—that of October 23 lasting 26 seconds over 622½ feet. They were ready to install a motor.

As Wilbur had concluded early on, the basic principle of power in powered flight had been well established. But it is one thing to start from a principle and quite another to make the leap to practical application. As Wilbur had earlier reduced the problem of flight to satisfying three basic requirements, so now the brothers subdivided the requirement of power into two parts: an engine that weighed no more than 180 pounds and would generate 8 to 9 horsepower, and a propeller. The brothers sent inquiries to ten manufacturers of engines and, while they awaited replies, turned to the matter of the propeller. To their surprise, they found that other aeronautical experimenters had devoted little thought to the propeller. Exercising common sense, the brothers made inquiries of ship designers, assuming that whatever principles governed marine propellers could be adapted to aeronautical propellers. But they soon discovered that shipwrights designed propellers not on the basis of theory derived from experimental observation and measurement, but simply according to prevailing tradition. There was nothing to adapt from marine experience because the data simply did not exist.

Instead of becoming discouraged by the lack of precedent, the Wright brothers were liberated by it. If they could not base their propeller on the nautical example, they decided to invent it anew. Ship builders and sailors called their propellers "screws," but the Wrights decided that an aircraft propeller was not a screw that somehow pulled the plane through the air. It was, as Orville wrote in 1913, "simply an aeroplane [wing] traveling in a spiral course." Without a usable nautical analog, the Wrights were left free to think in an entirely new way, and the insight was astounding. It led to what proved a difficult process of design, but it was a process guided by a purely aeronautical precedent: the wing.

As for the engine, the brothers soon learned that they were on their own here as well. No manufacturer could meet their weight-to-power ratio requirement and, furthermore, since no demand existed for a very light but very powerful gasoline engine, no manufacturer was interested in designing one. Teaming up with a machinist named Charlie Taylor, the Wrights designed their own engine, which weighed in at 200 pounds, but reliably produced more than 12 horsepower.

THE FINAL DECISION, which came after they had built the aircraft of 1903 and had installed its engine and fixed in place its two counter-rotating propellers, was which brother would make the first flight. Since the late 1890s, when they started serious work on flying, the Wright brothers had doggedly refused to leave anything to chance. They researched, they experimented, they compiled data, and they learned to question the data of others. Now, on the blustery Kitty Hawk morning of December 14, they let the toss of a coin decide who would fly first. Wilbur won, but he stalled the machine on takeoff, and it fell to earth barely sixty feet beyond the end of the rail that had been rigged for the launch. Repairs to the plane consumed the next day, and they were ready to fly again on December 16. But the wind was wrong.

It was right on the morning of the 17th, and Wilbur agreed it was Orville's turn. He covered 120 feet in 12 seconds—in the first powered and manned flight by a heavier-than-air craft. The brothers kept flying. By the fourth and final launch of December 17, 1903, Wilbur Wright flew 852 feet in 59 seconds: a 610 percent increase in distance, a 392 percent increase in duration, and a 44 percent increase in speed—all in the very first day of human flight.

Sigmund Freud and Sex (1905)

THE DECISION TO
DEFY THE MORALS OF AN AGE

Look at any photograph of Sigmund Freud, and what you see is a sober, even somber figure, impeccably attired in the suit coat, vest, and cravat of a turn-of-the-century businessman or professional. There is no trace of the unorthodox, let alone the subversive or revolutionary, about him, but rather a visual affirmation of the bourgeois values associated with prosperous propriety.

He was born in 1856, in Moravia—at the time a part of the Austrian empire and today a region of the Czech Republic—to a Jewish wool merchant and his wife, but he grew up in the cosmopolitan sophistication of Vienna, to which the family moved in 1860. Young Freud graduated from the Sperl Gymnasium in 1873. He emerged from his early education very much alive to the world and its intellectual currents. After attending a public reading of an essay on nature written by the great German romantic poet and philosopher Johann Wolfgang von Goethe, he suddenly decided on his life's work: medicine. Enrolled in the University of Vienna, he came under the tutelage of the influential physiologist Ernst von Brücke, an advocate of a school of biology and physiology strictly based on physics and chemistry.

With this rigorous scientific training behind him, Freud entered the General Hospital in Vienna in 1882 as a clinical assistant to Theodor Meynert, a renowned psychiatrist, and Hermann Nothnagel, a professor of internal medicine. A brilliant student, Freud was appointed lecturer in neuropathology in 1885. Later that same year, he left Vienna to continue his studies in neuropathology at the Salpêtrière Hospital in Paris under Jean-Martin Charcot.

Up to this point, Freud's training had been in the physical nature of the brain and the nervous system. As his earliest training in the Sperl Gymnasium had made him acutely receptive to the lecture that awakened him to the study of medicine, so now, having learned all he could from the physiologists, his nineteen weeks under Charcot turned him from the brain to the study of the mind. Charcot worked with patients whose disorders were classified as "hysteria," and what the Frenchman demonstrated is that manifestly physical hysterical symptoms—such as paralysis or blindness—had their source not in some physical defect of brain or nerves, but in the mind. Moreover, Charcot was able to use hypnosis—specifically, hypnotic suggestion—to influence and alter (at least temporarily) the links between the mind and the physical symptoms of his patients.

Freud the young physician saw in Charcot's work the possibility of relieving the suffering of an entire class of psychiatric patients whose fate had been given up as hopeless. Freud the emerging philosopher-scientist saw something even more profound. Thousands of years of Western civilization were based on two beliefs: that mind and body were entirely separate and that people exercise a high degree of control over their destinies via the mind in the form of conscious will. Charcot's work suggested to Freud that mind and body were really one, and that much of the mind was quite inaccessible to consciousness, let alone will. These implications, revolutionary and subversive, Freud decided to follow wherever they led him.

In February 1886, Freud returned to Vienna, where he began to practice medicine in the specialized area of neuropsychology and commenced a partnership with another physician, Josef Breuer. Breuer discussed with Freud the case of a patient he called Anna O. (her real name was Bertha Pappenheim), who was plagued by a variety of debilitating "hysterical" symptoms. Breuer explained to Freud that he had discovered that he could provide relief of her symptoms not through hypnosis, but by encouraging her to talk freely and randomly about her symptoms. This process of what Freud would later call "free association"—allowing the mind to wander and, without any conscious effort at censorship, verbalizing these mental meanderings—Breuer referred to as the "talking cure." It was, he said to Freud, as if verbalization produced a catharsis, or purging, of pent-up thoughts and emotions. Freud realized that this catharsis was not merely a purgation, but was the result of bringing to consciousness hitherto unconscious feelings. So now he had another idea. His work with Charcot had undermined the foundation of Western civilization itself by suggesting a seamless connection between body and mind and, simultaneously, revealing a universe of thought beneath or beyond consciousness and control. His work with Breuer now suggested that this unconscious realm, which could wreak havoc on the body in the form of hysterical symptoms, was not entirely inaccessible to consciousness after all. It could be reached.

Like Freud, Breuer was a Viennese physician, his patients drawn from the city's economic and social elite. Unlike Freud, who merely took on the appearance and trappings of bourgeois life, Breuer was a thoroughgoing and committed bourgeois. He soon found himself drawing back from some of the implications of his work with Anna O., the most important of which was his increasing awareness that his patient's symptoms were rooted in sexuality. In a later recollection, Breuer was quite candid: "I confess that the plunging into sexuality in theory and practice is not to my taste." The very fact that Breuer resisted exploring the sexual basis of Anna O.'s disease suggested all the more to Freud the great importance of sexuality.

Vienna, like much of the world toward the end of the nineteenth century, was governed by a collective moral attitude most often named after the long-reigning queen of England, Victoria. Victorian society exaggerated the age-old prejudices of Western civilization: the belief in the absolute separation of mind and body and the confidence that whatever one earnestly *willed* to do, one *could* do—because, even if civilized men and women could not always control their thoughts and feelings, they could always govern their actions. Part of this governance depended on excluding from public consideration—and even most private conversation—the entire topic of sexuality. To violate this taboo invited social censure and, for a physician struggling to earn or maintain a reputation for respectability, utter ruin. If Breuer was unwilling to risk the topic, Freud embraced it and quickly drifted away from his conventional medical associate.

Freud did not decide lightly to take this great social and professional risk. It was not merely a product of bravado, but a profound realization that the effort with which a society resists an idea is actually a measure of the ultimate truth and force of that idea. Freud reasoned that people develop hysterical symptoms because of the mental and physical energy required to suppress ideas and feelings that are intolerable to the conscious mind, which is, after all, influenced and shaped by social norms and social taboos. To help his patients, to render a great service to society, Freud decided, he would have to defy society itself.

Freud's first great book, *The Interpretation of Dreams*, was published in 1899 and dealt in great detail with dreams as "the royal road to a knowledge of the unconscious." Freud argued that the mind's energy—or libido, which Freud closely identified with the sexual drive—sought discharge to ensure pleasure and prevent pain. Social conventions and taboos often denied this pleasurable discharge of energy; therefore, the libido found release through indirect mental channels, most notably the imaginary fulfillment of wishes. Dreams, Freud contended, even nightmares, were ultimately the mental fulfillment of such wishes. Only rarely, however, did dreams express this fulfillment in obvious ways. More usually, the content of a dream was the disguised expression of wish fulfillments. In this, they resembled hysterical or neurotic symptoms. Like such symptoms, dreams were the products of compromises the psyche makes between its innermost desires and the prohibitions that are dictated from outside. Like symptoms, dreams have to be analyzed—in effect, decoded—in order to be understood. This decoding would be the basic work of the treatment Freud called psychoanalysis.

The Interpretation of Dreams was a revolutionary work, but, having written it, Freud did not cease his explorations. No sooner had the work been published than he wrote to his close friend Wilhelm Fliess that "things are working in the lowest floor" and "a theory of sexuality may become the next successor to the dream book." Over the next several years, Freud collected data "for the sexual theory . . . waiting until the piled-up material can be set aflame by a rousing spark." For Freud, decision was a matter of discovery and, by this stage in his career, he realized that discovery came to him on its own schedule. It could not be rushed. His task was to keep looking, compiling, and studying until the accumulated material reached a kind of critical mass. It was all a matter of patience, timing, and ripeness. He wrote to Fliess late in 1900 that "things . . . are probably going forward soundly on a subterranean level; but it is certainly not a time of harvest, of conscious mastery."

The harvest and conscious mastery came in 1905 with the publication of *Three Essays on the Theory of Sexuality*. As Freud's most perceptive modern biographer, Peter Gay, writes: "Freud the conventional bourgeois battled Freud the scientific conquistador every step of the way. His propositions on libido were little less scandalous to Freud than they were to most of his readers." Yet, unlike Breuer, Freud made the decision to overcome the resistance he felt and to tell the world—himself included—what it did not want to hear, but what it needed to be told because it was the truth. And the core element of Freud's theory of sexuality was the most socially subversive of all: infantile sexuality, the idea that infants and children, deemed innocent by the most cherished of social conventions, are in reality endowed with powerful sexual feelings, which profoundly shape their subsequent development.

PUBLISHING HIS THEORY OF INFANTILE SEXUALITY, which became a cornerstone of psychoanalysis and of Freud's entire picture of human psychology, was perhaps the most dangerous decision Freud ever made. How did he know it was the right decision? He explained in a 1908 letter to psychoanalytic disciple Karl Abraham: "The resistance to infantile sexuality strengthens me in my opinion that the three essays are an achievement of comparable value to the *Interpretation of Dreams.*" Often, the harder a decision, the greater its risk, the higher its price, the more valuable and valid it is. That is a truth as basic and as difficult to accept as any Sigmund Freud found and faced.

Frank X. McNamara and Diners Club (1950)

THE DECISION TO REMAKE THE BUSINESS OF BUYING AND SELLING

B y the middle of the twentieth century, the idea of credit was hardly new. The great fortunes of the Italian Renaissance were amassed by moneylenders who extended credit to the crowned heads of Europe, and, doubtless, people borrowed money from one another long before this time. But what the twentieth century introduced on an increasingly large scale was the routine, standardized extension of credit to ordinary individuals, and one of the tools by which credit was standardized was the credit card. As far as anyone can tell, the origin of the credit card may be traced to the practice of many American hotels, beginning in the early 1900s, of offering their customers cards they could use to charge rooms and other services. The idea of the cards was not only to provide a convenience for the guest, but also to keep guests coming back to the same hotel.

The advent of World War I made Americans familiar with "identity discs"—called dog tags by World War II—which doughboys wore around their necks as identification in the event of injury or death. The dog-tag idea inspired a growing number of large department stores to issue "charge plates" to select customers: metal plates stamped with the customer's name, which could be used to make credit purchases. (Even today, people of a certain age refer to their many *plastic* credit cards as charge plates.) By 1924, gas stations also began issuing credit cards, since travelers didn't like to be burdened with carrying extra cash. As with the hotel charge cards, these not only offered the customer a convenience; they encouraged repeat business as well as loyalty to a given brand of gasoline.

The rise of the credit card was slowed by the onset of the Great Depression in 1929. Interest on the cards fell so low that most merchants did not consider the financial rewards of the broad issuance of credit sufficient to compensate for the risk involved. Instead of buying on credit, customers were encouraged to pony up the cash or to make purchases on a layaway plan, in which the merchant retained (but reserved) the merchandise until it was paid for. With the return of prosperity as World War II approached, the credit card revived, only to suffer a new setback when wartime rationing and conservation efforts put restrictions on credit purchasing.

The end of World War II brought an influx of returning GIs who quickly set about the business of creating families. By the start of the 1950s, the baby boom was in full swing and, with it, came an enormous spike in consumer purchasing. That brought back the department store "charge plate" with a vengeance.

Into this emerging climate of consumer credit came Frank X. McNamara, who ran the Hamilton Credit Corporation, a small loan company in New York City. One afternoon in 1949, McNamara took two associates to lunch at Major's Cabin Grill, a favorite Manhattan watering hole next to the Empire State Building. His intention was to discuss with his attorney, Ralph Schneider, and longtime friend Alfred Bloomingdale, grandson of the founder of Bloomingdale's department store, a problem he was having with a Hamilton Credit customer. The difficulty was that the customer had borrowed more than he could pay. Now, that was hardly unusual in the credit business and certainly not worth discussing with Schneider and Bloomingdale. But the wrinkle in this particular case was that the customer had been, in effect, subletting his credit.

A number of his neighbors were too poor to secure oil-company and department-store credit cards on their own. McNamara's customer started regularly lending these folks his own charge cards, requiring that they pay him back, with additional modest interest, for any charges they made. There was, of course, a basic flaw in this arrangement: The man's neighbors were judged to be poor credit risks for good reason, and many of them were unable to pay him back before the credit card charges came due. As a result, he was forced to borrow money from Hamilton Credit to meet his obligations and soon, he couldn't pay, either. McNamara wanted to share this very interesting story, and he also needed practical advice on collection options.

At the end of the lunch, McNamara reached into his pocket for his wallet so that he could pay—in cash, naturally—for the meal. Patting his pockets, he was suddenly seized with a sinking feeling. No wallet. He had left it at home. Red-faced, he phoned his wife, who hopped in a cab with the cash. McNamara swore to himself that this would never happen again, but somehow, he couldn't quite get this little episode behind him. Over the next several days, the case of his delinquent customer and his own embarrassment mingled and merged in his mind until an idea took shape.

McNamara was not a big-time banker, but a small-time loan maker. By rights, his customer's shenanigans should have angered him. But McNamara decided to look beyond anger and annoyance. He decided that, at bottom, his customer's scheme was a sound concept. Sure, the guy was undercapitalized and couldn't carry it off. Nor was it practical (on any kind of meaningful scale) or, for that matter, legal to sublet to others a fistful of your own credit cards. However, McNamara reasoned, instead of lending a bunch of cards to a bunch of people, why not develop a *single* card that could be used in a wide variety of places and then market that card to a large number of people?

Perhaps because the idea had been born in a restaurant, McNamara decided that restaurants would be the best group of businesses to deal with. He called Schneider and Bloomingdale and explained his brainstorm. McNamara put up $25,000, and the other two staked $15,000 each. In February 1950, they opened an office in the Empire State Building, right next door to the fateful restaurant, and they persuaded a small number of New York City restaurants to serve meals, on credit, to members of what they called the Diners Club. Some sources say that the trio began with just fourteen restaurants, others report that twenty-two city restaurants as well as one hotel signed on initially. As to the first cards, McNamara distributed them to about two hundred of his business contacts, mostly salesmen who were obliged to dine frequently with clients.

The first year of business produced a $58,000 loss, but the very next year turned over $6 million in business, for an after-tax profit of a cool $60,000. Despite success, McNamara did not stay on long for the rest of the ride. He sold his share of the company in 1952, and Diners Club continued to grow, so that, by 1958, it had some 200,000 card-holding customers who dined at some 1,000 participating restaurants. The American Express company took notice and entered the travel-and-entertainment card business before the decade was out. Carte Blanche followed a short time later. By the middle 1960s, several banks began issuing revolving credit lines accessible by card, and before the end of the sixties, the idea of the bank card had taken full hold, made possible by the pooled resources of a network of financial institutions. These new cards were called "master charge cards," and they could be used to make purchases not just at businesses related to travel and entertainment, but from just about any store or service firm.

Master Charge, founded in 1967, was the first company devoted solely to issuing master charge cards and, within a year, the Interbank group—the banks behind Master Charge—boasted 16.7 million card-holders who had the power to make credit purchases from some 400,000 participating merchants. Master Charge became MasterCard, and soon other "major credit card" companies came into being, most notably Visa. As for the original, Diners Club, it continued to do business, becoming part of Citibank and expanding its coverage to include all types of merchants. Eventually, Diners Club joined the MasterCard network so that by 2005, Diners Club cardholders could use their cards at more than 24 million locations worldwide.

—

MCNAMARA'S LUNCHTIME DECISION created not only a massive international industry, it began the remaking of the economic universe. "The plastic" has encouraged a nation of consumers to consume even more, transforming the majority of Americans (and probably the majority of people living in the entire developed world) into borrowers, if not debtors. This in itself has created profound social as well as economic changes, intimately tied to technological and cultural transformations McNamara could not have possibly foreseen: the development of sophisticated computers linked via the Internet, the replacement of coin and currency with virtual money existing only as numbers noted in the electronic ether, and a whole new relationship between producers and consumers, defined by electronically stored and instantly available "data," allowing merchants, banks, and governments to monitor spending habits, travel habits, the types and quantities of purchases, and the promptness or tardiness of payments. With each swipe of the plastic through the machine on a merchant's counter, the cardholder simultaneously exercises, enhances, and relinquishes a certain share of freedom.

John F. Kennedy and the Moon (1961)
THE DECISION TO LEAVE THE EARTH

On October 4, 1957, televisions and radios in America and elsewhere in the world broadcast a series of beeps. Nothing spectacular about them—except their origin: the transmitter inside a 184-pound metal orb circling miles above and around the Earth. History's first artificial Earth satellite had not been invented, built, and launched by the world's great democratic capitalist superpower. On the contrary, *Sputnik I* was a triumph of Soviet Communist science. For many, each electronic beep came not as a song celebrating an achievement of humankind, but as a dirge for democracy.

Fat and happy, postwar America had been a largely prosperous and complacent place during most of the two-term administration of a smiling Dwight David Eisenhower. Suddenly, after *Sputnik*, there was less reason for satisfaction.

In 1960, by a razor-thin margin, Americans sent John F. Kennedy to the White House instead of Ike's vice president, Richard M. Nixon. Whereas Nixon was an agent of the status quo, the handsome, glamorous, and suavely idealistic Kennedy promised a new vigor and challenge in American life. Nevertheless, little more than three months into the new president's term, on April 12, 1961, the Soviet Union launched and orbited the first man in space, "cosmonaut" Yuri Gagarin.

First *Sputnik* and now Gagarin. Americans were stunned yet again—perhaps without knowing quite why. True, some military men worried that the Soviets were gaining the "high ground" of space, carving out a kind of platform from which any number of weapons might be aimed at the United States. But that was not what bothered most Americans. It was a deeper and more terrible fear. It was nothing less than doubt, doubt that a free, democratic society was inherently superior to communist totalitarianism and would inevitably triumph over it.

In 1961, the Cold War—that mostly ideological and economic struggle between the United States and the Soviet Union—was about a decade-and-a-half old. That there was no end in sight hardly mattered to most Americans, who were convinced that the United States, representing freedom and all that freedom implied and enabled, would ultimately prevail against the Soviet Union, which was founded on tyranny. Democracy and capitalism had built the modern world. Soviet Communism, on the other hand, was an aberration and could not, therefore, prevail. Yet the facts were that the Soviet Union, not the United States, had orbited *Sputnik* and, now, had orbited Yuri Gagarin as well.

On May 5, 1961, little less than a month after Gagarin's flight, the United States sent astronaut Alan B. Shepard into space, but, even so, his was a suborbital flight, a mere fifteen-minute foray beyond the atmosphere. Nevertheless, Shepard was hailed as a national hero, and JFK embraced him. Ever since the Gagarin mission, the young president had been getting advice to scrap the whole manned space program. The head of his powerful Science Advisory Committee, Jerome B. Wiesner, an MIT professor, wanted NASA to concentrate on aeronautics and relinquish space exploration to the Soviets. He advised Kennedy to cancel Project Mercury—the first phase of the manned space program—immediately and concentrate instead on general science, communications, and *military* satellites. These, Wiesner counseled, were the "winners," and the president should "go with the winners." Besides, if anyone got killed in Mercury, the blame would be laid at the feet of the president.

Kennedy listened, but now that Shepard had been at least to the edge of space and had gotten back alive, he was not about to leave the space race. JFK understood the risks, and he understood the costs, but he reasoned that, in this Cold War, the entire world judged the Soviet Union and the United States not by what they said they stood for, but by what they actually achieved, how they actually performed. He understood that, based on success in high-profile undertakings, the world would judge which nation, which system of government, offered more effective leadership. Strictly in terms of science, Wiesner might have been right: go with the winners, develop those areas that are most immediately useful. But the space race was not about science. It was about who would create the future, and JFK decided that ownership of the future was worth just about any risk.

Seen by many as an idealist, John F. Kennedy was also a realist. His desire not to give up the space race did not blind him to the fact that, so far, the United States was losing. In the contest to orbit a man around the earth, Kennedy conceded, the United States had already lost. Moreover, the Soviets had bigger, more powerful rocket boosters than the

United States, which meant that they were likely, in the near term, to orbit bigger and more impressive payloads—bigger space vehicles carrying more men—than the United States could manage. There would be no pulling ahead of the Soviets in the orbital contest. This led Kennedy to search for a new project, one with an obvious and obviously remarkable goal sufficient to capture the imagination of the world. He also needed to buy time to allow American technology to catch up to and surpass the Soviets. That meant, Kennedy realized, identifying a goal that would take time to achieve and that was at the end of a field in which the Soviets had no appreciable head start. The decision, although daunting, was almost obvious. A man had just orbited the Earth: a giant *Soviet* step. What was the next giant leap for mankind? JFK decided to go to the Moon.

JUST TWENTY DAYS after Shepard's fifteen-minute flight, on May 25, 1961, President Kennedy addressed Congress in a "Special Message on Urgent National Needs":

> If we are to win the battle that is now going on around the world between freedom and tyranny, the dramatic achievements in space which occurred in recent weeks should have made clear to us all, as did the *Sputnik* in 1957, the impact of this adventure on the minds of men everywhere, who are attempting to make a determination of which road they should take.
>
> Since early in my term, our efforts in space have been under review. . . . Now it is time to take longer strides—time for a great new American enterprise—time for this nation to take a clearly leading role in space achievement, which in many ways may hold the key to our future on Earth.
>
> I believe we possess all the resources and talents necessary. But the facts of the matter are that we have never made the national decisions or marshaled the national resources required

for such leadership. We have never specified long-range goals on an urgent time schedule, or managed our resources and our time so as to insure their fulfillment. Recognizing the head start obtained by the Soviets with their large rocket engines, which gives them many months of lead-time, and recognizing the likelihood that they will exploit this lead for some time to come in still more impressive successes, we nevertheless are required to make new efforts on our own. For while we cannot guarantee that we shall one day be first, we can guarantee that any failure to make this effort will be our last. We take an additional risk by making it in full view of the world, but as shown by the feat of astronaut Shepard, this very risk enhances our stature when we are successful. But this is not merely a race. Space is open to us now; and our eagerness to share its meaning is not governed by the efforts of others. We go into space because whatever mankind must undertake, free men must fully share.

With a single suborbital flight having been made—a baby step, compared to what the Soviets had already accomplished—Kennedy declared: "I believe that this nation should commit itself to achieving the goal, before this decade is out, of landing a man on the Moon and returning him safely to the Earth. No single space project in this period will be more impressive to mankind, or more important for the long-range exploration of space; and none will be so difficult or expensive to accomplish." And he asked Congress for the funds to make it possible to achieve the goal he had set.

The president faced questions from politicians, the public, and scientists about whether it was prudent to invest so much money in space when the Earth was confronted with so many urgent problems. They were valid questions. Kennedy, however, believed he was right, and he took comfort in a 1962 *Aviation Week* poll reporting that 56 percent of Americans thought the lunar mission was "questionable but perhaps necessary because of the Cold War." This was hardly an overwhelming popular mandate, but it was enough to suggest that a majority of the American people "got" what the Moon shot was all about. Congress got it, too, and voted the funds.

On September 12, 1962, in an address to the students and faculty of Rice University, President Kennedy put his decision, now officially a national goal, into eloquent context:

> William Bradford, speaking in 1630 of the founding of the Plymouth Bay Colony, said that all great and honorable actions are accompanied with great difficulties, and both must be enterprised and overcome with answerable courage. . . . The exploration of space will go ahead, whether we join in it or not, and it is one of the great adventures of all time, and no nation which expects to be the leader of other nations can expect to stay behind in the race for space.
>
> Those who came before us made certain that this country rode the first waves of the industrial revolutions, the first waves of modern invention, and the first wave of nuclear power, and this generation does not intend to founder in the backwash of the coming age of space. We mean to be a part of it—we mean to lead it. For the eyes of the world now look into space, to the moon and to the planets beyond, and we have vowed that we shall not see it governed by a hostile flag of conquest, but by a banner of freedom and peace. We have vowed that we shall not see space filled with weapons of mass destruction, but with instruments of knowledge and understanding.
>
> Yet the vows of this Nation can only be fulfilled if we in this Nation are first, and, therefore, we intend to be first. In short, our leadership in science and in industry, our hopes for peace and security, our obligations to ourselves as well as others, all require us to make this effort, to solve these mysteries, to solve them for the good of all men, and to become the world's leading spacefaring nation.

We set sail on this new sea because there is new knowledge to be gained, and new rights to be won, and they must be won and used for the progress of all people. For space science, like nuclear science and all technology, has no conscience of its own. Whether it will become a force for good or ill depends on man, and only if the United States occupies a position of preeminence can we help decide whether this new ocean will be a sea of peace or a new terrifying theater of war. . . .

There is no strife, no prejudice, no national conflict in outer space as yet. Its hazards are hostile to us all. Its conquest deserves the best of all mankind, and its opportunity for peaceful cooperation may never come again. But why, some say, the moon? Why choose this as our goal? And they may well ask why climb the highest mountain? Why, thirty-five years ago, fly the Atlantic? Why does Rice play Texas?

We choose to go to the moon. We choose to go to the moon in this decade and do the other things, not because they are easy, but because they are hard, because that goal will serve to organize and measure the best of our energies and skills, because that challenge is one that we are willing to accept, one we are unwilling to postpone, and one which we intend to win, and the others, too.

. . . To be sure, we are behind, and will be behind for some time in manned flight. But we do not intend to stay behind, and in this decade, we shall make up and move ahead.

. . . Many years ago the great British explorer George Mallory, who was to die on Mount Everest, was asked why did he want to climb it. He said, "Because it is there."

Well, space is there, and we're going to climb it, and the moon and the planets are there, and new hopes for knowledge and peace are there. And, therefore, as we set sail we ask God's blessing on the most hazardous and dangerous and greatest adventure on which man has ever embarked.

Ted Turner and CNN (1979)

THE DECISION TO NETWORK THE PLANET

F ew great decisions take place in a moment, but every decision, no matter how complex, does have its moment. For Ted Turner, the decision to risk his fortune and his media-and-sports empire on the unheard-of notion of creating a twenty-four-hour cable television news network crystallized in the moment he realized what it meant that a man named Bill Lucas was going to die.

Vice president of the Atlanta Braves baseball team, which Turner owned, Bill Lucas had suffered a massive hemorrhage of the brain. Initially, the news was devastating to Turner, who regarded the impending death of a young, strong former athlete as simply senseless. Then came the moment in which the death of Bill Lucas suddenly made a certain sense. It was a message.

For some years, Ted Turner had been thinking about creating a twenty-four-hour cable television news network. There were many obstacles, ranging from the infancy of the cable industry during the 1970s to the fact that just about everyone he talked to said it couldn't be done and, even more, that it shouldn't be done. But he kept thinking. When he floated the idea at a meeting of cable-service operators and failed to obtain subscription commitments from most of them, he hesitated, but he did not discard the idea. Now that Bill Lucas was about to die, Ted Turner called Reese Schonfeld, a television news journalist and executive with whom he had been formulating the idea. Hank Whittemore, in his 1990 book *CNN: The Inside Story*, relates the substance of the phone call:

> "Hey, Reese! Do you know what happened today to Bill Lucas?"
>
> "No. What happened?"
>
> "He's got a hemorrhage! He's gonna die! And guess what? *None* of us is gonna live forever! So listen, Reese, let's *do* this thing! With or *without* support!"

For Ted Turner, a moment of mortality was the tipping point. It was a classic moment of *If not now, when? If not me, who?* Behind it was a long string of insights and decisions, which combined all at once with essential elements of Ted Turner's personality and the state of television, communications, and satellite technology in the year 1979.

First, Ted Turner.

In a famous quote, he remarked that "I just love it when people say I can't do something. There's nothing that makes me feel better, because all my life people have said I wasn't going to make it."

Ted Turner was born Robert Edward Turner III in 1938 in Cincinnati, Ohio, the son of a man in the outdoor advertising business. When he was nine, the family moved to Savannah, Georgia, where prospects for the billboard business looked brighter. Young Ted was a handful, and his father a stern disciplinarian. He sent the boy to military schools, after which Ted enrolled in Brown University. In college, he became passionate about sailboat racing, but was suspended during his sophomore year for drunken misbehavior while visiting a nearby women's college. Turner joined the Coast Guard, served for six months, and then returned to Brown, where he pursued a course of liberal arts studies that struck his father as an acute waste of time. In the end, it didn't matter, because Ted Turner never graduated. He was expelled for "entertaining" female guests in his dorm room. After another interval with the Coast Guard, he went to work for his father, who, in 1960, made him general manager of the Turner Advertising branch in Macon, Georgia. On March 5, 1963, with his outdoor advertising business faltering, Ted Turner's father, deeply depressed, killed himself.

Surely, there must have been profound ambivalence in this father-son relationship, but the suicide of Ed Turner suddenly gave direction to the life of Ted Turner. As if determined both to redeem his father's memory and to outshine him, he set about rebuilding the advertising company, and used it as the foundation on which to build a much larger media empire. In an interview, Turner confessed to having had, as a young man, the "gnawing feeling" that he was not going to be a success.

"My father died when I was twenty-four and he was the one, really, that I had expected to be the judge of whether I was successful or not." When, years after his father's death, he appeared on the cover of *Success* magazine, Ted Turner held it up and said, "Dad? Do you see this? I made the cover of *Success* magazine! Is that *enough?*"

In 1970, Turner purchased Atlanta's financially ailing Channel 17, an independent UHF station, and renamed his company TBS (Turner Broadcasting System). Then, six months later, he bought the UHF Channel 36 in Charlotte, North Carolina. By 1972, he had made Channel 17 profitable and the next year acquired the rights to broadcast Atlanta Braves baseball games, beating out the city's far larger network affiliate, WSB. Turner had a talent for making weaknesses seem like strengths. In the early 1970s, UHF stations had far fewer viewers than the longer-established "standard" VHF stations; before the widespread advent of cable, UHF was harder to tune in, TVs required special UHF antennas, and older sets needed UHF converters as well. To potential advertisers who pointed this out, Ted Turner replied that fewer viewers meant more intelligent viewers, because anyone who could actually tune in to a UHF station *had* to be smart. And when those same advertisers next pointed out that much of Turner's programming, which consisted largely of rerun classic TV shows, was in black-and-white, Turner responded that this would serve to enhance the "shock value" of the color commercials and make people pay more attention to them.

Now, the technology.

In 1975, Ted Turner took notice when Home Box Office (HBO), a pioneer of cable television, announced that it would soon begin transmitting its signal to a new communications satellite. The satellite would bounce the signal back to receiving dishes owned by American cable distributors, who would, in turn, distribute the programming to cable subscribers all over the United States. In this way, HBO would be a *national* television presence. Inspired by this example, Turner decided to make WTCG Channel 17 the first local broadcast station to go national by sending its signal to a satellite and bouncing it to America's cable distributors. In 1976, he launched the enterprise, which he called a "superstation." As he saw it, whereas HBO showed *new* movies, he would offer the nation *old* movies from the large and growing library of films he was in the process of amassing. Having just purchased the Atlanta Braves, he now owned outright the broadcast rights to the club's games, and he beamed these to the nation along with other sports events (in 1977, he would buy the Atlanta Hawks basketball team) in addition to the reruns he had started with.

Although his superstation was feeding cable subscribers nationwide the kind of broadcast programming nobody else was giving them, Turner realized that one thing was still missing: news.

The traditional broadcast networks had news shows, of course, but the national news broadcasts occupied just one half-hour (twenty-two minutes plus commercials) each evening. Ted Turner proposed to use a satellite/cable station to give the nation what no one else was giving it: twenty-four hours of news.

Turner was aware of the success of radio stations that featured an all-news format. Nevertheless, the idea was unprecedented in television, and everyone said it would fail. The reason was obvious: As the major broadcast networks knew only too well, news lost money. People wanted entertainment. There was virtually no demand for news, let alone twenty-four hours of it, and elementary economics teaches that it is foolish to supply something for which there is no demand.

Precisely because the idea violated the commonest of common wisdom, it appealed to Ted Turner. In American business, market researchers asked people what they wanted; then, based on this information, companies supplied it. Turner argued that operating this way doomed you to unoriginality. Did the Wright brothers ask people whether or not they wanted an airplane *before* they invented it? Of course not. Turner's belief was that if you offered something wonderful, it would create the necessary demand. Build it, and they will come.

Over the next few years, Turner began to gather a small cadre of non-network, but television-savvy, news experts. Working with them, he put together the formula and the logistics of a twenty-four-hour news station. He understood that setting up the venture would require sinking into it virtually every dime his media and sports empire produced. He was willing to go into debt, because he believed that he was offering a unique value, which would ultimately create profits. He was also keenly aware that he occupied a critical moment in time: He had the idea, he was in touch with the right people to execute the idea, and a brand-new technology existed to make the idea a reality. Sure, people were laughing at the concept right now, but very soon, he believed, someone else would do this very thing, create a cable-television news network. "Once it's obvious to everybody that something is going to be successful, the opportunity is gone," he later explained. "Then anybody else can do it, too."

As Turner moved closer to the decision, those who worked with him noticed that he began asking people, ordinary people, "Don't you think an all-news TV channel would be terrific?" It was as if he were daring them to answer no. It was as if he were trying to find something wrong with the idea. He asked colleagues and he asked himself: "Am I crazy?" and "Why am I doing this?" But the more he asked, the more he became convinced of his decision. He stumbled and hesitated when, after presenting the idea to the cable operators, few were willing to pony up the modest subscription fee he asked for. But it was at this moment that Bill Lucas died, and Ted Turner became aware of his own mortality. He decided to follow his original instinct: to build the network in the confidence that the demand would follow.

ON MAY 21, 1979, TURNER ANNOUNCED to the convention of the National Cable Television Association that CNN, the Cable News Network, would be launched on June 1, 1980, and that it would be a national news network (with "overseas sources" around the world as well), broadcasting news and only news, twenty-four hours a day, seven days a week. He explained that his intention was to realize the promise of television that media philosopher Marshall McLuhan had written about in the 1960s: the transformation of the world into a "global village." Moved to action by Turner's bold announcement, the cable providers, including the many who had hesitated less than a year before, rushed to subscribe, and Ted Turner never looked back—or had reason to.

Bill Gates and MS-DOS (1981)

THE DECISION TO OWN
AN INDISPENSABLE TECHNOLOGY

It is rare that living, let alone middle-aged, people earn a place in the likes of *Encyclopaedia Britannica*—although, admittedly, that august publication does hedge its bet in its article on the founder of Microsoft. "It remains to be seen," *Britannica* says, "whether Gates's extraordinary success will guarantee him a lasting place in the pantheon of great Americans," but it concludes that, "at the very least, historians seem likely to view him as a business figure as important to computers as John D. Rockefeller was to oil."

Rockefeller had a most unpleasant side and created a great deal of controversy, but just as his importance to the oil industry is obvious, so is the role of oil in civilization, which officially began, let's say, with Ford's Model T of 1908. Like Rockefeller, Bill Gates also has an unpleasant side and has created a great deal of controversy, but his importance to the personal computer is obvious, as is the evolving role of the personal computer in civilization, beginning with the release of the IBM PC in 1981.

Gates's role in the creation of modern civilization was made possible in part through genetic predisposition, through being in the right place at a certain time in the evolution of information and information-processing technology, and through certain deliberate decisions he made.

The genetic part is clear from the fact that he wrote his first program at the age of thirteen. While he was still in high school, he became a charter member of a group of programmers who put the school's payroll system on computer, and, before graduating, he founded his first software company. Traf-O-Data grew out of a part-time data-processing job Gates took in 1971. A firm called Logic Simulation had been commissioned to study traffic on the streets of Kent, Washington, by means of strategically placed counting boxes, each attached to a hose laid across the street. Every time a car crossed the hose, the box registered a count, spitting out the results as holes punched into a paper tape—at the time the predominant medium for recording data. Gates had the tedious job of counting the holes and producing a report while also transcribing the results onto punch cards so that the data could be transferred to a computer that read punch cards rather than tape. To do the grunt work, Gates hired classmates from his high school, including a friend named Paul Allen who had recently graduated. This collaboration developed into Traf-O-Data, which was headquartered in Allen's dorm room at Washington State University.

Gates and Allen got jobs programming for defense contractor TRW and, while working for that company, developed computer hardware and software that enabled Traf-O-Data to perfect and market efficient traffic-counting systems to local governments. After graduating from high school, Gates enrolled in Harvard University in 1973, but by his sophomore year was again working with Paul Allen on software development—this time for the emerging microcomputer industry—beginning by adapting BASIC, an important mainframe language, for use on microcomputers. The success of this venture made Gates impatient with higher education, and, during his junior year, he left Harvard to found Microsoft with Allen.

Microsoft rapidly became a small-business success story, in part because Gates made the first of three turning-point decisions concerning his role in the emerging microcomputer industry. The first decision concerned the identity of his prime customers. Gates understood that, operating in an embryonic marketplace, he was in a position to shape the industry, becoming a major force in it. He would do this, he decided, not by serving individual consumers ("end users," as the industry called them), but by marketing his products to a host of emerging microcomputer manufacturers. Gates was determined that Microsoft would become the leader in OEM sales (sales to "original equipment manufacturers"), supplying microcomputer makers with the software needed to run their machines, including Microsoft-modified versions of the classic programming languages BASIC, COBOL, FORTRAN, and Pascal.

Gates worked closely with computer makers and chip manufacturers to ensure that his software would be optimally compatible with their hardware. He persuaded them—quite correctly—that while his company certainly needed them, they just as certainly needed him and that, ultimately, it would be software that would drive the emerging industry.

Things were going very well for Bill Gates and his small business. Beginning on July 21, 1980, they were about to go a lot better. On that day, Gates received a phone call from IBM, which resulted in a meeting at which the computer giant asked Microsoft to develop software for the microcomputer it intended to design and manufacture. Gates knew that, to the proverbial man on the street, the three initials *I-B-M* were synonymous with the word *computer*. If IBM made a microcomputer, there would be no turning back. The industry would be here to stay. With IBM's endorsement, Gates believed that a day would come when there would be a computer on every desk and in every home. He was also aware, however, that his company, with about forty employees, was too small even to be considered a David to IBM's Goliath. Companies like "Big Blue" ate small fry for lunch and didn't break a sweat. Even if getting swallowed up hadn't been a danger, there existed a vast cultural gulf between the suit-and-wingtips computer giant and the jeans-and-sandals entrepreneurs at Microsoft. But Gates was not content to remain a small business, and, despite the risks, here was a chance to create a market, shape an industry, and remake the world. He decided to take it. It was his second turning-point decision.

As the ink dried on the initial deal with IBM, Gates sensed that something was missing from his company's portfolio. IBM wanted software to bundle with the machine that was about to come into the world as the "personal computer." Gates was happy that IBM had come to his company for the software, but he also understood that soon there would be many companies capable of supplying a wide variety of software to IBM and to other hardware makers. There was, however, one essential piece of software IBM and everyone else would need, regardless of whatever else they bundled with a machine. It was an operating system, the software layer between the machine itself and any useful programs the user wanted to run. An operating system performed the basic tasks, including recognizing input from the keyboard, sending output to the display screen, keeping track of files and directories, and controlling such peripheral devices as disk drives and printers. Initially, IBM merely asked Gates to supply an off-the-shelf operating system that Microsoft had licensed from another company. It was called CP/M ("Control Program for Microcomputers"), and, in the infancy of the microcomputer industry, it came closest to being the standard operating system— although the term "standard" meant little at the time, since CP/M existed in a variety of mutually incompatible flavors.

Gates had struck a terrific deal with Digital Research, the creator of CP/M, which allowed Microsoft wide latitude in licensing the product. Microsoft would certainly make money supplying a version of CP/M to IBM. At present, however, CP/M was a very limited program, designed to operate with the 8-bit microchip, which, even by 1980, was an obsolescent piece of processing hardware. Gates encouraged IBM to base its forthcoming PC on the emerging 16-bit chip architecture, which could do a lot more a lot faster. Trouble was that CP/M-86, the Digital Research operating system intended for the 16-bit chips, was still in the works and was progressing very slowly. Moreover, the corporate culture of Digital Research more closely resembled that of Microsoft than it did IBM, but whereas Bill Gates decided to bridge the cultural divide and work with the suits at Big Blue, DR's leadership found the going much rougher. The deal for the still-unfinished CP/M-86 couldn't get off the ground.

In the meantime, Gates negotiated an increasingly sweet deal with IBM. With Digital Research receding from the picture, however, he was facing a situation that could either become an unmitigated disaster or a spectacular opportunity. Gates had pushed IBM to back a 16-bit machine; however, Digital Research, the source for the 16-bit operating system, increasingly seemed to be a nonstarter. Without a 16-bit operating system, the Microsoft-IBM deal would fall through, and either the microcomputer industry would stumble—badly—or somebody else would step in to partner with IBM.

At this point, Paul Allen thought of Tim Paterson, a computer engineer he knew. Paterson's company, Seattle Computer Products, had a little-known product called QDOS: Quick and Dirty Operating System. A connection was made between Paterson and Gates, and QDOS quickly evolved into 86-DOS, a 16-bit operating system. At the time, Seattle Computer wanted to license Microsoft's bread-and-butter programming language, BASIC, to use with its 86-DOS product. Paterson suggested a swap: in exchange for the right to license Microsoft's languages (including BASIC), Seattle Computer would give Microsoft the right to license 86-DOS. Now Gates could continue working with IBM, confident at last that he had an operating system for them.

For $10,000, Gates secured the nonexclusive right to distribute 86-DOS to an unlimited number of end users. For another $10,000 per company, he could sublicense 86-DOS to OEM customers. For $15,000 each, he could sublicense 86-DOS complete with the source code—the very guts of the operating system. Moreover, Seattle Computer agreed to work diligently to improve the operating system and make any improvements available as well.

It was, of course, an extraordinary deal, with plenty of margin for Microsoft profit when that company exercised its sublicense to IBM and any other customers. According to Stephen Manes and Paul Andrews, in their 1994 *Gates,* Microsoft received from IBM an up-front advance of about $400,000 for what was now being called simply DOS against a royalty of anywhere from one to fifteen dollars per copy of DOS, in addition to other large amounts of money for language software also sublicensed to IBM. Moreover, the contract was unilaterally nonexclusive: While IBM was barred from licensing DOS and other Microsoft programs to third parties, Microsoft was free to sell DOS (and its other programs) to anyone at any time.

But this wasn't the end of the deal.

In the months that followed the DOS contract between IBM and Microsoft, and even before the IBM PC hit the shelves, other manufacturers, especially from Japan, approached Microsoft about DOS. Thanks to the terms of his IBM contract, Gates was free to sublicense it to them. Great news. Even more exciting was an offer from Lifeboat Associates, the leading independent distributor of the biggest competitor of DOS, CP/M. Lifeboat wanted to make DOS, not CP/M, its standard 16-bit product, and it offered Microsoft hundreds of thousands of dollars for the right to do so.

Bill Gates had understood the significance of selling an operating system to IBM, but he had understood it mainly as a means of getting the IBM PC off the ground, thereby ensuring the future of the microcomputer industry and thereby providing a market for Microsoft's other software products, especially its array of programming languages. The operating system was vitally important, but, as Gates had seen it, it was primarily a means to an end. Now, amid a cascade of additional offers for DOS, he saw the operating system not just as a means to an end, but as an end in itself—the key to dominance of the microcomputer software industry.

This insight motivated his third turning-point decision. Gates, with Allen, decided to acquire DOS—outright—from Seattle Computer. As another Microsoft principal, Steve Ballmer, put it: "Bill's judgment and gut told him that the best thing is for this to be something that's clearly ours and clearly unencumbered and something where we could have flexibility to do whatever we wanted to do with it." Ultimately, Microsoft acquired full ownership of DOS for $75,000.

From the perspective of today, with Bill Gates one of the richest men in the world and Microsoft one of the world's most powerful companies, the deal seems akin to Peter Minuit buying Manhattan for twenty-four dollars. But this was by no means clear to industry pundits in 1981. Many said that IBM had made a huge mistake by hitching their about-to-be-introduced PC to this "new" operating system instead of latching on to what they called the "industry standard," CP/M. What they did not realize—and what Gates realized above all else—is that IBM's endorsement of DOS would render CP/M irrelevant. Gates had persuaded IBM to go with DOS—now called MS-DOS, for *Microsoft* DOS—thereby recruiting IBM as the mighty muscle by which CP/M would be pummeled and swept away. As Gates had predicted, the IBM PC *made* the personal computer market, and since it ran on MS-DOS, it also made the market for microcomputer operating systems—the market that Microsoft was in a uniquely powerful position to supply. And when IBM's many emerging competitors prepared to introduce their own machines, Gates was now in a position to ask each of them: Do you want to go with CP/M, a dying operating system a few small-timers cling to, or MS-DOS, the one endorsed by IBM? The answer was obvious.

THE ANSWER NOT ONLY PROMOTED Microsoft's explosive expansion of business; it promoted the establishment of software and hardware standards that ended the issues of incompatibility that had threatened to strangle the microcomputer industry in its infancy. The widespread adoption of MS-DOS promoted standards that made a PC a PC, whether it was manufactured by IBM or some other company. Gates fully realized the great power of standards. They "increase the basic machine we can sell into," he declared. "I really shouldn't say this, but in some ways [standards lead] . . . to a natural monopoly: where somebody properly documents, properly trains, properly promotes a particular package and through momentum, user loyalty, reputation, sales force, and prices builds a very strong position within the product." That phrase, "natural monopoly," would come back to haunt Bill Gates in the mid-1990s, when Microsoft became embroiled in massive and costly federal litigation over charges of violation of antitrust laws, but the phrase nevertheless described the universe created by Bill Gates's decision to own a technology he himself had worked to make indispensable. As *Britannica* says: Gates is to personal computers what Rockefeller was to oil, and as the encyclopedia implies, this fact, and the decisions that made it fact, propelled him to a central role in our society and civilization.

PART THREE

The Decision
of Conscience

Joan of Arc and the Dauphin (1429)

THE DECISION TO ACT ON INSPIRATION

The story of Joan of Arc has fascinated and inspired generations since 1431, when her nineteen-year life ended in flames. Her devotees have included even the most unlikely of people, among them Mark Twain. A man capable of penning such acid observations as "If you pick up a starving dog and make him prosperous, he will not bite you. This is the principal difference between a dog and a man," wrote adoringly of Joan, "There is no blemish in that rounded and beautiful character." He thought so highly of her that, in 1896, he devoted a long and rather tedious novel to the life of Joan of Arc. The author of *Life on the Mississippi* and *Adventures of Huckleberry Finn*, Twain believed his greatest work to have been *Personal Recollections of Joan of Arc by the Sieur Louis de Conte*, which few read during his lifetime and no one reads today.

In a magazine article written around the time of his novel, Twain encapsulated the achievement of this girl of medieval France and accounted for the enduring power she exercised over his imagination and that of so many others. An uneducated peasant raised "in a dull little village on the frontiers of civilization," Joan, "aged seventeen, . . . was

made Commander-in-Chief, with a prince of the royal house and the veteran generals of France for subordinates; at the head of the first army she
had ever seen, she marched to Orléans, carried the commanding
fortresses of the enemy by storm in three desperate assaults, and in ten
days raised a siege which defied the might of France for seven months."
The victories of this adolescent girl at Patay and elsewhere during 1429
and 1430 struck a blow, Twain and others have observed, from which
English power in France "was destined never to recover. It was the beginning of the end of an alien dominion which had ridden France intermit-
tently for three hundred years" and it "broke the back" of the
interminable Hundred Years' War. The price she paid, of course, was terrible. Captured by the pro-English Burgundians, she was sold to the English, who set up an ecclesiastical kangaroo court that convicted her of
heresy and sent her to the stake at Rouen. Years later, the Church "reha-
bilitated" her, France came to revere her as its national hero, and Pope
Benedict XV canonized her as Saint Joan in 1920.

Some may regard the transformation of an unlettered and innocent
peasant girl into the savior of France as nothing more or less than a divine
miracle. Others may dismiss the story as history clouded by religious
mythology. For both these factions, the story of Joan of Arc holds little
human interest. Nevertheless, as Mark Twain and so many others have
discovered, whatever else it may be, the story of Joan is an intensely
human story. It is about the power of a decision.

Joan of Arc—Jeanne d'Arc or Jehanne Darc—was born about 1412
in the village of Domrémy in the valley of the Meuse. At the time of her
birth, Domrémy was in the Duchy of Bar, a part of France loyal to Burgundy, which, in turn, favored the hegemony of the English and opposed
the Armagnacs, who wanted to expel the English and bring the dauphin,
Charles VII, to the French throne. In 1420, however, after years of
combat, the Treaty of Troyes gave the throne to the heirs of the English
king Henry V, disinheriting Charles. Accordingly, after Henry V's death in
1422, the infant Henry VI became—at least in name—king of France.
A little more than two years after this event, "in my father's garden,"

thirteen-year-old Joan of Arc began to see visions of Saint Michael the Archangel, Saint Catherine, and Saint Margaret.

"And the first time," she later said, "I was very much afraid." She explained: "I heard the voice on my right, in the direction of the [little church near her father's house], and rarely do I hear it without a light. This light comes from the same side as the voice." Frightened though she was, Joan concluded: "It seemed to me a worthy voice, and I believed it was sent to me by God . . ."

Joan was a girl, not a divine being. Her first response to the voice was fear, but this was followed by a judgment—apparently based in part on the direction of the voice and the light that accompanied it—that the voice was "worthy." From this conclusion, Joan decided to *believe*.

At first the voice told her simply "to be good, to go regularly to church." But, over a period of about four years, the voice, or really, voices—those of Saints Michael, Catherine, and Margaret—became more specific in what they asked. By 1428, when Joan was sixteen, the English had made extensive inroads into more of France and were about to begin a campaign aimed at conquering the entire south of the country. It was now that the voices told Joan she "should come into France"—that is, the territory still loyal to the dauphin. "This voice told me, two or three times a week, that I must go away and that I must come to France." The voice gave explicit instructions as to how she was to begin this task, telling her that "I should go to Robert de Baudricourt at the town of Vaucouleurs, who was the captain of the town, and he would provide people [a military escort] to go with me" to Chinon, the seat of the dauphin's court. There she was to persuade the dauphin, Charles VII, to commence an aggressive campaign to reclaim his throne.

Joan objected to all of this by pointing out the obvious: "I replied that I was a poor girl who knew neither how to ride nor lead in war." To this, Saint Michael responded that Saints Catherine and Margaret would come to her "and that I should act on their advice; that they were instructed to lead and advise me in what I had to do; and that I should believe in what they would say to me, for it was by God's order."

We may rightly ask whether Joan of Arc actually made any decisions at all. Perhaps she was mentally ill and did not so much decide to act as she was moved to action by her delusions. But even if we grant her sanity, even if we believe that she was visited by the saints, can one decide to refuse a task assigned by the messengers of the Lord?

Luckily, we don't need the answers. All that is important is that Joan believed herself to be sane, and she believed that she had spoken with the angels. Most important of all, she did *not* believe that she had been *commanded* to do anything, at least not in her early experience of the voices. By her own account, through all of her early "conversations," no order, no divine commandment, was ever issued. Instead, Saint Michael's voice appealed to the girl's reason, assuring her that she would be given instructions and that she would be carrying out God's will. Free will is key to faith, and Joan's saints never asked her to relinquish that. Whatever instructions she might receive, it would still be up to Joan to decide whether to act in accordance with her voices.

The French crisis of 1428 seems to have persuaded her to do just that. But how would she persuade others?

On or about May 13, 1428, Joan told her father that she was off to visit relatives in Burey-le-Petit, a village near Vaucouleurs. She managed to persuade her uncle there, Durand Lassois, to take her to Robert de Baudricourt at Vaucouleurs. Presumably, she told Robert what she had told her uncle: that "she wanted to go to France, to the dauphin, to have him crowned, saying: 'Has it not been said that France would be ruined by a woman and later restored by a virgin?'" Robert's response was to tell Lassois "several times to take her back to her father's house and slap her." At this, Joan clearly became discouraged, withdrew from the audience with Robert, and returned to Domrémy.

In July 1428, two months after her disappointing audience, the Anglo-Burgundians attacked Vaucouleurs and other villages, including Domrémy. Then, on October 12, the English laid siege to Orléans, which controlled a crucial bridge over the Loire, gateway to all southern France. At this time, Joan's voices told her "that I should raise the siege laid [by the Anglo-Burgundians] to the city of Orléans," and she was accordingly moved to make a second journey to Vaucouleurs.

In January 1429, she left her home village forever, having now at last decided that she was definitely acting in accordance with a commandment of God, and since he had "commanded it, it was necessary that I do it. Since God commanded it, even if I had a hundred fathers and mothers, even if I had been a king's daughter, I would have gone nevertheless."

Once again, she talked her uncle into taking her to Vaucouleurs, and for three weeks she repeatedly asked Robert de Baudricourt to escort her to the dauphin. "Have you not heard," she pleaded with him, "that it has been prophesied that France will be ruined by a woman and restored by a virgin from the borders of Lorraine?" Robert remained unimpressed, even as stories of Joan were spreading. Though Robert continued to do his best to ignore her, a lord in the distant city of Nancy, in Lorraine (at the time part of the Holy Roman Empire), sent a message to Joan, asking that she meet with Duke Charles II of Lorraine. Aged and ailing, the duke hoped that this visionary of whom he had heard could cure him. Eager to find anyone with the power possibly to help her, she traveled to Nancy and told the duke "that I wanted to go to France. The Duke questioned me about the recovery of his health, but I said I knew nothing about that. . . . I nevertheless said . . . that he should send his son and some men to take me into France, and that I would pray to God for his health."

Duke Charles II did nothing but give Joan safe conduct back to Vaucouleurs, and, on or about February 12, she appeared before Robert de Baudricourt yet again. Before she called on him this time, she spoke to Jean de Metz, one of Robert's soldiers. "My friend," he asked her, "what are you doing here? Will not the King be expelled from the kingdom and we become English?"

Joan replied: "I have come to this Royal town to speak to Robert de Baudricourt, so that he might wish to bring me, or have me brought, to the King; but he pays no attention to me or my words." Despairing though this sounded, Joan continued: "Nevertheless, before mid-Lent I must be before the King even if I must wear down my feet to the knees. For truly no one in the world, neither kings, nor dukes, nor the King of Scotland's daughter, or anyone else can regain the Kingdom of France; there is no aid except myself, although I would prefer to spin wool beside my poor mother, because [leading an army] is not my social station; but it is necessary that I go, and do this, for my Lord wishes that I do it."

Jean de Metz asked her when she wanted to leave.

"Rather now than tomorrow, and tomorrow rather than later."

The interest Duke Charles of Lorraine had taken in her must have impressed Robert, because this time he granted her the escort she wanted. As she left, he bade: "Go, and let come what may."

These parting words are significant; for they clearly reveal that Robert did not share Joan's faith. But, then, neither did the dauphin, Charles VII. A feckless young man, his own people called him *le falot*, "the comical one," because of his awkward and ungainly appearance. He had no driving ambition to be king of France, and he was plagued by doubts over the very legitimacy of his birth. This passionless, even apathetic dauphin was about to meet a girl driven by a sense of mission she believed heaven-sent. Like her encounter with Robert de Baudricourt, it would be yet another contest between the forward force of faith and the backward force of doubt.

With her escort of soldiers—whom she seems to have won over completely during the long journey to the dauphin's seat in Chinon— Joan of Arc arrived on March 4, 1429. She wanted to meet with Charles VII instantly, but had to wait two days while the dithering young man held counsel with his advisers, who frenetically debated the prudence of allowing the meeting. At length, she was admitted to an audience, which was witnessed by some hundreds of the dauphin's supporters.

"Noble Dauphin, I am called Jehanne the Maiden and the King of the Heavens sends word to you through me, that you will be anointed and crowned in the town of Rheims, and you will be the lieutenant of the King of Heaven, who is King of France."

Who could resist her conviction? A witness reported that, "having heard her, the King looked joyful." Yet Charles VII was not the person of faith Joan of Arc was, and, even having joyfully heard her, he decided to send her to Poitiers for three weeks of questioning and examination by clerics and theologians, as one noble recalled, "in order to know if he should or could rightfully believe in her."

Joan did her best to answer patiently all of the questions. When one examiner asked her to produce a sign of the legitimacy of her mission, she replied, "In God's name, I did not come to Poitiers to produce signs; but send me to Orléans; I will show you the signs for which I was sent." At length, the clerics and theologians advised Charles VII to send her.

The rest of the familiar story can be quickly told. Joan reached the besieged city on April 29, 1429. She led the army in taking a number of English fortifications between May 4 and May 7, forcing the English to lift the siege on May 8. This event was widely accepted by the French clergy as verification of her legitimacy as a visionary, and it greatly inspired the dauphin's army, which, under Joan's continued leadership, set about evicting the English from the rest of the Loire Valley. A great victory at Patay on June 18, in which 2,200 English soldiers were killed for the loss of about twenty French and allied Scots, allowed the dauphin's forces to march toward Rheims for the coronation of Charles VII. This occurred on the morning of July 17, 1429.

Joan and her top commanders wanted to maintain the momentum of victory with an immediate march on Paris, but Charles, though crowned, once again demonstrated his deficiency of faith and passion. Rather than take his rightful place boldly, he favored a negotiated peace with the Duke of Burgundy. Hostilities were renewed after a brief truce, and Charles's army at last slowly advanced on Paris. It did not attack the city until September 8, but when an arrow pierced Joan's leg, the attack—against her urgent pleading—was instantly called off. Terrified, Charles ordered the army to withdraw on the tenth. Lacking royal support, subsequent attacks elsewhere in November and December failed. A new truce went into effect, and Joan did not return to the field

until March 14, 1430. While leading an attempt to lift the siege of
Compiègne on May 23, she was captured by Burgundian troops and
ultimately handed over to the English, who saw to her conviction and
execution as a heretic.

———

REALLY, IT IS HARD TO IMAGINE that it could have ended any other way.
Joan of Arc's is a story of what happens when a decision is built on faith
and absolute conviction. It was not an easy decision for her to reach, and
it came from nothing in her background or education (she had no education) and even less from any inborn desire for glory. Once the decision
had been reached, however, it became easier for Joan to decide to accept
the mission she believed had been assigned to her. Driven by these
cumulative decisions, she overcame the resistance of a world populated
by the undecided and the unfaithful. Despite the prodigies she achieved,
Joan of Arc could not long exist in such a world. The dauphin proved
unworthy of the height to which her faith had elevated him, and it was
Joan of Arc who paid the price for his unworthiness.

Lincoln and Emancipation (1862)
THE DECISION FOR FREEDOM

In a world painted mostly in shades of moral gray, very few issues
present themselves in the stark contrast of simple right versus simple
wrong. For us, in the twenty-first century, slavery is just such an issue. About
it there is only wrong and can be no right—which is why what Abraham
Lincoln wrote of slavery on August 22, 1862, still has the power to stun us:

> My paramount object in this [Civil War] struggle is to save the
> Union, and is not either to save or destroy Slavery. If I could save
> the Union without freeing any slave, I would do it; and if I could

save it by freeing all the slaves, I would do it; and if I could do it by freeing some and leaving others alone, I would also do that. What I do about Slavery and the colored race, I do because I believe it helps to save this Union; and what I forbear, I forbear because I do not believe it would help to save the Union.

This was the president's response to an open letter that *New York Tribune* editor Horace Greeley addressed to him in the pages of his paper, a critical letter written (Greeley declared) on behalf of the twenty million citizens of the loyal states. Although Lincoln's response shocks us, it probably did not surprise those who had voted for him or had even followed his career. It is true that, in the 1850s, when he debated Stephen Douglas in an unsuccessful campaign for a Senate seat, Lincoln called slavery "an unqualified evil to the negro, the white man, and the State," yet, less than a decade later, in his first inaugural address, he disavowed any "purpose, directly or indirectly, to interfere with slavery in the States where it exists," and, in his first message to Congress on July 4, 1861, three months into the Civil War, he said much the same thing.

What appears to us today as a moral issue with but a single, self-evident right side, presented an agony of ambiguity to Lincoln. As president, he had sworn an oath to "preserve, protect, and defend" the Constitution, and the Constitution in 1861 clearly protected slavery. Most members of Lincoln's own Republican Party, an antislavery party, believed this, and only a radical minority argued that the outbreak of the war gave the president the legal authority to abolish slavery.

Lincoln certainly did not think so. In May 1861, Major General Benjamin F. Butler, commanding Fort Monroe, Virginia, gave asylum to runaway slaves at his fort, refusing to return them to their owners. Lincoln thought Butler was acting contrary to the Constitution but, on the advice of his cabinet, chose not to reprimand him. However, three months later, when Major General John C. Frémont—commanding Union army forces in St. Louis—took it upon himself to proclaim the freedom of all slaves owned by Confederates in Missouri, Lincoln ordered him to restrict his proclamation to slaves owned by Missourians actively working for the South. When Frémont refused, Lincoln summarily removed him from command. "Can it be pretended," he wrote to Frémont, "that it is any longer the government of the U.S.—any government of Constitution and laws—wherein a General, or a President, may make permanent rules of property by proclamation?"

In May 1862, General David Hunter began enlisting black soldiers in the occupied coastal areas of Georgia, Florida, and South Carolina that were under his control. He then declared free all slaves owned by Confederates in this region. Lincoln responded by ordering Hunter to disband the regiment he had created and to retract his proclamation. It was this order that prompted Greeley's open letter.

What all of these controversies obscure is the fact that Lincoln personally hated slavery: "As I would not be a *slave*," he wrote in 1858, "so I would not be a *master*. This expresses my idea of democracy." And he did very much want to bring an end to slavery—but not at the expense of the Constitution, the rule of law, and the Union.

Before he took office as president, before the Civil War began, Lincoln contemplated a policy of gradual emancipation, which would be conducted in accordance with the Constitution by compensating slave owners for freeing their "property." Moreover, because the Constitution left the issue of slavery to the states, he would go to each of the states, beginning with those where slavery was already weak—northern slave-holding states, such as Delaware. He planned to persuade the legislatures of these states to change their laws so as to abolish slavery. This, he hoped, would not only stave off civil war, it would also keep the issue of emancipation out of the federal courts—which might well decide to block permanently any attempt to abolish slavery.

Even after seven southern states seceded from the Union, Lincoln did not abandon hope for legislated emancipation. As Lincoln's first term began, Senator Thomas Crittenden of Kentucky proposed a constitutional amendment explicitly barring the federal government from interfering with the institution of slavery, even by some future amendment. In the hope that it would bring the errant states back into the Union, Lincoln offered no objection to the proposal. At the same time, however, he absolutely refused to compromise on the expansion of slavery. His belief, his hope, was that by containing slavery while also preventing its expansion into the federal territories and prevailing upon state legislatures to introduce gradual, compensated emancipation, he could wear down the "peculiar institution"—ultimately into nonexistence. This, he believed, was precisely what the Founding Fathers had anticipated and intended.

If secession did not end Lincoln's hopes, neither did the outbreak of the war itself—at least, not at first. Lincoln clung to the idea of persuading the legislatures of the loyal slaveholding states, the so-called border states, to agree to compensated emancipation. Owners would be paid to free their slaves. Once the viability of this scheme had been demonstrated in these states, Lincoln believed, there was a chance that the rebellion would end, the Union would be restored, and slave owners in the states of the former Confederacy would begin to accept compensation to part with their slaves. If this did not work, Lincoln hoped that the combination of Union military success against the Confederacy and compensated emancipation in the loyal slave states would cause the rebellion to collapse. In either case, once war had broken out, Lincoln felt that his best chance for both ending slavery and restoring the Union lay with the border states. He could not afford to alienate, or worse, lose them. For that reason, he could not simply take slaves away from their owners—personally gratifying as that action might have been.

Thus Lincoln's first hard decision was *not* to free the slaves, much as he may have wanted to. Yet circumstances—or, rather, the *failure* of circumstances—caused him to make another decision.

The border state legislatures turned down Lincoln's proposals for compensated emancipation, and, even worse, the Union army under George B. McClellan failed to cripple, let alone kill, the Confederacy. Time, Lincoln decided, was running out. The slaveholding border states had rejected legislated, compensated emancipation, and the Union was not winning the war. If Lincoln failed to act, failed to issue an emancipation proclamation—and soon—the entire issue of emancipation could well die. If, however, he issued the proclamation, it might just supply a moral impetus sufficient to stir Union passions and create victories at long last.

That, admittedly, was a long shot, and the dangers of an emancipation proclamation seemed like much more of a sure thing. First, proclaiming emancipation might throw the issue into the federal courts, which, given their conservative tenor, could very well end up guaranteeing the existence of slavery forever. Second, even liberally construed, emancipation was quite possibly unconstitutional, and therefore open to legal challenge even *after* a successful conclusion to the war. Third, an emancipation proclamation might alienate the border states, sending them into the Confederate camp. Fourth, while emancipation would give the war a powerful moral dimension, Lincoln was acutely aware that there were plenty of people in the North, soldiers included, who were willing to fight a war to preserve the Union but had no desire to bleed and die for the freedom of "negroes."

Despite all of these dangers, Lincoln consulted William Whiting, a War Department lawyer, on the question of the president's legal authority to declare emancipation. Whiting believed that the chief executive's war powers gave him the necessary authority. After consulting his vice president, Hannibal Hamlin, Lincoln decided to attempt to craft an emancipation proclamation that would claim the moral high ground without losing the border states, or anyone else, and without injuring the Constitution.

It was not easy. Major Thomas Thompson Eckert, the chief of the War Department's telegraph staff, frequently saw the president when he came to the War Department building to await telegraphed news of battles. On one of these occasions, during the first week of July 1862, Lincoln asked Eckert for some paper. He wanted to write something special, he explained. Eckert offered the president his own desk and handed him a piece of fine foolscap. He recalled how Lincoln gazed out of the window before putting his Gillot small-barrel pen to the paper. The president wrote a few words, stopped, then wrote a few more. There were long, silent pauses between the words, the phrases, the sentences.

Over the next couple of weeks, Lincoln returned to Eckert's office and desk to work on this document. Only when he had finished did Lincoln tell him that he had been laboring over an order that gave freedom to the slaves in the South. In the White House, he explained, someone was always interrupting him. Here, he could work quietly and with the intense concentration the document required.

On July 22, Lincoln first told his cabinet that he meant to issue a proclamation freeing the slaves in the unconquered Confederacy. Postmaster General Montgomery Blair was horrified. He argued that if the president went ahead, the result would be a collapse of power for the Republican Party. Secretary of State William Seward disagreed with Blair and supported the idea of emancipation, but, he warned, it would come as a hollow gesture hard on the heels of so many military disappointments. No one in the North or the South would take it seriously. He advised President Lincoln not to issue the proclamation until the Union Army had won a major military victory.

So Lincoln waited. At last on September 17, 1862, the Union and Confederate armies clashed at Antietam, Maryland, in the bloodiest single day of the war: the Union army lost 2,108 killed, 9,549 wounded, and 753 missing; the Confederate army, some 2,700 killed, 9,024 wounded, and 2,000 missing. Lincoln called it a victory, and, on September 22, he convened his cabinet. Secretary of the Treasury Salmon P. Chase wrote down what he said, excerpted below:

> Gentlemen, I have, as you are aware, thought a great deal about the relation of this war to slavery, and you all remember that, several weeks ago, I read to you an order I had prepared upon the subject, which, on account of objections made by some of you, was not issued. Ever since then my mind has been much occupied with this subject, and I have thought all along that the time for acting on it might probably come. I think the time has come now. I wish it was a better time. I wish that we were in a better condition. The action of the army against the Rebels has not

been quite what I should have liked best. But they have been driven out of Maryland, and Pennsylvania is no longer in danger of invasion. . . . I have got you together to hear what I have written down. I do not wish your advice about the main matter, for that I have determined for myself. . . . What I have written is that which my reflections have determined me to say.

Lincoln had decided. Even at that, he hedged his bet in an effort to avoid legal challenge now or in the future and, most of all, to avoid alienating anyone who was still willing to be considered loyal. The document Lincoln published on September 23, 1862, was called the Preliminary Emancipation Proclamation. It freed not a single slave, but merely served warning on slave owners living in states "still in rebellion on January 1, 1863" that their living property would be declared "forever free."

Only after the January 1 deadline had passed did Lincoln issue the "final" Emancipation Proclamation, which freed only those slaves in areas still "in rebellion"—that is, those living in parts of the Confederacy that were not yet under the control of the Union army. Lincoln did not want to provoke Union-occupied areas of Confederate states to rise up against the occupiers, so he ensured that the Emancipation Proclamation did not apply to them. Nor was he willing to send the border states scrambling into the enemy camp. So, in Delaware, Kentucky, Maryland, and Missouri—slave states still loyal to the Union—slavery continued to flourish. West Virginia, which had broken away from Virginia when that state seceded, was not officially admitted to the Union until June 20, 1863—and then on condition that its slaves would be emancipated gradually. As for the Confederacy, the irony of the Emancipation Proclamation is that slavery prevailed wherever the Union army had been victorious. The slaves were proclaimed free only in those parts of the Confederacy the Union did not control. Of course, it was in those very places that the Emancipation Proclamation could not yet be enforced.

TIMID AS THE EMANCIPATION PROCLAMATION may seem from the perspective of our century, it did what Lincoln hoped it would, giving to the
war new moral force. For those who chose to see it this way, the Civil
War became a struggle to make men free, yet the proclamation was
sufficiently cautious to avoid inflaming the occupied South or alienating
the border states. Even before the war was over, Congress would take
action beyond the modest confines of the Emancipation Proclamation.
On April 8, 1864, the Thirteenth Amendment was passed by the Senate
and, on January 31, 1865, by the House as well. By December 18, 1865,
with the Civil War ended and Abraham Lincoln dead by an assassin's
hand, the amendment had been ratified by the states: "Neither slavery
nor involuntary servitude, except as a punishment for crime whereof the
party shall have been duly convicted, shall exist within the United States,
or any place subject to their jurisdiction."

Clara Barton and the Soldiers (1861–62)

THE DECISION TO CARE

On April 19, 1861, the 6th Massachusetts Regiment, Colonel
Edward F. Jones commanding, was riding the rails. The troops
were bound for Washington, D.C., to garrison the national capital, now
under threat by a rebel army. As the southbound soldiers changed trains
in Baltimore—an ostensibly loyal city with nevertheless powerful Confederate sympathies—rioters, part of a gang of ruffians known as the
"Plug Uglies," hurled stones and brickbats at the bluecoats. Four soldiers
were killed and others injured. The troops opened fire, killing a dozen
Plug Uglies and wounding many more.

Naturally, the Baltimore riot was traumatic for all northerners, but
its impact hit one woman, a thirty-nine-year-old unmarried U.S. Patent

Office clerk named Clara Barton, with particular intensity. She herself was from Massachusetts—North Oxford—and she knew that a number of her childhood friends were now soldiers in the 6th. What's more, Barton was a Republican and a patriot, the daughter, she proudly said, of Captain Stephen Barton, who had served under Mad Anthony Wayne in the Indian wars of the Old Northwest. The rebellion of the South enraged and inflamed her, and when she heard of the Baltimore riots, she headed to the Washington railroad station to greet the arrival of the battered regiment. Among the troops who descended to the platform were about thirty wounded. With a few other women, Barton instinctively moved forward to aid these men, giving them water, a comforting word, and even dressing a wound as best she could with her handkerchief.

Barton recognized among the hurt a few familiar faces from North Oxford. The sight touched her heart, already heated with patriotic fervor. But this emotion was soon supplanted by a growing outrage: outrage directed against the rebels, and outrage directed against her own government, which had provided virtually no medical care for the troops. They had been through nothing more than a riot, and their wounds, relatively few in number, went untended. What would happen when the *real* fighting began?

Clarissa Harlowe Barton—Clara Barton—was petite even by the standards of the mid-nineteenth century. Barely five feet tall, she had a round face that contrasted strikingly with her slender frame. From most tintypes and daguerreotypes of the period, eyes stare fixedly in expressions stern and stiff. Photographs of Barton, however, reveal a woman with large, soft eyes, a woman who looked much younger than middle aged and on whose wide mouth a benign half smile plays. It is a face of great gentleness. Indeed, much about Clara Barton was gentle. At the age of twelve, she fainted dead away at the sight of an ox being butchered, and from that day on she was a strict vegetarian.

Quiet and studious, Barton was trained as a teacher. She taught school for a time, but then claimed to have "outgrown" the profession. Unmarried by choice, she sought something truly useful to do—but the best she could find was work in the patent office. Now, amid the bugles and the drums that were insistent throughout Washington, this work was no longer sufficient to satisfy her.

Gentle though she was, Clara Barton had been raised (as her father said) "more boy than girl" along with older brothers, who taught her to ride a horse as hard and as fast as any man and to shoot a revolver with the skill of an expert marksman. Indeed, she now wanted nothing more than to be a soldier. But she knew that could not be. Doubtless, she was aware that a handful of women had joined the ranks by dressing as men, but such a masquerade was far too strange for her. Although raised like a boy, she looked and always behaved like a proper New England lady.

There was one other obvious option for her. Dorothea Dix, who had earned renown as a leading reformer of the nation's prisons and asylums, was organizing an army nursing corps, for which she was actively recruiting women. Like Barton, Dix was a Massachusetts Unionist with uncompromising ideals. But where Barton, for all her zeal, radiated a quiet and gentle warmth, the sixty-year-old Dix, iron-jawed and ramrod straight, was something of a terror. "Dragon Dix," they called her, and there is no evidence that she objected to the name. She called for nurse recruits who were "sober, earnest, self-sacrificing, and self-sustained; who can bear the presence of suffering and exercise entire self-control, of speech and manner; who can be calm, gentle, quiet, active, and stead-fast in duty." That certainly described Clara Barton, but Dix also specified "plain-looking women"—which Barton was not—over the age of thirty. Dix was acutely aware of the dangers involved in putting a few women among a large number of men. Except for Florence Nightingale in the Crimean War, which ended in the previous decade, female nursing was virtually unknown in the military, and the only women who were regularly found in the company of troops were "camp followers," "soldiers' women"—*whores.*

Perhaps Barton was put off by Dix's prudery, or perhaps she instinc-tively knew that she could never happily serve under a woman dubbed the Dragon. Besides, Barton had always gone her own way. When she first began at the patent office in 1854, she was one of just four women employed in *any* public building in the city of Washington. She was determined to find another means of serving in this war.

The arrival of the 6th Massachusetts Regiment in Washington had taken place in April. By June, seventy-five thousand Union troops were massed in and around the city. Everything was in short supply. While those around her shook their heads over this situation, Barton decided to act. This was her key decision—not to appeal to an authority for a task or a job, not to join some official organization, not to beg for permission to be appointed to this or that office. But simply to act. If she could not be a soldier or even a nurse working for Dorothea Dix, no one could stop her from working on her own to help supply the troops.

With her meager patent office salary, Barton bought up stores of food, concentrating on what the soldiers did not get with their regular rations: homemade jellies, cakes, and pies. She also bought and distributed tobacco and whiskey—something Dix, doubtless, would never have allowed. While she did not drink hard liquor herself, Barton believed that "our men's nerves require their accustomed narcotics," and so she would see to it that they had them.

In company with a male escort or her fifty-year-old married sister, Barton made the rounds of the local encampments, distributing her supplies. She did this throughout the remainder of 1861, even managing in the process to make a few influential government connections, which enabled her to enlarge her operation. She started to receive contributions of food and supplies, and so she had to rent space in three warehouses in addition to stuffing her own apartment with cartons and crates. At the end of the year, she was visited by a self-appointed delegation of soldiers who were passing through Washington en route to battle on the North Carolina coast. They had been students of hers when she was a teacher. She was proud of them as well as deeply anxious for them, and after they left the capital, her empathetic imagination was more deeply engaged than ever. Barton continued to work at the patent office, and she continued to devote a large part of her salary to supplies. After work each

day, she visited the makeshift hospitals in and around Washington, beginning with the one that had been set up on the top floor of the patent
office itself. Here the sick and the wounded languished amid models and
prototypes of machines submitted for patent protection.

Early in 1862, Barton's father fell ill, and she returned to North
Oxford to nurse him. The old warrior wanted to hear news of the war, so
Barton read him newspaper accounts of the combat in North Carolina.
She confessed to her father that she wanted to go there, but she was
afraid—afraid not of battle, but of being perceived as a camp follower.

Stephen Barton looked into his daughter's eyes. "I know soldiers," he
said, "and they will respect you and your errand."

He reminded her that she was the daughter of a soldier and a patriot,
and he told her that, if she was inclined to go, it was her duty to do so.

On the wings of these words, she wrote to Massachusetts governor
John A. Andrew, seeking permission to go to Roanoke, Virginia, to nurse
the Massachusetts troops who were under the command of General
Ambrose Burnside: "I ask neither pay or praise, simply a soldier's fare and
the sanction of your Excellency to go and do with my might, what ever
my hands find to do."

Her father died on March 21, 1862, shortly after which Governor
Andrew granted his permission to make the journey—only to rescind it
almost immediately because the chief surgeon serving with Burnside,
Dr. Alfred Hitchcock, disapproved.

Once again, Barton found herself in limbo. With nothing more to do
than accumulate, store, pack, and distribute supplies, she was active but
she never felt that she was truly *in* the war. Yet on the heels of this latest
disappointment, Barton learned that Frederick Law Olmsted, the
pioneering landscape architect, had organized the Sanitary Commission,
a privately funded effort to provide nursing care for Union soldiers.
Olmsted recruited about fifteen women to serve as nurses on ships
converted to hospitals, which were dispatched to the Virginia peninsula
during George B. McClellan's seemingly interminable Peninsula
Campaign. About serving in the Olmsted organization, Barton felt

much the same as she had felt about working under Dragon Dix: her essential independence would not let her do it. But the work of the Sanitary Commission inspired her, and her determination to become an *independent* nurse in service to the Army of the Potomac was rekindled.

In June 1862, when masses of wounded from the Peninsula Campaign began flowing into Washington hospitals, Barton did what she could in these overcrowded, understaffed, and pestilential institutions. The volume of the wounded and the sick was so great that the job of caring for them seemed overwhelming. "I am sick at heart and yet not weak," Barton wrote to her friend Mary Norton. "I have no right to these easy comfortable days and our poor men suffering and dying thirsting in this hot sun and I so quiet here in want of nothing, it is not rightly distributed, my lot is too easy and I am sorry for it."

Clara Barton decided that the army that needed her supplies and succor most urgently now was the one just organized under General John Pope in the Shenandoah Valley and down toward Fredericksburg. On July 11, 1862, she called on Colonel Daniel H. Rucker, commander of the Quartermaster Depot in Washington. Rucker received her with a look of annoyance.

"Well, what do you want?" he demanded.

Suddenly choked with emotion, Barton burst into tears.

Taken aback, Rucker instantly softened and invited her to sit down and "tell me all about it."

"I want," she said, "to go to the front."

Rucker told her that the front was no place for a lady, but Barton replied that she had "no fear of the battlefield," and she explained that she had three warehouses full of supplies of all kinds. All she needed, she said, were some wagons and a pass. Impressed, Rucker immediately wrote out the pass and the necessary orders, which authorized her "to go upon the sick transports in any direction for the purpose of distributing comforts to the sick and wounded, and nursing them, always subject to the direction of the Surgeon in charge."

Clara Barton was thrilled—but not so blinded by elation that she failed to exercise political acumen. Anticipating that the Sanitary Commission might object to her invading their bailiwick, she paid a visit to the commission's Washington headquarters and explained to the assistant secretary there that her work would complement that of the commission and by no means interfere or compete with it. This resulted in a letter of endorsement from the assistant secretary.

Clara Barton took to the field in the summer of 1862. Laboring in a zone of active combat, she distributed her supplies and she nursed the wounded. Warned that she was in danger of being killed or captured, she replied simply, "I fail to see any more danger to me than for our disabled men."

It was not bravado. Clara Barton, truly, was unafraid. As for the sights and sounds of the charnel houses that were the field hospitals of the period—they indeed horrified her, this woman who would not eat meat because the sight of a slaughtered ox had sickened her. Yet, somehow, she was neither deterred nor impeded. The weapons of the Civil War were the products of a new industrial age. New explosives, new projectiles, new artillery were producing wounds the like of which had never been seen in war before: limbs shattered or torn away, torsos split wide, viscera exposed, and all caused with such speed that death hardly had time to catch up. Medical technology lagged far behind the technology of destruction. Men wallowed in their own blood and gore. Barton faced all of this, and she offered what aid and comfort she could, from seeing to it that the slippery filth of hospital floors was continually scrubbed clean, to changing dressings, to administering a sip of water or a bite of food, to simply sitting with a dying boy through his last, terrible night.

"Miss Barton," one captain surgeon said to her, "this is a rough and unseemly position for you, a woman, to occupy."

"Is it not as rough and unseemly for these pain-wracked men?" she replied quietly.

Others saw her for what she was: the "angel of the battlefield."

From this point on, Barton divided her time between distributing supplies, nursing the wounded, and doing all she could to make the public aware of the great need for more aid to the sick and the wounded. In June 1864, she received a formal appointment as superintendent of nurses for the Army of the James, and early in 1865, President Abraham Lincoln asked her to create and direct a bureau of records to search for the missing and the dead.

FOR THE REST OF HER LIFE SHE REMAINED TRUE to her credo—*to act*. Barton's work with the bureau consumed several years. In 1869, mentally and physically exhausted, she went to Europe to rest, but while she was there, war broke out between France and Germany. Not surprisingly, Barton began distributing relief supplies to the victims of combat. This woman whose independence had made it difficult for her to work with large organizations now became associated with the new International Red Cross, which had been founded by Swiss humanitarians. Back in the United States, she campaigned to secure the U.S. government's endorsement of the Geneva Convention, which the Red Cross had formulated to promote the humane treatment of soldiers wounded or captured in war. In 1881, Barton organized the American Association of the Red Cross, which became the American Red Cross; like other national Red Cross organizations, it was an independent affiliate of the International Red Cross. Under her leadership—which lasted until 1904—she composed and engineered passage of the "American Amendment" to the constitution of the International Red Cross, which expanded the brief of the institution from relief in war to relief in other times of major emergency, including floods, earthquakes, hurricanes, tornadoes, epidemics, and famines. Never content to remain merely an administrator, she took to the field at age seventy-six during the 1898 Spanish-American War in Cuba.

Ultimately, the self-reliant Barton was deemed unable or unwilling to delegate responsibility as an executive; this, along with her age and political infighting, led to her forced resignation as president of the

American Red Cross in 1904, when she was eighty-two. Although deeply hurt, she remained active in the cause of organized relief work until virtually the day of her death, April 12, 1912, having transformed humanitarianism from a philosophy to a vocation practiced on a scale both intimate and universal.

Gandhi and Nonviolent Revolution (1893)

THE DECISION TO PREVAIL
WITHOUT BLOODSHED

Mohandas Gandhi is better known by the name his followers gave him: *Mahatma*—"Great Soul"—Gandhi. Most of his Indian countrymen called him, more simply, *Bapu* (father). He was the father of India's independence from Great Britain and, beyond this, the leading twentieth-century exponent of nonviolent revolutionary social change. Passionate about social justice, the greatest lesson he sought to impart was that those who struggle for their rights must never forsake their own respect for life.

How did Gandhi not only arrive at his sweeping philosophy, but decide to put it into practical operation?

There was nothing unusual about the circumstances of his birth. He was born on October 2, 1869, in the Indian province of Gujarat, into a family of the Hindu *Bania*, or merchant, caste. His father was the *diwan* (prime minister) of a small Indian state, and his mother—the fourth wife of his father—was a devout member of a small sect known as the *pranamis*, who mingled Hindu and Muslim beliefs and practices. From her, young Gandhi absorbed the Hindu concept of *ahimsa*, which encompasses universal religious tolerance, a duty to harm no living being, the practice of vegetarianism, and the observance of fasts as a means of self-purification. He was also greatly influenced by the religious traditions of Jainism— which once flourished in Gujarat—including its central tenet of nonviolence.

In keeping with religious tradition, Gandhi was betrothed at age seven, to Kasturba Makharji, and the couple was wed when he was fourteen. Gandhi received a fine education in India, then, in 1888, at age nineteen, he traveled to London. There he studied law at the Inner Temple, and in 1891 was admitted to the bar. He returned to India and started a practice, but soon found it impossible to earn a living. In search of greener pastures, he moved in 1893 to South Africa—which had a substantial Indian community—and went to work for an Indian firm there.

It was in South Africa that Gandhi's life changed forever. In India and in England, he had seen social inequality, but it was in May 1893, in Natal, that he suddenly awoke to the realities of colonial and racial oppression. Years later, he put his awakening in a single sentence: "I discovered that as a man and as an Indian I had no rights."

Gandhi landed at Durban, Natal, on assignment to prosecute a law-suit for a Muslim businessman named Dada Abdulla Sheth. As a young, London-trained barrister, Gandhi was attired in European frock coat, trousers, and cravat, though he also wore a turban. When the case required that he travel to Pretoria, capital of Transvaal, his firm booked a first-class train compartment for him. The journey from Durban to Pre-toria was an overnight haul, and, at about 9:00 P.M., the train stopped at Maritzburg, capital of Natal. Here a white man entered Gandhi's com-partment. "He saw," Gandhi wrote later, "that I was a 'colored' man. This disturbed him. Out he went and came in with one or two officials. They all kept quiet, when another official came to me and said, 'Come along, you must go to the van [third-class] compartment.'"

Gandhi protested calmly: "But I have a first-class ticket."

The official was unimpressed. "That doesn't matter. I tell you, you must go to the van compartment."

Gandhi persisted: "I tell you, I was permitted to travel in this com-partment in Durban and I insist on going on in it."

At this the official again ordered him to leave, "or else I shall have to call a police constable to push you out."

Gandhi found himself replying, with perfect calm, "Yes you may. I refuse to get out voluntarily."

In his later memoirs and recollections, Gandhi left no clue as to whether he was, at the time, fully aware of the profound nature of his refusal. The refusal was not outraged, or abusive, or threatening, or even impolite. The simple sentence "Yes you may" could have been spoken in reply to an offer of some civilized service—"May I pour you a cup of tea?" "Yes you may"—but instead it granted the railway worker unsought permission to fetch a constable. With these three simple words, Gandhi utterly preempted the coercive authority of an agent of unjust oppression.

Had he consciously decided to use these words? Or had they just come to him, unbidden, out of a background of Jainism, Hinduism, and colonial injustice? Gandhi did not say. But the words came, and, once they had come, he decided to work through their consequences, moving with them wherever they led.

"I refuse to get out voluntarily," Gandhi also said. It was another declaration with a very precise meaning. "I refuse to get out" would have been weak by comparison, since the refusal could easily be negated by physical force. But "I refuse to get out voluntarily" presented a different case altogether. To be sure, by physical force, Gandhi could still be ejected from the train, but, no matter how much force was used, the action could never be made voluntary. "I refuse to get out" expressed a stand beyond Gandhi's power, whereas "I refuse to get out voluntarily" declared the basic power of the individual to resist coercion, no matter how forceful. No one, including the state itself, could compel voluntary action.

Having made this simple but profoundly complex declaration, Gandhi waited for the constable. He came, seized Gandhi's hand, and pushed him off the train, sending his luggage out behind him. As the train steamed away, Gandhi sat in the waiting room of the Maritzburg station.

It was winter—"and winter in the higher regions of South Africa is severely cold." Gandhi's overcoat was in his luggage, which had been taken by the station attendants. He did not dare ask for it, "lest I might

160 PROFILES IN AUDACITY

be insulted and assaulted once again." He sat, and he shivered. "There was no light in the room," but "sleep was out of the question." Cold, alone, sleepless, "I began to think of my duty." As Gandhi saw it, he had three options. He could fight for his rights. He could go back to India. Or he could ignore what had happened, and go on to Pretoria. "It would," he decided that night, "be cowardice to run back to India without fulfilling my obligation." So he would finish the case. But what about fighting for his rights? "The hardship to which I was subjected was superficial—only a symptom of the deep disease of color prejudice." Having made this analysis, he decided not simply to fight for *his* rights, but to "try, if possible, to root out the disease and suffer hardships in the process." He did not want revenge or simply that an exception be made in his case. "Redress for wrongs I should seek only to the extent that would be necessary for the removal of the color prejudice."

Unjustly thrown off a train, Gandhi decided to change the world—at least, for the present, the world of South Africa.

"This resolution somewhat pacified and strengthened me," he wrote later, and when he "suffered further insults and received more beatings on the way to Pretoria," they served only to confirm him in his newborn determination. "Thus . . . I obtained full experience of the condition of Indians in South Africa."

Driven not only by his experience on the journey to Pretoria, but by his analysis of its larger meaning, its meaning beyond himself, Gandhi began a career as a social activist and moral reformer in the South African Indian community. He was guided by three unbreakable rules, which he also enforced upon his followers. There was his absolute belief in *satyagraha*, or the truth-force. Gandhi described it as "the method of securing rights by personal suffering; . . . it is the reverse of resistance by arms." Second came *ahimsa*, the doctrine of nonviolence he had learned in childhood. The third came a bit later: sexual abstinence, or *brahmacharya*, a Hindu doctrine that conferred strength. A "man or woman completely practicing Brahmacharya is absolutely free from passion," Gandhi said. "Such a one therefore lives nigh unto God, is Godlike."

Gandhi soon became well established in South Africa as a lawyer and politician. With the money he made, he established a number of communes, or ashrams, the best known of which were Phoenix Settlement, near Durban, and Tolstoy Farm, near Johannesburg. In 1894, he organized the Natal Indian Congress and, in 1903, he founded the *Indian Opinion,* a weekly newspaper. Three years after this, Gandhi led his first full-scale experiment in nonviolent resistance or civil disobedience. Intended to begin the process of overcoming discrimination against Indians in South Africa, the campaign brought prison sentences and beatings down on Gandhi and his followers, but it also drew the attention of the world, set South Africa's Indians on a course of liberation, and transformed Mohandas Gandhi into an internationally recognized leader for Indian rights.

Gandhi left South Africa in July 1914, and returned to India. There he founded a new ashram, which he intended to serve as a model community in which neither class nor caste played any part. To demonstrate the values of the ashram, Gandhi invited as residents a family of "untouchables"—the lowest caste in Hindu society, traditionally considered a source of spiritual pollution. The untouchables lived side by side with upper-caste Hindus. It was far more than a symbolic gesture. Gandhi understood that a principal source of Hindu prejudice against Muslims in India was the fact that many Muslims were descendants of untouchable converts to Islam. Gandhi pushed the demonstration to the limit. In Hindu-dominated Indian society, untouchables performed work no Hindu would defile himself with, such as disposing of human waste. At Gandhi's direction, everyone in the ashram, including himself, took turns raking the latrines.

Gandhi campaigned on behalf of Indian peasants and mill workers, successfully employing a hunger-strike protest in 1918. In 1919, he organized the first all-India nonviolent protest campaign. Despite his efforts, the campaign gave rise to mob violence, to which British colonial administrators responded with utmost savagery in the infamous Amritsar Massacre. Three hundred seventy-nine Indian men, women, and children were cut down by British bullets. Amritsar badly shook Gandhi, who now questioned his own nonviolent methods. He emerged, however, from a period of reflection with even greater determination to use nonviolence against the British. Violence, he reasoned, was not only wrong in and of itself; it was also ineffective, because it would beget more violence. Worse, violence on the part of the Indians would justify violence on the part of the British. Clearly, only nonviolence could expose to the world and to the British themselves the injustice and illegitimacy of British rule by force. "Nonviolence and truth (*satya*)," Gandhi wrote, "are inseparable and presuppose one another. There is no god higher than truth."

Gandhi believed that an appeal made to common sense and morality—even the common sense and morality of the oppressor—would ultimately win the day, especially if it was supplemented by what he called "noncooperation" with the oppressors. Accordingly, he organized practical movements of noncooperation. Oppression requires an oppressor as well as a people willing to "cooperate" with the oppression. Cease the cooperation, and the oppression cannot long continue.

Gandhi organized a boycott of British cloth by encouraging Indians to weave on their traditional hand looms. As a result, British textile exports suffered. Encouraged by this result, Gandhi extended the boycott to all British goods. From goods, he expanded noncooperation to institutions. Indian lawyers refused to practice in the British-run courts, and Indian students stopped attending British-run universities. Colonial authorities responded by imprisoning Gandhi in 1922. Released in 1924, he was elected to the presidency of the Indian National Congress and announced that he would seek nothing less than home rule for India, leading, ultimately, to complete independence. Even as he conducted this campaign, Gandhi campaigned for minority rights, for the rights of untouchables and women, and for the proliferation of education, the development of village industries, and the improvement of public health and hygiene.

In 1930, Gandhi led a 240-mile march against the British monopoly on salt manufacture. His object was to take the marchers to the sea, to the coastal village of Dandi, Gujarat, where they would illegally extract salt from the seawater. Gandhi set off from the ashram with a handful of followers, but, as the procession crossed India, more and more people joined the protest, including foreign newspaper reporters and newsreel crews. Reported worldwide, the Salt Campaign brought much support to the cause of Indian independence. Again imprisoned in 1932, Gandhi fasted for six days in protest of the treatment of the untouchables. In 1933, he fasted for twenty-one days, an action that secured his release from prison by officials fearful of an insurrection if Gandhi should die in custody.

ALTHOUGH GANDHI WAS ANTI-NAZI during World War II, he did not let up on what was now called the "Quit India" campaign, the campaign to end British rule of India. Both Gandhi and his wife, Kasturba, were imprisoned. Kasturba fell ill in captivity and died. Devastated by the loss, Gandhi rapidly declined in health and spirit and was released from prison in May 1944. He revived, determined now to prepare India for the independence he believed was inevitable. His focus was to bring about Hindu-Muslim harmony, which proved all but hopeless.

In July 1947, the British Parliament passed the Indian Independence Act, which granted Indian independence, but also partitioned the country into a separate, predominantly Hindu India and a predominantly Muslim Pakistan. Although profoundly disheartened by the partition, Gandhi threw himself into a campaign to heal the bloody communal conflict between Muslims and Hindus. It was during this work, on January 30, 1948, while he was walking to prayers, that Mohandas Gandhi fell to the bullet of a Hindu extremist. His final act was to pronounce a blessing on his assassin.

W. E. B. Du Bois and the NAACP (1909)

THE DECISION AGAINST COMPROMISE

On September 18, 1895, Booker T. Washington, regarded almost universally among whites as well as blacks as the leader and voice of the nation's African Americans, spoke before a white audience at the Atlanta Cotton States and International Exposition. The speech marked an epoch in race relations in the United States. Washington expressed willingness to accept social inequality, political disfranchisement, and segregation in exchange for white encouragement of black progress in economic opportunity and vocational education. He held out his hand, fingers spread before him. "In all things that are purely social we can be as separate as the fingers," Washington said, "yet one as the hand in all things essential to mutual progress." He continued:

> The wisest among my race understand that the agitation of questions of social equality is the extremist folly, and that progress in the enjoyment of all the privileges that will come to us must be the result of severe and constant struggle rather than of artificial forcing. No race that has anything to contribute to the markets of the world is long in any degree ostracized. It is important and right that all privileges of the law be ours, but it is vastly more important that we be prepared for the exercises of these privileges. The opportunity to earn a dollar in a factory just now is worth infinitely more than the opportunity to spend a dollar in an opera house.

Washington's audience applauded the speech, and soon the entire nation spoke of the "Atlanta Compromise" as the only viable formula for productive race relations and as the earnest desire of the majority of black people—people (according to Washington) who did not want social or political rights equal to those of the white race, but who wanted only to work and, what is more, to work at jobs useful to white employers.

Booker T. Washington produced extraordinary results in his long life. He founded a major black vocational school in the Tuskegee Institute, there is no question that he won a significant measure of economic opportunity for African Americans, and he did make himself and other black leaders of like mind heard by the white majority. He was a mighty figure among black as well as white reformers. The policy of compromise—or accommodation, as it was also called—became something akin to gospel, an article of faith, a kind of social contract between black and white society, which few dared to question, let alone challenge.

One who did both question and challenge it was William Edward Burghardt Du Bois. His very life was an affront to the racial stereotypes and minimal expectations imposed on blacks by blacks as well as whites—and to the assumptions behind the Atlanta Compromise.

Born in Great Barrington, Massachusetts, in 1868, Du Bois became the first African American to receive a Ph.D. from Harvard University in 1895, and between 1897 and 1914 he researched and wrote several landmark sociological studies of black America. Initially, he hoped that through the rational application of social science, he could begin to crack the hard shell of irrational racial inequality in America. But even as he continued his sociological studies, he became increasingly convinced that racism and racially based injustice were so deeply ingrained in American culture and institutions that only through vigorous and unrelenting social activism, including agitation and protest, could black Americans begin to claim their rights under the Constitution.

Like Booker T. Washington, Du Bois supported the idea of black capitalism, and, as the nineteenth century came to an end, he was even willing to see, with Washington, black economic self-sufficiency as a necessary precursor to social equality. But what increasingly concerned him was Washington's almost casual willingness to put off social equality indefinitely in order to gain economic support from white America. How long would black America have to wait? Booker T. Washington wasn't saying.

At last, in his most important early book, *The Souls of Black Folk,* published in 1903, Du Bois made the decision to break publicly and sharply with Booker T. Washington and what he called "Mr. Washington's cult."

It is time, Du Bois wrote, to "speak in all sincerity and utter courtesy of the mistakes and shortcomings of Mr. Washington's career . . . without forgetting that it is easier to do ill than well in the world." Du Bois had come to realize that to accept delay in the achievement of equality was to deny the importance of equality. Ultimately, it meant giving up on equality—in exchange for a measure of economic opportunity. Du Bois decided that this was a very bad bargain. Booker T. Washington, he wrote, demanded too little and conceded far too much in his distressingly successful effort to maneuver white America into saying, "If that is all you and your race ask, take it." Du Bois condemned Washington as a representative "in Negro thought [of] the old attitude of adjustment and submission," now put into the service of a "gospel of Work and Money to such an extent as apparently almost completely to overshadow the higher aims of life."

Du Bois decided not to accept the Atlanta Compromise as the solution to race relations. He rejected the gospel of Work and Money, and he looked critically at the implications of Washington's program. It "practically accepts the alleged inferiority of the Negro races," he concluded, and it "withdraws many of the high demands of Negroes as men and American citizens." Du Bois believed that America was entering a period of heightened racism, a period of crisis, yet whereas "in other periods of intensified prejudice all the Negro's tendency to self-assertion has been called forth, at this period a policy of submission is advocated. In the history of nearly all other races and peoples the doctrine preached at such crises has been that manly self-respect is worth more than lands and houses, and that a people who voluntarily surrender such respect, or cease striving for it, are not worth civilizing" Yet, the followers of Booker T. Washington, it seemed to Du Bois, "claimed that the Negro can survive only through submission."

In *The Souls of Black Folk*, Du Bois listed his objections to the Atlanta Compromise:

> Mr. Washington distinctly asks that black people give up, at least for the present, three things—
>
>> First, political power,
>>
>> Second, insistence on civil rights,
>>
>> Third, higher education of Negro youth—
>
> And concentrate all their energies on industrial education, the accumulation of wealth, and the conciliation of the South.

The result of this compromise, Du Bois had come to feel, was:

> 1. The disenfranchisement of the Negro.
> 2. The legal creation of a distinct status of civil inferiority for the Negro.
> 3. The steady withdrawal of aid from institutions for the higher training of the Negro.

Du Bois decided that the Atlanta Compromise was a mistake perpetuated by Washington's propaganda, and that the duty of the "black men of America . . . a duty stern and delicate" was to lead "a forward movement to oppose a part of the work of their greatest leader."

> So far as Mr. Washington preaches Thrift, Patience, and Industrial Training for the masses, we must hold up his hands and strive with him. . . . But so far as Mr. Washington apologizes for injustice, North or South, does not rightly value the privilege and duty of voting, belittles the emasculating effects of caste distinctions, and opposes the higher training and ambition of our brighter minds—so far as he, the South, or the Nation, does this—we must unceasingly and firmly oppose them. By every civilized and peaceful method we must strive for the rights which the world accords to men.

In a 1904 *Outlook* magazine article, "The Parting of the Ways," Du Bois was even more emphatic in his rejection of compromise: "We refuse to kiss the hands that smite us, but rather insist on striving by all civilized methods to keep wide educational opportunity, to keep the right to vote, to insist on equal civil rights and to gain every right and privilege open to a free American citizen." To those who denied the possibility of ever achieving these things, to those who were saying, "America will never spell opportunity for black men," Du Bois answered, "Simply: I do not believe it."

Determined not merely to object to compromise, but to offer an organized alternative to it, Du Bois, in the summer of 1905, led a group of twenty-nine other social activists, including African Americans and whites, to a secret meeting in Niagara Falls, Ontario. There they formulated an explicit response to the Atlanta Compromise in the form of a set of resolutions, which resulted in the founding of the Niagara Movement and the composition of a manifesto demanding full civil liberties for African Americans, an end to racial discrimination, and acknowledgment of brotherhood among all races.

WITH GREAT RAPIDITY, the Niagara Movement spawned thirty branches nationwide. Yet, almost as quickly, it began to fall apart for lack of funding and organization. What saved it was an act of racial terrorism. In August 1908, thousands of white residents of Springfield, Illinois, descended upon the black community of that town after a black prisoner charged with the rape of a white woman was transferred to another prison. The white mob randomly assaulted and even killed black residents, burned homes and buildings, and lynched two elderly black men before the Illinois state militia intervened to restore order. The riot evoked no remorse from white leaders, and some even voiced approval of an action that might do much to keep blacks "in their place"—even after charges against the accused rapist were dropped as groundless.

The riot, which the press called a "Race War of the North," prompted a number of prominent white liberals to join with members of the Niagara group, including W. E. B. Du Bois, to create the National Association for the Advancement of Colored People, the NAACP, in 1909. The NAACP formally supplanted the Niagara Movement the following year.

From the founding of the NAACP until 1934, Du Bois served as the association's director of research and the editor of its extremely influential magazine, the *Crisis*. He saw the NAACP as an antidote to the propaganda and cultism of the Atlanta Compromise, and for all his brilliance and love of social analysis and political disputation, he declared that the association had but one great purpose—"to fight the wrong of race prejudice."

Marshall and the Marshall Plan (1947)

THE DECISION TO RESCUE EUROPE

Six years of World War II had devastated Europe. Cities were leveled, industry all but destroyed, millions were homeless, and national treasuries exhausted. Two problems were especially acute: the shortage of food and the scarcity of coal for heating. In 1946–47, the daily nutritional intake of the average German was just 1,800 calories, a figure that prompted U.S. state department official William Clayton to remark that "millions of people are slowly starving." But they were also freezing, at a much more rapid pace. In Germany, hundreds, perhaps thousands, died in their unheated homes during the exceptionally brutal winters of 1945, 1946, and 1947.

The United States had begun sending aid and relief to Europe well before the war ended, amounting to some $9 billion by early 1947. There was also hope that Britain and France would recover sufficiently not only to care for their own populations, but to aid others. This quickly proved wildly optimistic. The war had not only shattered individual lives and physical infrastructure, it had deeply disrupted the basics of trade. Farmers could still produce food, but city dwellers had no way to pay for it. Industrial plants could be rebuilt, but neither urbanites nor farmers could pay for the goods produced. The cycle of the European economy was stalled and needed a massive infusion of capital to restart.

There were various plans on the table. President Truman's secretary of state James F. Byrnes proposed an aid plan in a speech at the Stuttgart Opera House in Germany on September 6, 1946, and General Lucius D. Clay took steps to create a plan for the reindustrialization of Germany. At about this time, Undersecretary of State Dean Acheson and Vice President Alben W. Barkley formulated the broad outline of their own relief plans. All worked against the background of an opposing plan, which had been introduced as early as 1944 by Secretary of the Treasury Henry Morgenthau, Jr. In the "Morgenthau Plan," Germany would pay for most of the rebuilding of Europe through massive war reparations, which (by design) would also prevent Germany from ever being rebuilt as an industrial power. Morgenthau wanted the nation reduced to a preindustrial agricultural state.

Initially, the Morgenthau Plan had appealed to President Franklin Roosevelt, but, after Roosevelt's death, President Truman revisited the proposal and saw in it nothing but disaster. An earnest student of history, Truman was keenly aware of how the punitive reparations imposed by the Allies after World War I had created in Germany a universal despair, anger, and desperation that was fertile soil for the growth of Adolf Hitler and his Nazi regime. The harsh peace following World War I had done nothing less than create World War II.

George Catlett Marshall, who, as U.S. Army chief of staff during the war had been one of the architects of the Allied military victory, replaced Byrnes as secretary of state in January 1947. Like Truman, he heeded the lessons of World War I, including how the punitive terms of the Treaty of Versailles had made another war inevitable. He was also aware that, because Germany had been the most powerful industrial force in Europe before World War II, its current devastation was holding back the economic recovery of all Europe. Both Marshall and Truman vowed to avoid repeating the terrible errors of the past—the first decision toward what became the Marshall Plan. The second was a decision to surmount national passions, including the passion for vengeance. Marshall and Truman agreed that, in order to recover, Europe would have to act with a unity it had never known before.

Yet another motive helped propel these decisions into action. Acutely aware of the humanitarian and economic crisis ongoing in Europe, Marshall also came into office with an understanding of the political crisis looming there. The Soviet Union had been hailed as a heroic ally of the West during the war, but in February 1946, George F. Kennan, an American diplomat stationed in Moscow, sent a long cablegram to Washington predicting the Soviets' postwar strategy of aggressive expansion and advocating for the United States a policy of "containment," a confrontation of the Soviets wherever and whenever they attempted to interfere in the affairs of another nation.

Kennan elucidated these remarks in a highly influential article that appeared in *Foreign Affairs* magazine in July 1947. Marshall agreed with Kennan's analysis, and he saw an American-financed plan of aid as an important means of containing the spread of Soviet influence. Indeed, Marshall hoped that such a plan would serve as an alternative to confronting the Soviets militarily. He even hoped that the Soviets might be encouraged to cooperate with the plan. This hope was dashed by the Foreign Ministers' Conference held in Moscow from March 10 to April 24, 1947. Meeting on the subject of European recovery, the diplomats of the West and of the Soviet Union quickly discovered that they could agree on virtually nothing. It became clear to Marshall that the Soviets were purposely stalling any effort at reconstruction, because they believed that the continued disintegration of European economies and governments created a vacuum that Soviet influence could fill.

In a 1952 interview, Marshall identified "disillusionment over the Moscow Conference," which "proved conclusively that the Soviet Union . . . could not be induced to cooperate in achieving European recovery," as the final element that prompted his decision to propose an expansive plan of U.S.-funded European aid. Marshall put the State Department—

especially William L. Clayton and George F. Kennan—to work on the nuts and bolts of the plan. The next task would be to win acceptance for it, and that required another series of decisions.

First, there was the matter of which nations would be involved in introducing the plan. The Soviets were out, of course, but Marshall boldly chose to exclude as well America's closest wartime ally, Great Britain, because of differences over the question of war reparations. The plan, therefore, would be a wholly American initiative.

And that led to another decision. Once the *American* initiative was taken, Marshall decided that it would be essential to make *Europe* responsible for allocating how the funds would be used. Marshall proposed that the states of Europe would have to get together and formulate, cooperatively and collaboratively, a plan for all the nations that wanted to receive aid. Indeed, release of the promised funds would be conditioned on such a unified plan.

Now Marshall had yet another formidable hurdle to clear: gaining acceptance of the plan at home. He believed that this was chiefly an issue of timing. As he remarked to interviewers in 1952, "The cardinal consideration . . . was to time properly the offer of U.S. assistance so as to assure domestic acceptance of the proposal." Marshall decided that the key was to "'spring the plan with explosive force' in order not to dissipate the chance of U.S. acceptance by premature political debate." As for possible European debate, Marshall remarked that "little consideration" was given to it because "it was believed that [Europe] was sufficiently desperate to accept any reasonable offer of U.S. aid."

Timing proved to be a very ticklish matter. "The greatest fear was of an adverse reaction from the Mid-West," where the conservative press— especially the *Chicago Tribune*—held sway and was a powerful force in moving national public opinion. Marshall at first thought that he would "spring the 'plan' in the heartland of expected opposition" by announcing it in a speech at the University of Michigan. But this gave Kennan and Clayton insufficient time to work out key details, so Marshall decided to put off the announcement until June 16, 1947, when he was to give a speech accepting an honorary degree from Amherst. Conditions in Europe became so urgent, however, that Marshall "reversed an earlier decision not to accept [an honorary] degree from Harvard" and decided to present the plan in a speech at Cambridge on June 5, 1947.

Secretary Marshall "took only a few intimate advisors into my confidence during the preparation of the European Recovery Program plan." He asked Kennan and another advisor, Charles Bohlen, "to present separate memoranda concerning means of meeting the European crisis," and he prepared his own paper on the subject. Marshall found Kennan's memorandum "the most succinct and useful," and he gave it, along with his own paper, to Bohlen, who drafted the actual speech Marshall delivered at Harvard. Marshall insisted on noting explicitly in the speech that the "U.S. proposal was aimed at hunger, poverty, and chaos and not against any group" or ideology. Kennan objected to this, as he did to offering aid to "all Europe including the Soviet Union and her satellites." Despite the objection from the advisor whose work he had found of greatest value, Marshall "insisted on formulating the speech as it was finally delivered."

The nature and content of the momentous Harvard speech involved yet another key decision: The speech contained no details and not a single number. Purposely vague, it was also bold and absolute. Disavowing any political or ideological purpose, Marshall called on Europeans to meet and to create their own plan for European recovery, which the United States would fund. That—and only that—was the sum and substance of the speech that launched an aid program unprecedented in the history of the nation and of the world. Truman and Marshall assumed that the aid plan would be unpopular among many, perhaps most, Americans. For that reason, journalists were not contacted to attend the Harvard ceremony. Truman even called a press conference on other topics, precisely to draw journalistic attention away from Cambridge. As for European journalists, Undersecretary of State Dean Acheson was detailed to contact media outlets there. The president and secretary of state wanted full coverage in Europe. They wanted to make a public promise, which American politicians would then be hard pressed to retract.

If European journalists were alerted, European governments were not. "The plan," Marshall reported, "had not been discussed with Europe in advance." Marshall and Truman wanted a quick response, unencumbered by political debate. As for "selling . . . the ERP [European Recovery Plan] to the American people," shortly after the Harvard address, Marshall set off on a nationwide speaking tour that "almost seemed as though I were running for office."

—

PRESIDENT TRUMAN WAS RIGHT to have sent George Marshall to campaign for the plan. At the time, perhaps no other American was as widely respected as he. When Truman's young aide Clark Clifford suggested that the European Recovery Plan be dubbed the "Truman Plan," the president snapped back: "Are you crazy? If we sent it up to that Republican Congress with my name on it, they'd tear it apart. We're going to call it the Marshall Plan." And, in the end, Americans accepted the Marshall Plan for what Prime Minister Winston Churchill called it: "the most unsordid political act in history." It saved countless lives, made possible the economic recovery of Europe, and proved to be the single most effective "weapon" in the struggle between the forces of Western democracy and Soviet communism in what would soon be called the Cold War.

Branch Rickey and Jackie Robinson (1945–47)

THE DECISION TO CROSS THE COLOR LINE

Branch Rickey started playing professional baseball while he was still a student at Ohio Wesleyan University, spending three seasons during 1905–7 in the American League as a catcher. After graduating from Ohio Wesleyan, he went on to the University of Michigan Law School, which he paid for by coaching the baseball team. In 1910, while he was on the road with the team, a hotel manager in South Bend,

Indiana, refused to provide a room for Rickey's one black player, Charley Thomas. Rickey pleaded and cajoled, finally persuading the manager to allow Thomas to share his own room. Years later, Rickey recalled how Charley Thomas would rub and rub his hands, as if he were trying to wash the color out of them. Rickey remembered pointing to the man's hands and making a promise: "Charley, the day will come when they won't have to be white."

Rickey graduated from law school in 1911, but decided to return to the diamond rather than enter the courtroom. He was field manager of the American League's St. Louis Browns from 1913 to 1915, then joined the National League's St. Louis Cardinals, serving as club president from 1917 to 1919, field manager from 1919 to 1925, and general manager from 1925 to 1942. He left the Cards to become president and general manager of the Brooklyn Dodgers in 1943.

One of his first decisions as president of the team was to "cross the color line" by signing up a black ballplayer. For Rickey, the decision had two sources. The first was a matter of personal morality. Rickey had never forgotten Charley Thomas, in whom the pain caused by racial prejudice was heartbreaking. If Jim Crow could do this to a fine athlete like Thomas, it was just plain wrong. The second source was more broadly practical. Rickey knew that there were extraordinarily promising players in the all-black Negro League, and it distressed him to pass up the talent for his team. In some ways, Rickey believed, the times were turning ripe for crossing the line. Late in 1943, longtime baseball commissioner Kenesaw Mountain Landis brought together members of the Black Publishers Association, social-activist singer Paul Robeson, and all sixteen team owners as well as the presidents of both leagues in a meeting. He gave Robeson the floor. "Because baseball is a national game," Robeson said, "it is up to baseball to see that discrimination does not become an American pattern." Rickey was impressed, but Landis continued publicly to oppose the integration of baseball.

Late the next year, Landis died and was succeeded as commissioner by Albert B. "Happy" Chandler, formerly the governor of Kentucky. When

Rickey told him what he planned to do, Chandler said simply, "If they can fight and die on Okinawa [and] Guadalcanal . . . they can play ball in America." Moreover, Rickey was aware that New York had just passed the Quinn-Ives Act, barring racial discrimination in hiring, and he himself enthusiastically endorsed New York mayor Fiorello LaGuardia's brand-new "End Jim Crow in Baseball" committee. Yet when Rickey petitioned the owners to allow him to integrate the National League, the vote was 15 to 1—against.

Although Commissioner Chandler had the moral courage to override the vote, Rickey was all too aware that, even with the commissioner's permission, recruiting a black player would meet with ugly resistance. He decided, therefore, to proceed via a back door of his own making.

In the spring of 1945, Branch Rickey created the United States League as a new "negro league." This drew shocked criticism from social activists, who accused Rickey of turning against the cause of integration by establishing a league that would encourage continued segregation in sports. The fact is, however, that the United States League never played a single game. It was nothing more than a feint, a maneuver to allow Rickey openly but quietly to scout black ballplayers. Out of about a hundred, he asked one, Jackie Robinson, to meet with him on August 28, 1945.

"Are you under contract to the Kansas City Monarchs?" Rickey asked the twenty-six-year-old Robinson, referring to the original Negro American League team on which he played.

"No, sir. We don't have contracts. . . . I just work from payday to payday."

"Do you know why you were brought here?"

"Not exactly. I heard something about a colored team at Ebbets Field. That it?"

"No . . . that isn't it. You were brought here, Jackie, to play for the Brooklyn organization. Perhaps on Montreal to start with—"

"Me? Play for Montreal?" the player gasped.

Rickey's plan was to start Robinson in the minors in Canada, where Jim Crow racism was far less of an issue than it was in the States. Not only would this prove Robinson's merits as a player, it would ease his transition into U.S. major-league play.

"If you can make it, yes. Later on—also if you can make it—you'll have a chance with the Brooklyn Dodgers."

Robinson nodded in stunned silence.

At length, Rickey broke the silence. "I want to win pennants and we need ballplayers!"

In the course of what stretched to a three-hour meeting, Rickey explained that he had not merely scouted Robinson on the diamond, but had employed private investigators to look into his past. He knew that Robinson went to church regularly, that he didn't drink and didn't smoke. He had no criminal record. He had attended UCLA, but had withdrawn in his third year to help his mother take care of their family. Rickey knew that, in 1942, Robinson had enlisted in the U.S. Army and enrolled in Officer Candidate School, and had been commissioned a second lieutenant in 1943. And he knew, too, that he and boxer Joe Louis had faced court-martial in 1944 for refusing to follow an order to sit in the back of a military bus. The charges were dismissed and, at the end of the war, Robinson was honorably discharged.

"Do you think you can do it? Make good in organized baseball?"

"If . . . if I got the chance," Robinson replied.

"There's more here than just playing, Jackie. I wish it meant only hits, runs, and errors—things you can see in a box score. . . . Can you do it?"

Rickey warned him that it wouldn't be pretty. Fans would shout insults, slurs, and threats—and so would some opponents. Runners would come in spikes first. Pitchers would throw at his head.

"Mr. Rickey, they've been throwing at my head for a long time."

Rickey suddenly shifted the discussion from the abstract to the concrete.

"Suppose I'm a player. . . . Suppose I collide with you at second base. When I get up, I yell, 'You dirty, black son of a— '" Rickey paused. "What do you do?"

This, at last, seemed to shake Robinson's resolve: "Mr. Rickey, do you want a ballplayer who's afraid to fight back?"

Rickey explained: "I want a ballplayer with guts enough not to fight back! You've got to do this job with base hits and stolen bases and fielding ground balls, Jackie. Nothing else!"

Rickey continued. He role-played a hotel clerk in the Deep South, a racist sportswriter, a prejudiced waiter.

"Now I'm playing against you in a World Series! I'm a hotheaded player. I want to win that game, so I go into you spikes first, but you don't give ground. You stand there and you jab the ball into my ribs and the umpire yells, 'Out!' I flare up—all I see is your face—that black face right on top of me. So I haul off and punch you right in the cheek!

"What do you do?"

"Mr. Rickey," Robinson replied, "I've got two cheeks." Then he paused. "That it?"

It was clear to Branch Rickey that Jackie Robinson understood— that he understood him and, more important, that he understood the stakes in what he was being asked to do. Robinson later explained that, in this moment, he realized he was being offered two opportunities: one was to play in Major League baseball; the other was to begin to change the world. For that, Jackie Robinson decided he *had* to turn the other cheek. He had to endure, and he had to play like hell in each and every game.

Rickey signed Jackie Robinson to a $600-a-month contract with a $3,500 signing bonus to play with the Montreal Royals, then moved him up to the Brooklyn Dodgers at the start of the 1947 season.

⁃

BRANCH RICKEY'S SCOUTING WAS RIGHT ON THE MONEY. With the Dodgers, Robinson was an immediate and spectacular success, leading the National League in stolen bases and earning the title of Rookie of the Year. In 1949, he won the batting championship with a .342 average and was voted league MVP. His lifetime batting average was .311, and he led Brooklyn to a total of six league championships and one World Series victory.

But Rickey was also right when he told Robinson that his career would mean more than "hits, runs, and errors—things you can see in a box score." Fans did hurl bottles as well as curses at Jackie Robinson. Some of his own teammates protested against having to play with him. Opposing pitchers did, at times, shoot for his head, and runners did, at times, come in spikes first. In the South, Jim Crow kept him out of the hotels that accommodated his teammates and out of the restaurants that fed them.

"Plenty of times," Robinson later said, "I wanted to haul off when somebody insulted me for the color of my skin, but I had to hold to myself. I knew I was kind of an experiment. The whole thing was bigger than me."

Rosa Parks and the Right to Sit (1955)

THE DECISION THAT LAUNCHED
THE CIVIL RIGHTS MOVEMENT

At the end of the workday, on Thursday, December 1, 1955, Rosa Parks, an African-American department-store tailor and seamstress, boarded a Montgomery, Alabama, city bus. She walked past seats marked "Whites Only" and sat with three other blacks in the fifth row, the first row that blacks, by city ordinance, were permitted to occupy—provided that no white person was left standing. After a few more stops, the front four rows filled with whites. One white man was left standing.

The same Montgomery city ordinance that barred African Americans from the first four rows of the bus seats also forbade blacks and whites from occupying the same row. Accordingly, the bus driver directed all four of the passengers seated in the fifth row to move.

Three did. Parks refused.

What went through her mind?

As the driver shouted at her, Parks remembered that, twelve years earlier, this very man had made her get off the bus and enter through the rear door. As she recalled this, Parks continued to say no, she would not move. Exasperated, the driver left the bus and returned with a policeman, who arrested Rosa Parks for violating segregation laws.

On various later occasions, Parks tried to recall exactly what she had been thinking at the time. "My only concern was to get home after a hard day's work," she remarked on one occasion, and also: "I didn't want to pay my fare and then go around the back door, because many times, even if you did that, you might not get on the bus at all. They'd probably shut the door, drive off, and leave you standing there." But, on another occasion, she explained: "The only tired I was, was tired of giving in." She also said: "Our mistreatment was just not right, and I was tired of it," and "I knew someone had to take the first step and I made up my mind not to move."

Neither the driver nor the police officer had intimidated her. "I have learned over the years that when one's mind is made up, this diminishes fear; knowing what must be done does away with fear."

Parks had not planned the bus confrontation, but the decision that led to her arrest was no accident, either. For one thing, she had a personal history of activism. A supporter of the Scottsboro Boys (the infamous case of nine African-American youths, ages thirteen to nineteen, who, on the shallowest possible evidence, were hurriedly convicted by an all-white Alabama jury of raping two white women in 1931), she joined the NAACP in 1943 and was secretary to E. D. Nixon, head of the organization's Montgomery chapter. Parks worked with the Montgomery Voters League, which sponsored voter registration campaigns, and, in the summer of 1955, she had attended a human rights workshop held at the Highlander Folk School in Tennessee. She boarded the bus that evening not with the intention to challenge an immoral law, but primed to do just that.

The activist community of Montgomery was likewise primed. It had long been contemplating testing the city's segregation ordinances by deliberately defying the bus-seating ban. There had even been discussion of organizing a boycott of Montgomery buses to force a change in the law, and when E. D. Nixon heard of Parks's arrest, he and the NAACP were ready to make the most of it.

Nixon posted bond for Parks, then enlisted her cooperation in organizing the boycott. Another NAACP activist, Jo Ann Robinson, mimeographed and distributed flyers appealing for a one-day boycott of the buses on the day that the Parks case was to be heard, and local black ministers, including Martin Luther King, Jr., agreed to spread the word in their Sunday sermons. King had hoped optimistically for 60 percent of Montgomery's black community to observe the boycott. To his amazement, Montgomery buses were almost completely empty on the day of the hearing, Monday, December 5, 1955.

Parks appeared before the local magistrate, who found her guilty of breaking the city segregation ordinance and fined her fourteen dollars. Her lawyer responded that he would appeal the case to the United States Supreme Court. That evening, thousands gathered in a Montgomery church to hear Dr. King speak on the boycott. He said that it must continue, explaining that "There comes a time that people get tired. We are here this evening to say to those who have mistreated us for so long, that we are tired, tired of being segregated and humiliated, tired of being kicked about by the brutal feet of oppression. . . . One of the great glories of democracy is the right to protest for right."

On the fourth day of the boycott, December 8, King and others, organized as the Montgomery Improvement Association (MIA), met with representatives of the bus company and city commissioners. The MIA presented a desegregation plan, which the bus company summarily rejected. The city commissioners also warned King and the others that any city cab driver who charged less than the authorized forty-five-cent minimum fare would be prosecuted. (African American taxi operators had begun charging blacks a dime, the same as the bus fare.) In response, the MIA devised what they called a "private taxi" service in the form of a well-organized system of car pools.

THE BOYCOTT THAT ROSA PARKS'S DEFIANCE had initiated proved hard, and it proved dangerous. King's home was bombed on January 30, 1956, and Nixon's on February 1. When this failed to end the boycott, officials secured the indictment of eighty-nine black activists under a rarely used statute prohibiting boycotts. King, the first to be tried, was convicted and given the choice of paying a $500 fine plus $500 in court costs or spending 386 days in the state penitentiary. He chose imprisonment. During this period, white insurance companies attacked the "private taxis" by canceling the liability policies covering church-owned station wagons. In response, an African American agent in Atlanta obtained underwriting directly from Lloyd's of London. The police ruthlessly harassed black drivers for minor or trumped-up traffic offenses, yet the boycott continued.

Bus ridership fell by 75 percent, and downtown businesses suffered, as African Americans, unwilling to ride the bus, stopped patronizing the stores. Moved by economic necessity, business owners formed a group called the Men of Montgomery and opened negotiations directly with the MIA. These soon broke down, but, in the meantime, boycott representatives sued the city and the bus company in federal court, securing a ruling that held segregation on buses unconstitutional. When the city appealed, the U.S. Supreme Court upheld the ruling on November 13, 1956. It was this decision that officially ended the Montgomery Bus Boycott, although black riders refused to return to the buses until December 21, 1956, when the court's mandate came into force. Even then, threats and violence continued. There were sniper incidents, which forced the temporary suspension of bus operations after 5:00 P.M. There was an attempt by one white group to start a privately funded white-only bus service. The homes of three black families were bombed, together with four Baptist churches and the People's Service Station and Cab Stand. An unexploded bomb was removed from King's front porch. Of seven white men arrested for the bombings, five were indicted. Two of these were found not guilty, despite their having signed confessions, and the other cases were dismissed in a compromise agreement that dropped the cases against blacks arrested under the antiboycott laws. Despite the violence and the threats of violence, the boycott triumphed, the Civil Rights movement began in earnest, and, for blacks as well as whites, life in the United States would never be the same.

Betty Friedan and a Woman's Place (1963)

THE DECISION TO REVALUE VALUES

Bettye Naomi Goldstein was born in the American heartland city of Peoria, Illinois, in 1921, and in 1942, graduated with a psychology degree from Smith College, the prestigious East Coast school for women. She pursued graduate work at the University of California, Berkeley, for a year, then moved to New York City, where she worked at a variety of jobs until she married Carl Friedan in 1947. For the next decade, Betty Friedan was primarily a housewife and a mother, although she also freelanced as a journalist for women's magazines.

Ten years into her marriage, family, and freelancing, Friedan became (as she reported) "strangely bored with writing articles about breast feeding and the like for *Redbook* and *Ladies' Home Journal.*" At the time, she could not account for her boredom, although she did feel that something was vaguely wrong. She assumed that the problem had to do with *her.* As she put it, "I . . . thought there was something wrong with *me* because I didn't have an orgasm waxing the kitchen floor" as the television commercials seemed to promise.

Nevertheless, Friedan had a hunch that other women might have feelings similar to hers and, in 1957, she composed a long and detailed questionnaire designed to probe the lives led by her Smith College classmates since they graduated in 1942. Friedan intended to use the results of the questionnaire to write a magazine article disproving the notion that "education had fitted us ill for our role as women." In fact, the results raised more questions than they answered. Based on the responses she received from her classmates, it was apparent that the education she and they received had not exactly "geared us to the role women were trying to play." That led Freidan to ask whether the education was wrong—or the role. As she wrote the article, the answer became surprisingly clear.

McCall's, for which the questionnaire-based article was intended, rejected Friedan's finished piece. The senior editors of this women's magazine were men, and, although the lower-level female editors supported the article, the men prevailed, claiming that its surprising conclusion— that the best and brightest women were fundamentally unsuited to the accepted roles of women in American society—simply could not be true.

Ladies' Home Journal accepted the article, but then edited it to "say just the opposite of what, in fact, I was trying to say." Friedan therefore withdrew it and submitted it to *Redbook,* whose editor complained to Freidan's agent that the writer had clearly "gone off her rocker." The results presented in the article, he said, were such that "only the most neurotic housewife could identify" with them.

In the meantime, as she suffered one rejection after another, Betty Friedan continued to pursue her investigation. She interviewed more women, as well as psychologists, marriage counselors, and sociologists, certain that she was on to something, something important, although she was not quite sure just what. It had no name.

In analyzing her accumulating data and thinking about herself as well, Friedan concluded that the nameless problem was a feeling of vague guilt that came over most women whenever they did anything outside of their role as husbands' wives or children's mothers—that is, whenever they did anything for themselves, as people. This was different from the old Victorian guilt women felt about sexual desires and needs. It was not sexual guilt, but guilt over needs that did not fit the sexual or social definition of women, a definition Friedan called the "mystique of feminine fulfillment." With that phrase, she suddenly had a name for the nameless problem. It was *the feminine mystique.*

But the magazines weren't buying it. Friedan now understood why. The concept of the feminine mystique was the very basis on which women's magazines functioned. They were built upon the feminine mystique, they promoted the feminine mystique, and they thrived by it. Understandably, they were not about to print something that threatened their very reason for being. With this insight, Friedan decided that the only way she was going to get her ideas into print was to write a book.

She estimated that the writing would take a year. It took five. And although she continued to be a wife and a mother, she recalled later that the "book took me over, obsessed me, wanted to write itself." It came not just from what was now a mountain of research, but from somewhere within herself, from a depth of feeling and experience, including her memories of her own mother's chronic discontent, her college training in psychology, her guilt over having sacrificed academic and intellectual opportunities because they somehow did not fit what she had perceived as a woman's role, and her journalistic background, which (she said) taught her "to follow clues to the hidden economic underside of reality." She thought, too, about her present life—about what it meant to be married, to have children, to live in the suburbs, to shop with other mothers in suburban supermarkets, to entertain the children in company with other mothers, to spend free time in coffee klatches, and to have devoted years of her life writing for women's magazines whose gospel was that "normal" women could not legitimately identify with anything that lay outside of the home unless such issues could be filtered through their experience as a wife or a mother.

Having decided to write a book, the book-in-progress pushed Friedan to a whole new set of decisions based on the conclusion that this problem, this "feminine mystique," was a force that unnaturally confined the energies and vision of American women. It was a most unsettling sensation for her at first, but it led to a "growing feeling of calm, strong, gut-sureness as the clues fitted together."

Published in 1963, *The Feminine Mystique* became an instant best seller and catapulted Betty Friedan to the forefront of the emerging women's movement of the 1960s. Three years after the book was published, she was instrumental in founding the National Organization for Women (NOW) and served as its first president. As the book raised the consciousness of many women and men, NOW campaigned on the political front for liberalized abortion laws, the passage of the Equal Rights Amendment, and legislation to mandate workplace equality for men and women. From the publication of *The Feminine Mystique*, a new culture arose among principally college-educated, liberal women, who began to make their way into economic and political spheres that were previously the exclusive domain of men.

FRIEDAN'S DECISION TO EXPLORE THE SOURCES of her own discontent, boredom, and guilt had led to a decision to ask other women about these things, which resulted in an article and then the decision to write a book. This set of modest decisions, in turn, started a process that, with remarkable speed, transformed American culture, economy, morality, and collective psychology.

Lyndon Johnson
and the Civil Rights Act (1964)

THE DECISION TO CREATE RACIAL JUSTICE

Lyndon Baines Johnson was born in 1908 in a three-room house in the hills of southwest Texas, the first of five children. His father was a member of the Texas House of Representatives, and his mother was the daughter of a state legislator. Despite this measure of prominence, the family was poor and often struggled. Young LBJ graduated from high school in 1924 then went to work for three years to earn enough money to enroll in Southwest Texas State Teachers College. Taking a year off during 1928–29, he taught in a mostly Mexican-American school in

Cotulla, Texas, and here became acquainted firsthand with a poverty much greater than that of his family.

As a child of the South, LBJ imbibed the racial attitudes of the region, but he also saw African Americans, like Mexican Americans, as people—*poor* people—and he never became an ardent segregationist. Nevertheless, as he edged his way into politics—beginning as a campaign worker for Democratic congressional candidate Welly Hopkins in 1931, and continuing as the legislative assistant to Texas Congressman Richard Kleberg in Washington—Johnson clung to the southern party line on racial matters. Did he want to behave differently? Perhaps, perhaps not. As a practical matter, however, speaking out on racial justice would have ended his political career in the 1930s before it had properly begun.

In Washington, Johnson was befriended by Sam Rayburn, a fellow Texan and the influential chairman of the Committee on Interstate and Foreign Commerce. Through Rayburn, LBJ became connected with the administration of President Franklin D. Roosevelt and was named director of the Texas Division of the National Youth Administration (1935–37). Next, he won a seat in the House of Representatives as an enthusiastic supporter of the New Deal and became increasingly identified with the cause of social justice—though, as always, he drew the line at racial matters. A stint overseas as a lieutenant commander in the navy during World War II interrupted his legislative duties for seven months. In 1941, he had lost a bid for the United States Senate in a special election, but he won the seat in 1948.

Over the next dozen years he built an extraordinary career in the Senate, becoming Democratic whip in 1951 and minority leader in 1953. With the return of a Democratic majority in 1955, forty-six-year-old Johnson became the youngest majority leader in history. He was by this time a driven man. He wanted power and influence. He wanted to become president. And he also wanted to improve the lot of the poor and disenfranchised, whom Johnson always felt were "his" people. In addition to all of this, Johnson was also aware, as he often remarked, that "Johnson men do not live long," and in July 1955 LBJ suffered a heart attack he would later describe as "the worst a man could have and still live." Acute consciousness of his mortality seems to have pushed him to increasingly bold action.

From the point of view of the Democratic Party, LBJ's greatest talent was his ability to bring the party, typically torn along the North-South axis, together in a disciplined bloc. His influence was well-nigh irresistible. He would buttonhole, wheedle, and cajole fellow senators, but most of all, he would approach them with his father's favorite quotation from the New Testament: "Let us reason together."

In 1957, President Dwight D. Eisenhower's justice department drafted a bill, the Civil Rights Act of 1957, designed principally to ensure that all African Americans could exercise their right to vote. The bill also called for the writing of a joint report on race relations by representatives of both major political parties and the creation of an agency within the justice department to monitor civil rights abuses. The most controversial feature of the bill was a provision that certain violations of the Civil Rights Act could be tried in court without a jury. The provision was designed to circumvent the certainty that, in the South, a white jury would never convict a white person accused of violating a civil rights law, but even liberals found it hard to stomach an assault on the right to a jury trial.

Facing the bill, Johnson found himself in a difficult situation. He believed that the demands of social justice required the new law. He believed that southern knee-jerk opposition to civil rights was not only wrong and bad for the country, but also bad for the South itself and ultimately destructive to the Democratic Party. On the other hand, he knew that he could not ask southerners to support suspension of trial by jury, especially in civil rights matters. LBJ set about shepherding the bill through the Senate, ensuring first that jury trials would not be excluded under any circumstances and providing for civil rather than criminal penalties for many violations of the law. Some historians of civil rights have accused LBJ of gutting the bill before obtaining its passage. Such criticism is justified. The Civil Rights Act of 1957 was weak legislation— but it was the first federal civil rights legislation in eighty-two years, and

LBJ had found a way to make it palatable to a majority of his party without tearing the party apart. He believed, moreover, that it was merely an overture and opening to additional legislation.

The next civil rights act came in 1960, which introduced penalties for obstruction or attempted obstruction of anyone's attempt to register to vote, or to actually vote. It also created a Civil Rights Commission. An incremental step beyond the 1957 law, it was still tepid legislation, but, even so, it would never have passed without LBJ's skillful engineering in the Senate.

Anxious to maintain his own power and make himself viable for a run at the White House, anxious to advance his party socially but to keep it from breaking apart along the regional-cultural fault line separating North and South, anxious as well to begin the evolution toward racial justice, LBJ moved cautiously on civil rights. Yet by the election of John F. Kennedy as president, with LBJ as vice president, the nation was clearly moving in the direction of a more forceful federal stand on the issue.

Although Kennedy was no southerner, he moved, like Johnson, cautiously in the area of civil rights. His relations with Congress were not warm, and he was not eager to ask that body for strong legislation on matters of race. Events, however, moved his hand. As a national civil rights movement gathered momentum, on May 2, 1963, television newsreel cameras captured police violence against African American protestors in Birmingham, Alabama. Dogs, nightsticks, and powerful fire hoses were brought to bear on black men, women, and schoolchildren. With these ugly images, a line had been crossed, and in response to a national groundswell, a hitherto reluctant JFK announced on June 11 that he was sending a new, tough, comprehensive civil rights bill to Congress. That very evening, Medgar Evers, director of the Mississippi chapter of the NAACP was gunned down in the driveway of his house.

Kennedy appeared to be transformed, and he began to lobby vigorously for the bill. Yet, even now, his motives were divided. JFK was especially anxious to gain passage of a tax-reduction bill, which he believed would give the national economy a needed boost and stand him in good stead for the 1964 reelection campaign. He met secretly with Emanuel Cellar, who chaired the House committee debating the civil rights bill, and asked him to hold the bill until the tax cut passed. JFK feared that, if the civil rights bill came out first, the powerful head of the House Ways and Means Committee, Wilbur Mills of Arkansas, would retaliate by killing the tax cut. Thus the civil rights bill languished, even as the organized civil rights movement turned up the pressure for its passage, culminating in the March on Washington in August 1963 and Martin Luther King, Jr.'s stirring "I Have a Dream" speech from the steps of the Lincoln Memorial on August 28.

Approval of the tax cut by the House Ways and Means Committee on September 10 cleared the way for the "mark up" of the civil rights bill. That process took weeks of wrangling, but on November 19, the bill was ready to be scheduled by the Rules Committee for debate on the House floor. Three days later, John F. Kennedy was assassinated in Dallas.

Within hours of JFK's death, Lyndon Johnson, aboard Air Force One, was sworn in as the new president. Twelve hours later, he was in his Texas home in Spring Valley, surrounded by three trusted aides, Cliff Carter, Bill Moyers, and Jack Valenti. Valenti later recalled how LBJ lay in his bed watching television coverage of the assassination aftermath and discussing with them plans for the days ahead. "Though none of us who listened realized it at the time," Valenti wrote, "he was revealing the design of the Great Society. He had not yet given it a name, but he knew with stunning precision the mountaintop to which he was going to summon the people."

Perhaps.

Perhaps in the hours following the young president's murder, the new president saw clearly and, in a flash of moral vision, what he had to do. Others believe he was more politically calculating. JFK's staff was intensely loyal to Kennedy, not to Johnson, whom many did not even like. LBJ wanted to keep the staff intact. For the good of the country as well as the viability of the administration, he wanted at all costs to avoid a mass stampede from the White House. Since Kennedy had set the civil rights act in motion, LBJ believed it was politically expedient to keep it in motion. Moreover, he wanted to run for the presidency in 1964 and was determined to capture all of the black vote.

Perhaps those were the chief reasons for his wanting passage of the new civil rights act. More likely, though, it was a combination of vision and political savvy that moved LBJ in the days and weeks following the assassination. He had been driven not merely to be president, but to be a great president. He was president now, and here, now, was his chance to be a great president. As FDR had introduced the New Deal, so he would author the Great Society—and he knew instinctively that no society could be great if it denied civil rights to any of its members.

Like his fellow Americans, Johnson was horrified by the murder of JFK. But he also saw it as an opportunity. Martyrs have propelled many righteous but difficult movements. On November 27, 1963, LBJ addressed Congress: "Let us continue," he said. "I urge you again, as I did in 1957 and again in 1960, to enact a civil rights law so that we can move forward to eliminate from this Nation every trace of discrimination and oppression that is based on race or color. There could be no greater source of strength to this Nation both at home and abroad." It was, he implied, the unfinished work of the slain president.

Yet LBJ knew it would still be an uphill fight. He kept Congress in session after the winter recess was long overdue. When the bill became mired in the House Rules Committee, where the chairman, Howard Smith, would not give it a hearing, LBJ quietly enlisted the aid of Katharine Graham, publisher of the *Washington Post*, to bring pressure on individual congressmen with articles demanding to know "Why are you against a hearing?" LBJ also appealed to Republicans to sign a petition to get the bill out of committee: "We've only got 150 Democrats; the rest of them are southerners. So we've got to make every Republican [sign]. We ought to say, 'Here is the party of Lincoln. Here is the image of Lincoln, and whoever it is that is against a hearing and against a vote in the House of Representatives, is not a man who believes in giving humanity a fair shake.'"

ULTIMATELY, SMITH RELEASED THE BILL, and the committee, after three more weeks of delay, voted it to the floor. In the meantime, under a barrage of LBJ phone calls, the nation's clergy, black and white, began voicing their support for civil rights. The president turned next to the Senate, where he engineered bipartisan support for the bill by enlisting the aid of the weightiest Republican in that chamber, Everett McKinley Dirksen of Illinois. The powerful southern Democratic bloc was outmaneuvered and outvoted. On June 19, the Senate passed the civil rights bill, 73 to 27, and on July 2, the House voted 289 to 126 to accept the Senate version of the bill.

On the very day of its House passage, President Johnson signed the Civil Rights Act of 1964 in the East Room of the White House.

Daniel Ellsberg
and the Pentagon Papers (1971)
THE DECISION TO TELL THE TRUTH

In June 1971, the *New York Times* published one of the most shocking series of articles ever carried in an American newspaper. They concerned a top secret government study officially titled the "History of the U.S. Decision Making Process in Vietnam" and dubbed by *Times* editors the "Pentagon Papers." Ordered by Secretary of Defense Robert S. McNamara, the 47-volume document (consisting of 3,000 pages of narrative and 4,000 pages of original documents) on which the articles were based had been compiled between 1967 and 1969 by Defense Department analysts. The study meticulously chronicled how the administration of Harry S. Truman had aided France in its colonial war against the Communist-led Vietminh, thereby drawing the United States into the growing conflict in Vietnam. It revealed that in 1954 President Dwight D.

Eisenhower resolved to prevent a Communist takeover of South Vietnam and to use limited military means to undermine the emerging communist regime of North Vietnam. It detailed the decisions by which President John F. Kennedy transformed a policy of limited involvement into a "broad commitment," which included covert action by the CIA to bring about the overthrow and assassination of the corrupt and unpopular South Vietnamese president Ngo Dinh Diem, a longtime U.S. ally. Even more damningly, the Pentagon Papers exposed the questionable timing of the Gulf of Tonkin Resolution, which was passed by Congress in 1964 after reported North Vietnamese attacks on two American destroyers, the USS *Maddox* and USS *Turner Joy*. The resolution, which gave President Lyndon B. Johnson virtually unlimited war-making powers in Vietnam, was actually drafted months before the attacks. One of the attacks proved to be a false report; the other, a distortion. Moreover, the documents revealed that President Johnson had ordered the bombing of North Vietnam in 1965 even though it was the consensus of the American intelligence community that the air raids, no matter how massive, would fail to prevent North Vietnam from continuing to support the Viet Cong insurgency in South Vietnam. Publication of the Pentagon Papers not only brought to light the twisted story of America's tragic involvement in Vietnam; it chronicled three decades of government bungling and deliberate deceit in the formulation and execution of a foreign policy based on poor intelligence, flawed interpretation, and outright lies.

Among those who had compiled the original top secret "History of the U.S. Decision Making Process in Vietnam" was Daniel Ellsberg, a brilliant young senior research associate at the Massachusetts Institute of Technology's Center for International Studies and an employee of the RAND Corporation, the famous Pentagon "think tank." Ellsberg had been a U.S. Marine Corps company commander and Cold War-era "Cold Warrior," dedicated to helping the U.S. government formulate effective policies to oppose Communist aggression in the world. His work as a government analyst during the Vietnam Era was motivated by an intense desire to help his country prevail against Communist expansion in Southeast Asia. Yet the more he researched evolving American policy and the more he assessed the U.S. and South Vietnamese conduct of the escalating war—including in his research a trip to Vietnam to see the war close up and firsthand without the filter of official reports—the more he became convinced that the war was based on errors, delusions, and lies. It was not only impossible to win, Ellsberg became convinced—the effort was immoral, a wanton waste of American and Vietnamese lives.

What would he do about it? What could he do about it?

In a 2002 memoir entitled *Secrets*, Daniel Ellsberg detailed the moment of his decision to tell the truth.

He awoke on the morning of September 30, 1969, got out of bed, went to the front door of his house in Malibu, and picked up the *Los Angeles Times*. Relaxing in a bedroom that looked out upon the Pacific Ocean, Ellsberg read the paper. The lead story was about what was being called the Green Beret Murder Case. A Green Beret (Special Forces) colonel, Robert Rheault, and five intelligence officers under his command had been charged with the premeditated murder in Vietnam of one Thai Khac Chuyen, a Special Forces informant whom Rheault and his officers believed had betrayed them. After interrogation, on June 20, 1969, Chuyen was shot, his body placed in a weighted bag, and the bag tossed into the South China Sea. The story had been in the papers since July. Today's headline was "CHARGES AGAINST GREEN BERETS DROPPED BY ARMY." The story detailed how Secretary of the Army Stanley R. Resor, who just eleven days earlier had expressed his strong feeling that the case should be brought to trial, now overruled General Creighton Abrams, commander of U.S. forces in Vietnam, ordering that charges be dropped.

"I lay on my bed," Ellsberg wrote, "and listened to the ocean and the gulls and thought about what I read."

Secretary Resor claimed that the soldiers could not be given a fair trial because the CIA refused to make witnesses available. Ellsberg reasoned that the CIA could not "'refuse' to produce witnesses without the backing of the president." Although the Pentagon and the White House both denied involvement in the CIA refusal, the press "took it for granted that these denials were false"—and, in fact, the diary of H. R. Haldeman, President Nixon's chief of staff, published years later, confirmed that both Richard Nixon and his foreign policy adviser Henry Kissinger were directly involved in the CIA refusal. Ellsberg found himself suddenly amazed by the casualness with which the press accepted the inevitability of lying at the highest levels of government. He was also stunned by what Resor and Abrams had originally said, that the U.S. Army couldn't "condone murder," and yet, apparently, the president of the United States could.

Reading further in the newspaper account, Ellsberg discovered that incidents such as the summary execution of Thai Khac Chuyen were common in the Vietnam War, but that General Abrams had chosen to bring charges in this case because he had been lied to by Rheault or others, who had told him that Chuyen was on a "sensitive secret mission outside South Vietnam when he was already dead." Indeed, Rheault's lie seems to have had its origin in lies subordinates told *him*. The alleged triggerman, a Captain Robert F. Marasco, and other officers had apparently ordered their subordinates to conspire in a false cover story.

Of course, neither Resor nor Abrams spoke about lies. "Yet," Ellsberg wrote, "if they didn't personally condone an individual murder," they were not being honest about the reasons for bringing the charges or for dismissing them. They "were taking part in a lot of lying," and, Ellsberg continued, a "vision forming in my mind was what seemed to be the skeleton of [what] I had just read: a ladder of lies.

"I lay in bed that Tuesday morning and thought: This is the system that I have been working for, the system I have been part of, for a dozen years—fifteen, including the Marine Corps. It's a system that lies automatically, at every level from bottom to top—from sergeant to commander in chief—to conceal murder."

And Ellsberg kept thinking.

This same system had been lying "on an infinitely larger scale, continuously for a third of a century," about what it had been doing in Vietnam. "I thought: I'm not going to be part of it anymore."

Just outside was the timeless, peaceful truth of the ocean, the rhythmic rush of waves, the call of gulls, and in his hands was a story about lies, about people telling lies, and, even worse, about people outraged by lies but apparently willing to perpetuate those very lies. Ellsberg thought: "I'm not going to be part of this lying machine, this cover-up, the murder, anymore."

Often, a great decision materializes—unbidden, really—from the elements around us: a coincidence of ocean, news story, and a realization of who you are. The elements of the decision, when they materialize in this way, cannot be denied, but it requires a courageous exercise of positive will to act on the decision that has suddenly appeared to you.

Ellsberg realized that he had in his safe at the RAND Corporation seven thousand pages of "documentary evidence of lying, by four presidents and their administrations over twenty-three years, to conceal plans and actions of mass murder." He decided to "stop concealing that myself" and, somehow, to "get it out."

In an era before digital documents were stored on desktop computer hard drives, Ellsberg would have to smuggle out of his high-security office seven thousand sheets of paper and copy each page on the slow and cumbersome photocopiers of the time. The physical logistics involved were as labor-intensive as they were dangerous. To be caught with a single page of the top secret document would mean charges of espionage or even treason. Ellsberg knew that the best he could hope for was an end to his career, that, more likely, his actions would result in a criminal trial, conviction, and long imprisonment. This is what came with a decision to tell the truth when no one else would, and Ellsberg accepted all of it.

Over a long period, Ellsberg and a colleague copied the documents, then leaked major portions to the *New York Times* and the *Washington Post*. On June 13, 1971, the *Times* began publishing articles based on the documents. At first, President Richard Nixon was somewhat pleased to see chiefly Democratic administrations embarrassed, but it soon occurred to him that the leaks were undercutting a war he was still prosecuting and that allowing the circulation of top secret documents to go unchallenged was in and of itself a most dangerous precedent. Therefore, after the third daily installment appeared in the *Times*, the U.S. Department of Justice, at the president's direction, secured a temporary restraining order against further publication of the material on the grounds that continuing to disseminate the classified documents would cause immediate and irreparable harm to the national defense. For the next two weeks, the *Times* and the *Post* contested the order through the courts while publication of the rest of the series was suspended. On June 30, 1971, the U.S. Supreme Court handed down a six-to-three decision holding that the government had failed to justify restraint of publication, thereby freeing the newspapers to continue publishing the material. Associate Justice Hugo Black even commented that the newspapers "should be commended for serving the purpose that the Founding Fathers saw so clearly."

The Nixon White House responded to the Supreme Court's decision by taking action—illegal and covert—against Ellsberg himself. The president ordered a secret investigation of Ellsberg with the goal of discrediting him personally. A special unit secretly run from the Oval Office under the direction of former CIA agent E. Howard Hunt and ex-FBI special agent G. Gordon Liddy, with the guidance of the president's special counsel, Charles Colson, plotted against Ellsberg. This palace guard coterie was dubbed the Plumbers, because their mission was to stop leaks. There was a plan to intimidate Ellsberg by means of a physical assault, but the first step the Plumbers carried out was to burglarize the office of Ellsberg's psychiatrist in search of embarrassing revelations about the whistle-blower's private life. (A short time later, the Plumbers would be caught burglarizing Democratic National Headquarters at the Watergate office and apartment complex in Washington, D.C. With that, the downfall of Richard M. Nixon began.)

While pursuing covert action against Ellsberg, the Nixon Justice Department also chose to prosecute him on a dozen felony counts carrying possible sentences totaling 115 years. The charges, however, were dismissed on May 11, 1973, on grounds of the government's misconduct against him—misconduct that led to the trial and conviction of several White House aides and that figured prominently in the subsequent Watergate hearings and impeachment proceedings against the president.

—

PUBLICATION OF THE PENTAGON PAPERS simultaneously undermined Americans' confidence in their government even as it affirmed the power of the Constitution and the First Amendment guarantees of a free press—the tools by which American government corrects itself. More immediately, although the Pentagon Papers created a tidal wave of disillusionment, galvanized the anti–Vietnam War movement and surely hastened disengagement from a war in which victory was impossible and that had, for nearly a decade, torn the fabric of American society.

James Burke and the Tylenol Murders (1982)

THE DECISION FOR CORPORATE ETHICS

At dawn on September 29, 1982, in the Chicago suburb of Elk Grove Village, twelve-year-old Mary Kellerman awoke with a miserable cold. She called to her parents, who gave her one capsule of Extra-Strength Tylenol and tucked her back into bed. About an hour later, at seven, they were awakened again, this time by cries from the bathroom. There, on the floor, the Kellermans found their daughter, dying.

That same morning, in another suburb, Arlington Heights, twenty-seven-year-old Adam Janus was bothered by a mild pain in his chest. He reached for the Extra-Strength Tylenol, shook out two capsules, swallowed them, and, within an hour, suffered total cardiopulmonary collapse. In the evening, the young man's relatives, stunned by his death, gathered in the Janus home. To relieve his headache, Stanley Janus, Adam's twenty-five-year-old brother, took two Tylenol from the bottle his brother had used that morning. He passed the bottle to his wife, Theresa, age nineteen, who also took two capsules. Stanley and Theresa Janus were dead within forty-eight hours.

Mary Reiner of Winfield, Illinois, not far from Elk Grove Village and Arlington Heights, had just returned from the hospital after giving birth to her fourth child. She took two Tylenol and was pronounced dead at the local hospital a few hours later. Reiner was twenty-seven.

A short time later, in a lakefront neighborhood on Chicago's Near North Side, police were called to the apartment of thirty-five-year-old United Airlines flight attendant Paula Prince. She was dead, a bottle of Extra-Strength Tylenol near at hand. By that time, in Elmhurst, Illinois, Mary McFarland, thirty-one and healthy, had also died.

What could explain the sudden deaths of seven young persons, all apparently healthy, three from the same family?

The first to fit the events together were a pair of off-duty suburban fire fighters, Philip Cappitelli and Richard Keyworth. They were men who had a hard time putting their jobs on the shelf when they got home and so would "relax" by listening to calls on their police scanners.

Cappitelli phoned Keyworth—yes, he'd been listening to the scanner traffic, too. Yes, it was weird. The men compared notes, and what suddenly emerged was *Tylenol*. The product had been mentioned in each and every report. Cappitelli and Keyworth phoned their fire department captain, who contacted the police. Officials immediately ordered toxicological tests to be performed on the capsules in each case. It was quickly discovered that grayish crystalline potassium cyanide had been crudely stuffed into some of the capsules in the bottles found at each crime scene. In fact, so much cyanide had been used—65 to 100 or more milligrams per capsule—that the tainted capsules bulged with the substance.

As soon as the Tylenol connection was made, Chicago-area police drove loudspeaker-equipped squad cars through neighborhoods warning people not to take Tylenol. The story hit national television right away, but it took the U.S. Food and Drug Administration a full twenty-four hours to issue its advisory to avoid Tylenol capsules "until the series of deaths in the Chicago area can be clarified."

At the time, Johnson & Johnson, the maker of Tylenol, was headed by James Burke, a Harvard Business School graduate who had joined the company in 1953 as a product director after three years at Procter & Gamble. Eager to make his mark, Burke came out with a line of several over-the-counter medicines for children. One after another, the new products failed, and, at last, Burke was called in for a meeting with company chairman Robert Wood Johnson II. Burke assumed he was going to be fired. But instead, Johnson talked to him about the nature of business. He said, "Business is all about making decisions, and you don't make decisions without making mistakes. Don't make that mistake again, but please be sure you make others."

Burke recovered from his early mistakes and, in 1976, rose to the position of chairman and CEO of the company. Under his leadership, Johnson & Johnson became the nation's dominant health-care brand. At the time of the Tylenol murders, it was a consumer products empire valued at $9 billion dollars, including, in addition to the principal operating company, some fifty wholly owned subsidiaries.

Now it was under attack.

While medical examiners were still performing autopsies on the victims, Jerry Della Femina was quick to pronounce his postmortem on Johnson & Johnson's Tylenol. The goateed, shaven-headed advertising mogul, whose 1970 Madison Avenue memoir—*From Those Wonderful Folks Who Gave You Pearl Harbor*—earned him a reputation for pull-no-punches irreverence, told the *New York Times*: "I don't think they can ever sell another product under that name. There may be an advertising person who thinks he can solve this and if they find him, I want to hire him, because then I want him to turn our water cooler into a wine cooler."

It was natural that Della Femina would assume that the number one concern of Johnson & Johnson management would be "damage control" for the product. But he was wrong. It was far from the first thing on Burke's mind. As soon as he learned that the Chicago deaths were linked to Tylenol, Burke thought of his mentor, Robert Wood Johnson, and he looked to a corporate document Johnson had written in 1943. Titled

"Our Credo," it began, "We believe our first responsibility is to doctors, nurses and patients, to mothers and fathers and all others who use our products and services." Next in line, according to the Credo, were employees and the communities in which the firm operated. Occupying *last* place in the line of responsibility were shareholders.

No doubt, "Our Credo" was hopelessly out of date. The prevailing business philosophy of the decade was unapologetically investor centered, so much so that the typical company of 1982 no longer saw its primary business as producing useful, beneficial products for consumers, but producing returns for investors. It was to investors that corporate America held itself primarily accountable. Burke's decision was to put customers first and stockholders last. He made this decision not only in the belief that it was the right thing to do, but in the faith that the rest of "Our Credo" would also be borne out. "When we operate according to these principles," Robert Wood Johnson had written, "the stockholders should realize a fair return."

Officials at McNeil Consumer Products, the J & J subsidiary that manufactured Tylenol, were quick to point out that the tampering could not have taken place at either of the two plants producing the product. They cited strict quality-control procedures as well as the fact that cyanide-laced capsules had been discovered in shipments from *both* plants but had only been found in the Chicago area. It was clear, they argued, that any tampering must have occurred after the Tylenol reached the stores. They theorized that bottles had been obtained from one or more stores and five to ten capsules had been tainted in each bottle, which were then surreptitiously returned to shelves in five different Chicago-area stores—an act of reverse shoplifting. In legal terms, this scenario almost certainly cleared Johnson & Johnson of liability. The company could not be held accountable for the criminal acts some madman committed long after the product had passed into other hands.

But if J & J's lawyers sighed in some degree of relief, it was not absolution Burke was looking for. He decided to lead his company *ahead* of law enforcement officials, regulatory agencies, and the news media.

Burke seized the media and used it to tell consumers not to purchase or take *any* Tylenol product. Burke then ordered an immediate halt to production of Tylenol, and he pulled all advertising for it. Only after Burke had taken these voluntary and proactive steps did the FBI and the Food and Drug Administration order a recall—and only of those lots of the product actually implicated in the poisonings. Burke overrode the authorities, insisting that *all* Tylenol capsules be recalled. This meant a company buyback of 31 million bottles of the product, representing a retail value of $100 million. "We didn't care what it cost to fix the problem," Burke said later, and although the FBI and the FDA expressed fears that such a mass recall might serve to encourage the poisoner or increase public alarm, the chairman prevailed, and the massive recall commenced.

The stakes involved in Burke's decision could not have been higher. Beyond the cost of the 31 million capsules on store shelves, there was the future of a product that, at the time, owned 37 percent of the market for over-the-counter pain relievers. Burke's company was almost a hundred years old in 1982 and one of the best-known and most trusted American brands. Now that trust and that company were surely at stake, but whether or not Burke realized it, even more was in play. The poisonings represented the chaos of moral anarchy, against which those with authority, people like Burke, could choose to take a stand or to which they could simply yield.

Burke never looked back. Not only did he pull all Tylenol from stores; he decided not to resume production until specially designed triple-tamper-resistant packaging was available. Moreover, realizing that in addition to the millions of capsules on store shelves there were many more millions already in American homes, he authorized a large-scale extension of the recall campaign, offering to exchange all Tylenol capsules already purchased for Tylenol tablets. He also directed J & J to work closely with the media and law enforcement to aid in the investigation of the crime. The company posted a $100,000 reward for information leading to the arrest and conviction of the perpetrator. (He or she has yet to be found, and the company's reward offer still stands.)

After the first priority, public safety, had been fully addressed, Burke announced his company's intention to "restore Tylenol to its preeminent position." He acknowledged that doing so would "take time, . . . take money, and will be very difficult, but we consider it a moral imperative, as well as good business."

Tylenol capsules were reintroduced in November 1982 with triple-seal tamper-resistant packaging. For consumers, the company offered substantial $2.50 coupons good toward the purchase of *any* Tylenol product. For retailers, in order to reclaim the shelf space it had lost, J & J offered reduced pricing. This was coupled with an ambitious new advertising campaign. Finally, some 2,250 sales people were dispatched to make person-to-person presentations to medical professionals. At the end of the November, when Tylenol first reappeared in stores, its market share had dropped below 8 percent. By December 24, the *New York Times* reported, it had climbed back to 24 percent, well within striking distance of its original 37 percent market share, which it regained by the following spring. The company's stock, having plunged seven points immediately after the story of the murders broke, rebounded similarly, despite the generally weak stock market of this period.

COSTLY AS IT WAS IN THE SHORT TERM, the decision made by James Burke almost certainly saved lives and, in the longer term, not only rescued the company and one of its leading products, but greatly enhanced the reputations of both. For the industry and for government regulators, the decisions set a new standard for preventing and responding to issues of product tampering. Confronted by random terrorism, a corporate leader decided to reassert the rationality and rightness of ethical order, not merely by putting the social good before the apparent well-being of his company, but by refusing to divorce the future of his enterprise from the health of his community. The firm's approach to this crisis is a high point in the all-too-often dismal history of the ethics of big business, and it stands as one of the great emblematic decisions of the twentieth century.

PART FOUR

The Decision to Risk Everything

William the Conqueror
and the Norman Conquest (1066)

THE DECISION TO PREVAIL

By 1066, the year in which he decided on a most hazardous cross-Channel invasion of England, Duke William of Normandy was more securely in control of his own realm than any previous Norman ruler had ever been. He had subdued rebellions and defeated all competition for his throne. Between 1054 and 1060, he successfully resisted the combined efforts of King Henry I of France and Geoffrey Martel of Anjou to overthrow him. When both of these men died in 1060, they were succeeded by much weaker rulers. Seeing opportunity, William launched a successful conquest of Maine, Normandy's neighbor to the south, in 1063. In either 1064 or the year after that, Edward the Confessor, king of most of England, sent his brother-in-law, Harold, earl of Wessex, on an embassy to Normandy. William persuaded Harold to accompany him on a military campaign into Brittany, which bordered Normandy on the southeast. In company with Harold, William undertook the conquest of Brittany and quickly prevailed. With internal order established in Normandy and his borders expanded as well as secured, why would William risk it all to invade England?

William of Poitiers, a contemporary chronicler of William's reign, explained it this way: England was William's by right. In 1051, Edward the Confessor had promised William succession to the English throne. William of Poitiers further insisted that Edward, in 1064 or 1065, sent Harold to Normandy specifically to swear an oath to William affirming Edward's promised bequest of the English throne. But, the promise and the oath notwithstanding, when Edward died childless on January 5, 1066, it was Harold, backed by the earls and magnates of England, who ascended the throne. A ruler who overlooks a broken promise is not likely to long remain a ruler. Duke William, therefore, decided to go to war.

That, at any rate, is the version offered by William of Poitiers, and most modern historians believe that there is at least some truth in it. But it is by no means the full story of William of Normandy's decision to risk everything on the conquest of England.

The greater truth is that William's entire life pointed him toward this decision. He had been born about 1028, a bastard, the son of Robert I of Normandy and Herleva (also known as Arlette), the daughter of an undertaker in the village of Falaise. Although it was not uncommon for medieval rulers to have illegitimate heirs, and although Robert fully acknowledged William as his son and heir, the circumstances of his birth launched his life on a note of instability. But, then, instability was the prevailing feature of the world into which he had been born. Robert held the title of Duke of Normandy, but his actual rule was far from absolute. His duchy was perpetually menaced by numerous competing factions. When he died on a pilgrimage to Jerusalem, leaving seven-year-old William to succeed to the duchy, Normandy was plunged into utter chaos and outright civil war. Young William quickly became intimate with violent death. Three of the boy's guardians were killed before he grew up, and even his tutor was murdered. Relatives who should have protected him desired William's death, which surely would have come, had it not been for the vigilance of his mother.

"What does not kill me makes me stronger," the nineteenth-century German philosopher Friedrich Nietzsche wrote, and this seems to have been the case with William. He grew to adulthood determined to bring order and security to Normandy, but even when that had been largely achieved, he remained unsatisfied.

His childhood and early maturity had been about survival, which was largely a matter of suppressing internal rivals—and that, in turn, was typically a matter of utmost brutality. For instance, in 1051–52, William moved against the Count of Anjou, attacking the town of Alençon. As he laid siege to it, some citizens beat furs and pelts in mock allusion to William's heritage as the bastard descendant of undertakers—the skinned remains of the animals apparently suggesting the embalmer's trade. No sooner had William captured the town than he tracked down those who had mocked him and ordered their hands and feet to be lopped off. Hearing of this, the nearby town of Domfront surrendered to him without the hint of a fight.

His adulthood, in the years after his rivals had been defeated, was characterized not by mere survival, but by expansion—albeit as a means of permanently ensuring survival. First, as we have seen, William conquered his neighbors, then he looked across the Channel. Would the invasion of England, if unsuccessful, risk the immediate loss of Normandy? Yes. But William believed that failure to seize what he held as his by right of Edward's promise and Harold's pledge—and failure to push his empire across the Channel—would ensure the eventual loss of everything anyway. The lesson of his childhood was this: instability and disorder were to be controlled only by conquest of everything within reach. Whatever of the world was not his belonged to chaos.

William did not rely on terror alone to consolidate his power. In the run-up to the conquest of 1066, he wove a close-knit group of the most influential families of his duchy. The members of this coterie became William's loyal supporters, and were well rewarded for their support. He also created a great fortress city at Caen, which he transformed into a seat and symbol of his power. It outshone almost any other place in northern Europe, and it was evidence of a permanence of power previously unknown in most of the feudal world.

In 1066, he prepared for the invasion by calling a council at Lille-bonne to persuade the influential leaders of Normandy that the great risk was worth taking. He argued that Normandy, for all its might, was vulnerable to attack from England, and that the conquest of England would not only make the Norman realm safer, but also stronger and richer. William made his case persuasively, and he even recruited allies from Flanders, Brittany, and Aquitaine.

With support cemented among his vassals and followers as well as his neighbors, William decided to add a spiritual dimension to the enterprise by sending an embassy to Rome to secure the blessing of Pope Alexander II. Harold had the support of many powerful English earls and lords, who saw him as a legitimately ordained monarch. William wanted to ensure that the rest of the world would not share this view, but agree that Harold's overthrow was justified. He knew that the only justification required in the world of medieval Europe was a papal sanction. William therefore obtained it and, with it, transformed a power-grabbing invasion into a holy crusade to remove a usurping king. Having made his decision to risk all on an invasion, William moved earth as well as heaven to sup-port the step he was taking.

By July, the invasion fleet, ships carrying a total of perhaps seven thousand men, was assembled in the estuary of the River Dives and in the harbors of western Normandy. Contrary winds kept the fleet bottled up there for about a month before it could move up the coast to St-Valéry-sur-Somme in Ponthieu, where the Channel crossing would be shorter. During the delay, William frequently appeared among his men, exhorting them and encouraging them. When some men drowned on the voyage to Ponthieu, William exerted much effort to prevent the news of this misfortune from spreading. He was anxious to maintain the highest possible morale. During the crossing itself, when his own ship became separated from the fleet on the night of September 27, the next morning he prevented his crew from panicking by ostentatiously settling down to a hearty breakfast that included spiced wine. Landing at last at Pevensey, it is said that he stumbled and fell as he climbed down to the sandy shore. He transformed what might otherwise have been interpreted as an ill omen by gathering in his hand a clump of sandy earth, rising to his feet, and revealing to those around him his possession of English soil.

William did not rush into battle. Instead, he decided to draw Harold to him. He wanted to fight the decisive battle where he, not Harold, was strongest—and that meant as close to the coast as possible, where his supply lines were short and reliable but Harold's long and thin. Accordingly, William built earthwork castles at Pevensey, Hastings, and throughout the surrounding countryside, from which he launched raids of merciless pillage, burning down villages, killing men, and seizing their women and children, leaving Harold no choice but to come to the defense of his people.

When William landed in the south of England, Harold was fighting a Norse invasion at Stamford Bridge in the north. As soon as he succeeded in repelling the invaders, Harold led his army on a grueling forced march two hundred miles from York to London in just seven days. That was a remarkable achievement, and Harold was a skilled military leader. But his Saxons were exhausted as they deployed against William on the evening of October 13, along the slope of Senlac Hill. The hill occupied a strategic position seven miles north of Hastings, a village that barred the way to London.

William knew the Saxons would be tired and, for that reason, hastened to attack early on the morning of October 14. Harold occupied a good defensive hilltop position, yet it had the serious drawback of confining him and limiting his ability to maneuver. William sought to circumvent Harold's defensive advantages while exploiting his offensive liability. He used mobility—in the form of his cavalry—against Harold's more statically deployed infantry.

At first, the Saxons, wielding axes and spears, handily threw back William's mounted warriors, and when the Norman left flank started to retreat in disarray, the Saxon infantry left their strong defensive hilltop to give chase. William rallied the knights in his center, and they mowed down the now fully exposed Saxon attackers. Nevertheless, Harold exercised remarkable leadership to rally and reform his infantry line before William could organize a second attack. The Norman cavalry pounded the seemingly immovable mass of Saxon foot soldiers, who hour after bloody hour, held their ground.

—

DUSK DIMMED THE DAY, and William decided on a new approach. He suddenly feigned a general withdrawal of his cavalry. It was a daring gambit. Harold did not fall for it, but, despite his attempt to stop them, his frustrated Saxon soldiers took the bait. Breaking their ordered ranks, which had successfully resisted the Norman cavalry, they charged in mad pursuit. Halfway down the hill, William's knights, acting as one, wheeled 180 degrees to face the scattered onrush of infantrymen, whom they cut down in the field like so many sheaves of wheat.

With the battle now turned against Harold, his personal bodyguards closed round to protect their king. But their numbers were not thick enough to stop an errant arrow from piercing Harold through the eye. He fell and died. With that, the bodyguards panicked and melted away, and the rest of his soldiers gave up the fight. Having begun near dawn, the battle ended before sunset. William the Conqueror's way was clear to London, where, on Christmas Day, he was crowned king of England.

Washington and the Delaware Crossing (1776)

THE DECISION TO WIN

As far as anyone could tell, as Christmas 1776 approached, the American Revolution was lost. There had been some surprising Patriot successes at the beginning of the war, in Boston and upstate New York, but then General George Washington lost Long Island and Manhattan and was sent into retreat clear across New Jersey and into Pennsylvania. In New York, he had had about 20,000 men and, on paper, still commanded some 16,400, but most of these troops were scattered and many were underequipped, underfed, barely clothed, and barely sheltered. In the depths of a frigid winter, they were hardly in any condition to fight. The fact was that, in and around his New Jersey head-quarters, Washington's army consisted of just four thousand shivering soldiers. He had hoped for reinforcements from General Charles Lee, but Lee was days distant. On November 13, Lee sat in the tavern of the Widow White at Basking Ridge, New Jersey, writing a letter to General Horatio Gates complaining that "a certain great man"—that is, George Washington—"is most damnably deficient." Just as he finished his disparaging missive—"In short unless something which I do not expect turns up we are lost"—a detachment of British dragoons burst into the tavern and took General Charles Lee and four other American officers prisoner.

For their part, the British, under the overall command of General William Howe, were widely and thinly scattered in garrisons across New Jersey. Ordinarily, an attempt to cover so much territory with a relatively small army would be a very risky business, but Howe, with good reason, believed the American army had been defeated and no longer presented much of a threat. His principal commander in New Jersey, Major General James Grant, agreed, writing on December 17, "I can hardly believe that Washington would venture at this season of the year to pass the Delaware." Indeed, Grant had nothing but contempt for the army of Washington, and he felt particularly comfortable because Howe had dispatched three excellent Hessian regiments under Colonel Johann Rall to garrison the most vulnerable British position at Trenton, New Jersey. The Hessians, German mercenary troops in the employ of the British crown, were, in effect, instruments of terror, renowned for their discipline and infamous for their brutality toward enemy soldiers and civilians alike. Rall had a reputation as a particularly hard-bitten fighting commander. He, too, had nothing but contempt for the American army. As Hessian lieutenant Jakob Piel recalled, "It never struck him that the rebels might attack us, and therefore he made no preparations against an attack.

I must concede that on the whole we had a poor opinion of the rebels, who previously had never successfully opposed us." When several of Rall's officers urged him to erect some fortifications around their garrison at Trenton, he spat out a curse: "*Scheiszer bey Scheiz!* [Shit upon shit!] Let them come. . . . We will go at them with the bayonet."

But if Howe, Grant, and Rall thought little of Washington and his Continental Army, Rall did have his hands full with New Jersey locals and ad hoc militia troops. Whatever Washington did or did not do, the people of New Jersey deeply resented occupation by the British redcoats and, even more, by the Hessians. They were tired of being robbed and abused. While Howe's forces may have defeated Washington's army, New Jersey was in a chronic state of guerrilla warfare, which was taking its toll, especially on Rall's Hessians. Popular legend pictures these troops as fat, happy, and drunk in their Trenton garrison, but, in fact, they were cold, hungry, and tired—tired of continual skirmishes and the anxious necessity of ceaseless vigilance. This was not warfare as it was practiced in Europe, and their vaunted discipline had begun to fail.

Cracking discipline was not the only problem the Hessians faced. There was a fissure in the very heart of command. Colonel Rall distrusted and detested his superior, Colonel Carl von Donop, who had overall command of the Hessian forces along the Delaware River. The ill will was apparently reciprocated, and, as a result, Rall and Donop rarely communicated. For this reason, Donop had little idea of the situation among Rall's exhausted troops in unfortified Trenton. When Rall finally complained about increasing guerrilla attacks on the outskirts of Trenton, Donop offered no help but did advise him to build fortifications. Rall impatiently replied that these would do no good because "I have the enemy in all directions." He asked instead for reinforcements, a request Donop merely relayed to Major General Grant. That officer replied with a contempt for Rall that nearly equaled his contempt for Washington: "Tell the colonel he is safe. I will undertake to keep the peace in Jersey with a corporal's guard." To Rall directly, Grant wrote that he "may be assured that the rebel army in Pennsylvania . . . does not exceed eight thousand men, who have neither shoes nor stockings, are in fact almost naked, starving for cold, without Blankets, and very ill-supplied with provisions." No reinforcements would be sent.

About mid-December, the mind of George Washington was occupied with three things: First, the disintegration of his dwindling army. Second, the certainty of an impending British-Hessian invasion of Pennsylvania across the Delaware River. Third, an apparent opportunity to make a "counterstroke"—an offensive move against the British and Hessians. With a small and starving army—smaller and hungrier than even Grant thought—the prospects for such a counterstroke did not glow brightly, but, Washington reasoned, if it failed, the mere fact of taking *some* action would be beneficial to the army, reinvigorating its flagging spirits and necessarily reviving discipline among its faltering ranks.

Washington began thinking of crossing the Delaware and attacking one of the main Hessian garrisons there. He had been chased across New Jersey; now he would bring the war back to the enemy. The idea, however, was not some grand conception born of strategic genius. It was, rather, the recognition of prevailing circumstances, all of which were quite independent of the condition of Washington's army or his plans for the war. The commander-in-chief was getting encouraging news about popular resistance throughout New Jersey. At this very moment, a Pennsylvania militia force, without any orders from Washington or anyone else, was conducting hit-and-run raids against British installations along the Delaware. He was also aware that Colonel von Donop had led a large contingent of Hessians *away* from the Trenton area and down to Mount Holly, New Jersey, in pursuit of Patriot militia forces there. What Washington may or may not have known is that the militia was not his only target in Mount Holly. Donop was strongly attracted to a beautiful young widow there, who made him forget all about both of his enemies, Colonel Rall and General Washington.

On December 22, 1776, Washington's adjutant, Colonel Joseph Reed, sent his commander a message advising him about the Patriot militia near Mount Holly: "We can either give [the militia] a strong reinforcement—or make a separate attack—the latter bids fairest for producing the greatest and best effects. . . . We are all of the opinion my dear general that something must be attempted to revive our expiring credit, give our Cause some degree of reputation & prevent total depreciation of the Continental money which is coming very fast." Reed's thoughts anticipated and reinforced Washington's own, especially when Reed stated that "even a Failure cannot be more fatal than to remain in our present situation. In short some enterprize must be undertaken in our present Circumstances or we must give up the cause." Reed's recommendation, in view of the "scattered divided state of the enemy," was to stage an "offensive attack" on Trenton.

Doubtless, Reed was preaching to the converted. By this time, Washington had reached the same conclusion. Reed ended his message emphatically: "Delay is now equal to a total defeat," then excused himself for writing in such blunt language: "Pardon the Freedom I have used, the Love of my country, a Wife and four Children in the Enemys Hands, the Respect and Attachment I have to you—the Ruin and Poverty that must attend me & thousands of others will plead my Excuse for so much Freedom."

The very day he received Reed's dispatch, December 22, Washington called his commanders to a council of war. He presented Reed's proposal for crossing the Delaware and attacking one of the enemy's posts in New Jersey. With very little debate, the officers agreed on the operation. Washington now turned to Colonel John Glover, who led a regiment of rugged fishermen from Marblehead, Massachusetts. He was an expert in small boat handling. He looked Washington in the eye and told him not to "be troubled" about the crossing. His "boys could manage it." George Washington issued orders the next morning.

The same myth that portrays the Hessians as generally fat and happy depicts Colonel Rall and his men as reveling and drinking all Christmas day and night in Trenton, so that, when the attack came on the morning of December 26, they were too hungover to put up much of a fight. The truth is that Trenton was dismal and deserted, and Rall and his men had no celebration. They expected an attack—perhaps from Washington, certainly from rebel guerrillas. For the past week, there had been little sleep in the Hessian garrison. Nerves were frayed. However, when a storm began on Christmas night, Rall felt a sudden relief. After all, no one would try to cross the Delaware in a winter storm, let alone launch an attack in one. Loyalist spies had reported that Washington was forming up his troops on the other side of the river. Looking at the wind-driven ice and snow, Rall replied: "These clodhoppers will not attack us, and should they do so, we will simply fall on them and rout them."

The Delaware had indeed frozen. Then, under warm rains, it had melted again, only to refreeze, though not solid. On the night of December 25, the river's waters roiled with great sheets of broken ice whirling in the swift current. On this night, in this weather, Washington loaded 2,400 veteran troops and 18 cannon into large Durham boats, which were normally used for ferrying freight across the broad river. Washington made his crossing at McKonkey's Ferry (the modern Pennsylvania town of Washington Crossing), nine miles above Trenton. Simultaneously, about a thousand militiamen, commanded by General James Ewing, prepared to cross at Trenton Ferry, their mission to block any retreat of Hessians from Trenton. Also, as a diversion, Colonel John Cadwalader was to cross the Delaware at Bordentown.

That was the plan. But Ewing could not get across the treacherous river, and Cadwalader was so delayed that he was of no real help. Worse, Washington planned to disembark in New Jersey at midnight, under cover of darkness. The element of surprise was all important. The weather, however, had caused so many delays that his crossing was not completed until about 3:00 A.M. on the 26th. It was at least 4:00 A.M. by the time Washington's men were on the march. The attack, when it came, would not occur before daybreak.

Delay, Washington wrote, "made me despair of surprising the Town, as I well knew we could not reach it before the day was fairly broke." He began to think seriously of aborting the attack, but he decided, even as his boat tossed about in the middle of the half-frozen river, that he had passed the point of no return: "As I was certain there was no making a Retreat without being discovered, and harassed on repassing the River, I determined to push on at all Events."

Washington's decision to win was motivated not by the high spirits of a victor, but by the nothing-more-to-lose resignation of one who had suffered a series of devastating defeats. He could sit tight, do nothing, and surely lose. Or he could seize the opportunity current circumstances presented—a rebellious Jersey population, an exhausted and thinly distributed enemy—and quite probably be defeated, but possibly, just possibly, win. In the middle of the turbulent Delaware, he had determined that there was no return, only the slim opportunity offered by continuing to advance. But, really, he had already decided this very thing when he resolved to lead a "counterstroke" with a cold and hungry army almost everyone had written off as finished.

The night before the crossing, the physician and revolutionary patriot Benjamin Rush visited Washington as he was making final preparations for the crossing. The commander had wisely decided to protect the security of the operation by allowing no one to pass in or out of his army's encampment. When Rush saw him, he was busy writing a secret password on slips of paper to be distributed to all of his officers. As Rush spoke with the general, one of the slips "by accident fell upon the floor near my feet. I was struck with the inscription upon it. It was 'Victory or Death.'"

◆

WE CAN ONLY IMAGINE what it was like to march to battle nine miles along the Jersey side of the river through the frigid, stormy gloom of 4:00 A.M. that morning after Christmas. To preserve surprise as long as possible, Washington had ordered absolute silence, so there was none of the customary soldier's talk to ease the fatigue and the fear. Washington had also ordered that no lights be struck, so there was not even the comfort of a pipe. When it became clear that snow and freezing rain had rendered the muskets useless, Washington—affirming to his subordinate commander John Sullivan that "I am resolved to take Trenton"—directed him to order the men to fix bayonets. If they could not fire, they would thrust.

It was 7:30 A.M. by the time they reached the Hessian encampment and heard the German sentry's cry: *"Der Feind! Heraus! Heraus!"* ("The enemy! Get up! Get up!").

Rall did his best to rally his men, but was soon mortally wounded, and the Battle of Trenton, between a "defeated" army and some of the best troops of Europe, was over, according to some, in just under two hours. Others say it lasted little more than half an hour. Of the 1,200 Hessians engaged, 106 were killed or wounded and the rest captured, along with sorely needed equipment and stores. Washington's forces had suffered no more than four wounded, and some historians believe that no American was killed, while others report two killed in action and two frozen to death. With this victory, Trenton was redeemed and, with it, the revolution saved.

Woodrow Wilson and World War I (1917)

THE DECISION TO BECOME A WORLD POWER

"There's an old saying," John F. Kennedy remarked on April 21, 1961, when he accepted responsibility for the collapse of the Bay of Pigs invasion in Cuba, "that victory has a hundred fathers and defeat is an orphan." Woodrow Wilson knew he was taking a great risk in joining the catastrophe of the Great War in April 1917, and, like JFK some forty-four years later, he was willing to assume responsibility for the decision. Of course, unlike Kennedy and the Bay of Pigs fiasco, America's entry into World War I is generally counted a triumph. The nation entered the war at a low point for the Allies, who, exhausted and all but bled white by three years of stalemated slaughter, were reeling under the blows of a series of desperate German offensives. The arrival of some two million fresh troops—with millions more available after them—turned the tide by the autumn of 1918, and Wilson found himself fortunately counted among the fathers of victory.

Yet while no one doubts that Germany was defeated in World War I, a number of recent historians have challenged the simple calculus of victory versus defeat. President Wilson believed he could ensure that the Great War would be the "war to end all wars," but, as it turned out, a defeated Germany, crushed under the punitive terms of the Treaty of Versailles, became ripe for the rise of Adolf Hitler, and the Great War had to be renamed World War *I* after a second, even more horrific, world war began in September 1939. That it made World War *II* all but inevitable was the crowning, tragic irony of the "war to end all wars," which had been amply tragic in itself, costing the lives of 8,020,780 soldiers and 6,642,633 civilians. Apologists for Woodrow Wilson claim that, had he attained everything he had wanted at the peace talks that led to the Versailles treaty—had the treaty been less punitive and more conciliatory and had the Senate approved membership of the United States in the League of Nations—there might not have been a World War II or any other major war in the twentieth century. Perhaps. Yet the fact remains that Woodrow Wilson decided to take the nation into the most desperate and destructive war up to that time, a war for which the American army was woefully unprepared, and a war in which 50,300 American soldiers were killed and 198,059 were wounded during some two hundred days of combat. In addition, 62,668 succumbed to disease, and in 1930, the U.S. Veterans Bureau estimated that war-related maladies and wounds actually raised the total cost to 460,000 U.S. military dead.

It was a high price to pay even for an unambiguous victory. For a victory that, in essence, did not stick—that, in fact, brought on another, even costlier war—it was a cataclysmic price. What led Woodrow Wilson to decide on a risk with such stakes?

Thomas Woodrow Wilson was an unlikely warrior and, indeed, an unlikely American president. He was born in 1856 in the Shenandoah Valley town of Staunton, Virginia, the son of a Presbyterian minister. The bookish Wilson graduated from Princeton in 1879, studied law at the

University of Virginia, and practiced for a time in Atlanta. Bored and disillusioned with the legal profession, he returned to college, earning in 1886 a Ph.D. in government and history at Johns Hopkins. Wilson became a professor and author, turning out such books as *Congressional Government: A Study in American Politics* (1885), *The State: Elements of Historical and Practical Politics* (1889), *Division and Reunion, 1829–1889* (1893), a five-volume *History of the American People* (1902), and *Constitutional Government in the United States* (1908). In 1890, he became a professor at Princeton, and in 1902 was the unanimous faculty choice for president of the institution, which he set about transforming financially and intellectually, moving so vigorously that he drew the attention of Democratic Party bosses. Believing that Wilson would put a respectable face on spoils system politics while being quietly pliable himself, they offered him the 1910 nomination for governor of New Jersey. Wilson left Princeton, won the election, and, to the stunned consternation of the party bosses, introduced sweeping reforms into New Jersey government. These rapidly earned Wilson a national reputation, which won for him a hard-fought nomination as Democratic presidential candidate in 1912. In the general elections, Wilson prevailed against Republican incumbent William Howard Taft and third-party candidate and former president Theodore Roosevelt, in whose Progressive spirit he abundantly shared.

Wilson was the first—and so far, only—Ph.D.-holding college professor to become president, and although he was a fine orator, his manner was coolly professorial. Nevertheless, the many popular reforms he quickly introduced into American government, including a progressive income tax (introduced via the Sixteenth Amendment), the Federal Reserve Act, the Federal Trade Commission Act, the Clayton Antitrust Act, a farm loan act, labor reform legislation, and a child labor Act, won him much acclaim and a loyal constituency.

When Wilson was two years into his first term, on June 28, 1914, in Sarajevo, an obscure Balkan city of which few Americans had ever heard, a nineteen-year-old Serbian named Gavrilo Princip shot and killed

Archduke Franz Ferdinand of Austria and his wife, the Grand Duchess Sophie, as they toured the capital of Bosnia-Herzegovina, recently and unhappily annexed to the Austro-Hungarian Empire. Austria-Hungary accused Serbia of complicity in the act of Princip and delivered an ultimatum effectively stripping Serbia of its sovereignty. When that tiny nation balked, Austria-Hungary invaded, and a byzantine network of treaties, both secret and public, suddenly sprang into life, dragging Russia, France, Great Britain, and Germany into a war that quickly engulfed all of Europe, as well as the far-flung colonies of the European nations.

On balance, Austria-Hungary was the principal aggressor, but it was Germany that moved most aggressively, fighting on an Eastern as well as a Western front. Its strategy called for the defeat of France first, so that it could turn its full attention to Russia. This meant, on the Western Front, executing a swift, bold, and brutal strategy of ruthless advance guided by a grand war plan first conceived at the end of the nineteenth century by General Alfred von Schlieffen. The mass of the German army would not attack France head on, from the east, but instead swing through Belgium and Luxembourg to swoop down upon France from the north. Belgium held itself as a neutral, and it was the German violation of Belgian neutrality, in execution of the Schlieffen Plan, that brought Britain into the war.

The violation would also have another grave consequence for Germany. It would cast that nation, its army, and its emperor, Kaiser Wilhelm II, in the roles of oppressors and international criminals who brutally violated the neutrality of tiny nations that wanted nothing more than to live and let live. The entire world, including the United States, would hear accounts of the "rape of Belgium," stories that surely had a strong element of truth, but that were also amplified many fold by Britain's highly effective propaganda machine, which told tales liberally laced with literal rapes and the wanton bayoneting of children and babies.

The shooting war started on July 29, as Austrian artillery bombarded Belgrade, and just days later, on August 4, 1914, President Wilson firmly declared the absolute neutrality of the United States. It was during that month of August that Germany began execution of the Schlieffen Plan, crushing Belgium and deeply penetrating France before, as if losing nerve, its army stopped to dig in along the Marne. Trench works here soon developed into a network of trenches that stretched all the way from the English Channel in the north to the border of neutral Switzerland in the south. Along this continental scar, the armies of Germany and those of France and Britain slaughtered one another in exchange for so many yards of enemy territory, which, no sooner gained, were usually yielded as a result of counterattack. About this mindless meat grinder war, a French officer, Alfred Joubaire, later recorded in a 1916 diary entry: "Humanity is mad! It must be mad to do what it is doing. What a massacre! What bloody scenes of horror! Hell cannot be so terrible. Men are mad!" Joubaire was killed the next day.

America looked on in horror. After some eight months of the war, the *Literary Digest* polled some 367 U.S. writers and editors, of whom 105 favored the Allies and 20 the Germans, but a substantial majority, 242, called for the continuation of absolute neutrality.

Neutrality, in fact, was highly profitable. As a neutral, the United States had the right to trade with all sides—and it did. Indeed, President Wilson insisted that American industry and American financial institutions do business with all sides impartially. Yet, as the months passed, it became increasingly difficult to remain impartial. There were the atrocity stories coming out of Belgium, capped by the saga of Nurse Edith Cavell. An Englishwoman, she was a Red Cross nurse in German-occupied Belgium, who secretly worked with an underground group formed to help British, French, and Belgian soldiers escape to the neutral Netherlands. In August 1915, Cavell was arrested by German authorities, who, on October 9, sentenced her to death. Despite appeals from American and other diplomats, she was shot on October 12, an act interpreted as yet another example of German "barbarism."

Worst of all, however, was German submarine warfare, in which U-boats preyed upon Allied—especially British—ships, including commercial and passenger vessels. This in itself was not a violation of international law or the accepted conventions of warfare, especially because, initially at least, the German U-boats surfaced to give warning before an attack, allowing passengers sufficient time to abandon ship. Soon, however, Germany adopted a policy of "unrestricted submarine warfare," by which the U-boats attacked without warning.

On May 7, 1915, the British liner *Lusitania* was torpedoed by the U-20, with the loss of 1,198 lives, including 124 Americans. The fact was that the *Lusitania* carried more than passengers. It had been built before the war along lines established by the British Admiralty, which classified it as an "auxiliary cruiser," and on its fateful voyage from New York it carried American-made war materiel, including 10½ tons of rifle cartridges, 51 tons of shrapnel shells, and a large amount of gun cotton (which explodes on contact with water). There were also on board 67 soldiers of the 90th Regiment. Days before the *Lusitania* sailed, the German government secured permission from U.S. Secretary of State William Jennings Bryan to publish in New York newspapers a notice that the ship was leaving port with six million rounds of .303-caliber rifle ammunition and a warning to potential passengers that it was therefore subject to attack.

In the American outrage that followed the sinking of the *Lusitania*, none of the British violations of international law and the rules of warfare were noted. Instead, American newspapers condemned the attack as murder, plain and simple. Some prominent Americans, including Walter Hines Page, U.S. ambassador to Britain, called for an immediate U.S. declaration of war, lest the nation "forfeit European respect." Secretary of State Bryan was among the few government officials who pointed out that the *Lusitania* had carried contraband. For his part, Wilson condemned the attack as "unlawful and inhuman" and sent a strongly worded diplomatic protest to the German government on May 13. When he sent another note on June 9—even after the U.S. Customs Service had confirmed the presence of contraband onboard the *Lusitania*—Secretary Bryan resigned in protest.

While Wilson's notes were too much for Bryan, the president publicly continued to steer a neutral course, declaring in a famous speech just three days after the sinking that "there is such a thing as a man being too proud to fight." This statement drew criticism from American war hawks, including Theodore Roosevelt, but it is undeniable that Woodrow Wilson won reelection in November 1916 largely on the strength of his leading campaign slogan: *"He kept us out of war!"*

In the meantime, despite the president's stated policy of non-favoritism in trade, American industrialists and financiers increasingly backed the Allies while backing away from Germany. By the end of 1916, U.S. firms had done some $2 billion in business with the Allies and had made $2.5 billion in loans to them—in contrast to just $45 million loaned to Germany. Whether Wilson liked it or not, the U.S. economy was becoming wedded to the fate of the Allied cause. Were the Allies to lose, what would become of the loans? Increasingly, it came to seem as if American prosperity or financial disaster hung on Allied victory or defeat.

Wilson made repeated efforts to avoid U.S. entry into the war by bringing the war itself to an end. Early in 1916, he sent his closest adviser, Edward M. House, to London and Paris to sound out Allied leaders about the possibility of the United States acting as a mediator between the belligerents. This resulted in a memorandum drawn up with British foreign secretary Sir Edward Grey on February 22, 1916, which stipulated that the United States might enter the war if Germany rejected President Wilson's efforts at mediation, but that the right to initiate U.S. mediation rested with the government of Great Britain, not Wilson. It was a monumentally ambiguous document—on the one hand a genuine effort at bringing about binding mediation, but, on the other hand, a threat of U.S. entry into the war. As the 1916 elections approached, Wilson decided to suspend this peace initiative because he perceived that the threat of entry would conflict with his "he kept us out of war" platform. In any event, Germany had at this time agreed not to resume unrestricted submarine warfare, which Wilson saw as a hopeful sign that he might well be able to continue to keep the country out of the war.

Wilson did not resume an attempt at mediation until December 18, 1916, when he invited the Allies and the Germans to clear the air by stating their "war aims." This, however, resulted in nothing productive. On January 22, 1917, Wilson appealed for international conciliation based on achieving "peace without victory" on any side. War-weary Britain confidentially communicated its willingness to accept Wilson's mediation, as did Austria-Hungary. But Germany rejected the American president as a mediator and, worse, on January 31, 1917, announced the resumption of unrestricted submarine warfare. This prompted Wilson to take his first bold step toward war. On February 3, 1917, after a U.S. warship, the *Housatonic*, was torpedoed and sunk by a U-boat, Wilson severed diplomatic relations between the United States and Germany. Later in the month, on February 26, he asked Congress for the authority to arm U.S.-flagged merchant vessels and to take other military measures to protect American commerce. He called his new policy "armed neutrality."

It was the first official step in what had become an ongoing, if unofficial, military preparedness movement. Until Germany reinstated unrestricted submarine warfare, Wilson was careful to meet all calls for military preparedness with the response that America would remain the "champion of peace." Even after severing diplomatic relations with Germany, he declared, "I am not now preparing or contemplating war or any steps that need lead to it." Yet as early as the outbreak of war in Europe in 1914, such prominent individuals as former President Theodore Roosevelt, financier J. P. Morgan, and principal Wilson rival Senator Henry Cabot Lodge called for U.S. military preparedness. After the sinking of the *Lusitania*, the former army chief of staff Leonard Wood established the first so-called "businessmen's military training camps," in Plattsburg, New York. By the summer of 1916, well before the Selective Draft Act was signed in May of 1917, some forty thousand young men had been put through basic training in similar camps on a strictly unofficial basis—although the training was administered by personnel of the regular United States Army. And while he avoided sanctioning the

Plattsburg movement, Wilson did actively encourage American industry and commerce to assume a war footing.

Throughout late 1916 and early 1917, German attacks on British and American merchant ships continued; no fewer than three U.S. ships were sunk on March 18, 1917, alone. This came on top of a spectacular outrage that President Wilson had publicly revealed on March 1. It was the infamous "Zimmermann Telegram." On January 16, 1917, Alfred Zimmermann, Germany's foreign secretary, sent a coded telegram, via the German ambassador in Washington, D.C., to the German minister in Mexico. The telegram authorized the minister to propose a German-Mexican alliance to Mexican president Venustiano Carranza. If Mexico would declare war on the United States, Germany promised to lend its military support to help Mexico in the reconquest of its "lost territory in Texas, New Mexico, and Arizona." Carranza was also to be asked to invite Japan to join in on the anti-American alliance.

As it turned out, Carranza spurned the proposal and, all the worse for Germany, British agents intercepted the cable transmission, decoded it, and handed it to U.S. Ambassador Walter Page, who turned it over to President Wilson. "We can stand Germany's arrogance no longer," declared Wilson's secretary of the interior on March 31. His statement summarized the drift of public and political opinion. Although White House logs do not record his visit, Frank Cobb of the New York *World* reported talking with his old friend President Wilson on April 1. Cobb later wrote that he had "never seen him so worn down." Wilson, Cobb recalled, told him that entering the war would attack the soul of America: "The spirit of ruthless brutality will enter the very fiber of our national life, infecting Congress, the courts, the policeman on the beat, the man in the street. Conformity will be the only virtue. And every man who refuses to conform must pay the penalty." Nevertheless, the next day, the president sat down to write his war message, a request that Congress declare war on Germany and the other "Central Powers."

Before going to war, Woodrow Wilson went to war with himself. He had resolutely refused to prepare the nation militarily. Indeed, some historians believe that, even as he delivered his 32-minute war message to Congress beginning at 8:40 P.M. on April 2, 1917, he hoped the United States would not actually have to send troops to Europe. The mere threat, perhaps, would be sufficient to end the war. If this was indeed his hope, he wasn't alone. On April 6, after hearing testimony that the military might need appropriations for an army in France, Senator Thomas S. Martin of Virginia, chairman of the Senate Finance Comittee, exclaimed: "Good Lord! You're not going to send soldiers over there, are you?"

At some level, Wilson must have realized that his hope of mere intimidation was unrealistic. Wilson's personal secretary, Joseph Tumulty, recalled that at about 10:00 P.M., when Wilson returned to the White House after delivering the war speech, he slumped in a chair at the table in the empty cabinet room. Wilson looked at Tumulty and, reflecting on the thunderous applause that had greeted his war message, said, "Think what it was they were applauding. My message today was a message of death for our young men. How strange it seems to applaud that." Then, according to Tumulty, Woodrow Wilson put his head in his hands and sobbed uncontrollably.

Like most of his speeches, Wilson's war message had been eloquent and idealistic: "There is one choice we cannot make; we are incapable of making. We will not choose the path of submission!" He spoke, most famously, of fighting "for the ultimate peace of the world and the libera-tion of its people." He spoke of making the "world . . . safe for democracy."

WILSON MAY OR MAY NOT HAVE BEEN "WORN DOWN" by public opinion, accounts of German "atrocities," Germany's continual outrages on the high seas, and the Zimmermann telegram. (He chose, on the other hand to ignore Great Britain's flagrant violation of international law and the internationally accepted conventions of war in its maintenance of a naval blockade aimed at starving the German civilian population.) But by the time he asked Congress for a declaration, he had clearly also decided that war had a major advantage for the United States. It would transform the nation into a formidable world power. It would give him, the President of the United States, a seat at the table of other heads of state. It would allow him to guide the countries of the world in creating what he called a "scientific peace." He believed he could transform the Great War into a war that would end war itself.

This idealistic epiphany overpowered Wilson's long-held desire to avoid involvement in the European carnage. It also seems to have overwhelmed reason itself. For neither Wilson nor the majority of Congress stopped to examine the yawning gulf between the political-ideological decision to declare war and the nation's total inability, with its diminutive army of April 1917, to fight a war. Nevertheless, the nation—so recently pacifist and isolationist—found the will, for better or worse, to back the president's decision and, by the end of the war, in November 1918, the U.S. Army had grown from a mere 133,000 officers and men to 4.5 million, a force that proved indispensable to the Allied victory, that made the United States a world power, and that gave Woodrow Wilson a role in hammering out what emerged as a most imperfect and all-too-brief peace.

Jimmy Doolittle and the Tokyo Raid (1942)
THE DECISION TO STRIKE BACK

Two weeks after the Japanese attack on Pearl Harbor, and in the midst of one devastating Japanese victory after another, President Franklin D. Roosevelt summoned Army Chief of Staff General George C. Marshall, Chief of Staff of the Army Air Forces General Henry "Hap" Arnold, Chief of Naval Operations Admiral Ernest J. King, and others to the White House to receive an assignment. FDR wanted them to strike back at the Japanese, to hit their homeland with a bombing raid at the earliest possible moment. Such a raid, the president insisted, was essential to building the morale of the American people and the people of America's allies.

But how was such a raid possible when the United States and its allies were clearly losing the war in the Pacific? Japan was conquering one Pacific and Asian stronghold after another, pushing out from itself a great defensive ring, far beyond any place that could be used as a base from which to launch bombers. At this point in World War II, no combatant, including the United States, possessed bombers with transcontinental range, and so it seemed manifestly impossible to get bombers close enough to raid Japan itself. Each of the military leaders present left the meeting pondering the puzzle.

In the days that followed, FDR repeated his call to action. During the second week of January 1942, one of Admiral King's staff officers, Captain Francis Lowe, was inspecting the new aircraft carrier *Hornet* in Norfolk, Virginia. Nearby, he saw an airfield used by pilots to practice carrier take-offs and landings. On the airfield was painted the outline of a carrier flight deck. Something clicked in Lowe's mind: Could ground-based Army Air Forces bombers, big planes with far greater range than small carrier-based fighters, possibly take off from the deck of an aircraft carrier?

Lowe took the question to his air operations officer, Captain Donald Duncan. By January 16, Duncan came up with what he believed was a workable proposal to present to Admiral King. It called for twin-engine North American B-25 "Mitchell" medium bombers to take off from a carrier. Loaded with a ton of bombs and (thanks to extra tanks) enough fuel to fly two thousand miles, the bombers could—in theory—just barely make it off a carrier deck. *Landing* on that deck was another matter. It could not be done. But, Duncan declared, it would be possible for the aircraft to attack Japanese cities, then fly to friendly airfields in mainland China.

In great secrecy, Duncan worked with Captain Marc Mitscher, skipper of the *Hornet*, to transform theory into practice by testing the ability of the B-25 to take off in a very short space. By early February, the pair had developed a technique enabling the big plane to become airborne in as little as five hundred feet. The *Hornet*'s flight deck was well over eight hundred feet long.

When Lowe and Duncan called on Hap Arnold to report their findings and present their proposal, the air force chief of staff received them
enthusiastically. He did not tell them that, ever since the meeting with
FDR, he had had his staff working on much the same thing. After
meeting with the two navy men, Arnold brought in Colonel James
"Jimmy" Doolittle, the most thoroughly and uniquely experienced aviator
in the Army Air Forces. At Arnold's request, Doolittle had already been
studying short takeoffs with the B-25. He was very ready to hear what
Hap Arnold had to tell him.

Born in Alameda, California, and educated at Los Angeles Junior
College and the University of California, Doolittle had joined the Army
Reserve Corps in October 1917, shortly after the United States entered
World War I. He served as a flight instructor through 1919, then, still
flying for the army, captured national attention by making the first
transcontinental flight, doing this in less than fourteen hours on September 4, 1922. Doolittle enrolled in the aeronautical science program at
Massachusetts Institute of Technology and earned a doctorate of science
degree in 1925. Now the army's chief tester of new aircraft, he also par-
ticipated in high-profile air races. In September 1929, he gave a spectacular demonstration of the potential of instrument flying by making the
first-ever instruments-only ("blind") landing. Doolittle resigned his commission in 1930 to become aviation manager for Shell Oil, where he
worked on the development of new high-efficiency aviation fuels. He also
continued to race, winning the Harmon (1930) and Bendix (1931) tro-
phies, and in 1932, he set a world speed record. With war imminent, he
returned to active duty in the U.S. Army Air Corps in July 1940.

"Jim," Arnold said to him, referring to the still hazy idea of launching
a raid from the deck of an aircraft carrier, "I need someone to take this
job over . . ."

"And I know where you can get that someone," Doolittle answered.

For Doolittle, the decision was that simple. His own gut feeling that
it would be possible to take off from an aircraft carrier in a medium
bomber had been independently corroborated by two responsible naval

officers. Nevertheless, the mission would be as dangerous as they come. Given the fact that no round trip was possible, it was, in fact, nearly suicidal. But Doolittle was accustomed to taking risks when the risks were for sufficiently high stakes and there was at least a realistic possibility of success. It was instantly clear to him that such was the case now.

Doolittle went to work studying and implementing the necessary modifications—mostly provisions for additional fuel—to the B-25. He then engaged in a series of rigorous tests and called on Brigadier General Carl "Tooey" Spaatz, Arnold's deputy for intelligence, to come up with industrial targets in Tokyo, Yokohama, Kobe, Nagoya, and a half-dozen other cities. Doolittle trained himself to fly the mission, then set about recruiting additional volunteer aircrews. They were not told what they were going to do, but they were told, in no uncertain terms, that their mission would be extremely dangerous. Those who volunteered were run through a rigorous, highly specialized training program.

The newly launched *Hornet* sailed on April 2, 1942, and was joined en route by the carrier *Enterprise*, which would provide air cover during the approach to the planned launching point—a position about four hundred miles off the Japanese mainland, which was scheduled to be reached on April 18. Shortly before dawn on the eighteenth, however, enemy picket boats were sighted much farther east than expected. U.S. escort craft sank the pickets, but surely not before they had been able to transmit radio warnings. With the critical element of surprise now in jeopardy, Doolittle made a desperate decision. He would launch the raid immediately, not four hundred miles off the coast, but seven hundred. This put the aircraft at the extreme limit of their fuel supply and reduced the chances of reaching Chinese airfields. The alternative, however, was quite probably a preemptive Japanese attack on the *Hornet* that would end the mission before it had been launched. Doolittle understood that the risks were great under the best of circumstances. Now circumstances would hardly be the best. The mission was top secret, so the public would not know it had been aborted; however, to abort the mission would be a blow to the confidence of high command and the president, and it might well discourage them from waging war with boldness and daring. Besides, Doolittle had no desire to waste weeks of training and preparation. They were in position to make a strike, and that was what he intended to do.

At about 8:00 on the morning of April 18, Jimmy Doolittle's B-25 was the first to roll down the *Hornet's* flight deck, which pitched in the swell of moderately stormy weather. The storm winds, combined with the forward speed of the carrier, gave the pilots a stiff fifty-mile-per-hour headwind, which was essential for lift. Although the *Hornet's* flight deck was more than eight hundred feet long, less than five hundred feet of it was clear for the first planes, since all the large aircraft had to be parked on deck (they were too big to be stored on the hangar deck below and brought up by elevator). Doolittle had no trouble getting airborne, but some of the other planes came close to stalling on takeoff, dipping below the edge of the flight deck, then seeming to hang precariously over the waves before finally gaining altitude. There were sixteen five-man crews in all.

One bomber was sent to attack Kobe, another Nagoya, and a third, slated to bomb Osaka, instead dropped its ordnance on the Yokosuka naval yard and on Yokohama. A fourth plane suffered mechanical problems and was forced to divert to a landing at Vladivostok, Siberia. The twelve other raiders bombed Tokyo at noon.

As chance would have it, the Japanese civil defense was conducting a drill, a mock air raid, at the time. This may have diluted the immediate psychological effect of the raid, but it also provided a diversion that helped the bombers escape. Remarkably, no bomber was lost over Japan.

IN STRICTLY MILITARY TERMS, the damage inflicted by fifteen medium bombers was not great. Some fifty people were killed and one hundred houses damaged or destroyed. However, the damage done to the prestige, confidence, and sense of invulnerability that had pervaded the Japanese government and its military was far more serious. As a result of the raid, the Japanese high command was forced to retain a significant number of aircraft for home defense rather than combat. Also, the raid removed official objections to a plan proposed by Japan's Admiral Isoruku Yamamoto to draw out the American fleet to the area of Midway Island and deliver a fatal blow there. This plan, as it turned out, would play beautifully into American hands. The Battle of Midway proved to be a U.S. Navy triumph and the turning point of the war in the Pacific.

Having successfully completed the raid, the bombers were now critically short of fuel. The crews either crash landed them in China or abandoned them, bailing out wherever they could. Almost miraculously, Doolittle and seventy other mission members survived, and eventually found their way back home. One airman was killed in parachuting from his plane, two others in a crash, and eight were captured by the Japanese. Of this number, three were executed and one died in prison.

Truman and the Berlin Airlift (1948)

THE DECISION TO "CONTAIN" COMMUNISM

In the days following the surrender of Japan in August 1945, a popular slogan sweeping America summed up the combined relief and jubilation: *"Peace! Ain't it wonderful!"*

The feeling didn't last long.

Even before World War II was over, it became clear that the United States (and its Western allies) were squaring off against the Soviets, who were poised to gobble up as much of Europe as they could reach. Near the end of his tenure as deputy head of the U.S. mission in Moscow (he served from May 1944 to April 1946), George F. Kennan sent to his boss, President Harry S. Truman's secretary of state, James Byrnes, an eight-thousand-word telegram from the Soviet capital. It outlined what he proposed as a new strategy for handling diplomatic relations with the Soviet Union. Kennan argued that the Kremlin had a "neurotic view of world affairs," at the root of which was "the traditional and instinctive Russian sense of insecurity." This produced an inherent drive to expand the Soviet sphere of influence and control. The only way to counter this expansion, without waging World War III, was to take steps to "contain" the spread of Soviet influence in areas of vital strategic importance to the United States.

President Truman took notice, and the "containment of Communism" became the policy of his administration and the aim of the United States in what was soon being called the Cold War.

The first test of the new policy came during a civil war in Greece. A referendum in September 1946 returned King George II to the Greek throne, and when he died just six months later his brother, Paul, succeeded him. During the transition, the Greek Communist Party created the Democratic Army, which sought to overthrow the new king. The Greek Communists were a small minority, but they had the backing of the Soviet Union, which stood to gain control of Greece if the Communists won the civil war. On March 12, 1947, President Truman addressed a joint session of Congress, calling for the United States to confront and contain the Communists in Greece by sending direct aid to the elected majority government. He put this call in a larger context by proclaiming as the policy of the United States support for "free peoples" in their fight against Communist subversion. The press was quick to dub this the "Truman Doctrine," echoing the Monroe Doctrine of 1823, President James Monroe's defiant warning to European powers not to interfere in the affairs of the Western Hemisphere. Truman himself never liked the phrase, which he thought pretentious, but it stuck anyway.

Truman had agonized over the speech, because he was acutely aware of its great consequence. He rejected a first draft, recalling in a memoir that "the writers had filled the speech with all sorts of background data and statistical figures about Greece and made the whole thing sound like an investment prospectus." Taking the draft back to Under Secretary of State Dean Acheson, he asked for more emphasis on policy. Truman needed Congress as well as the American people to understand that he was proposing not merely helping Greece, but taking an enduring ideo-logical stand for the very highest stakes. Truman found Acheson's second draft "half-hearted." As the president later recalled, "The key sentence, for instance, read, 'I believe that it should be the policy of the United States . . .' I took my pencil, scratched out 'should' and wrote in 'must.'" He wanted "no hedging in this speech. This was America's answer to the surge of expansion of Communist tyranny. It had to be clear and free of hesitation or double talk."

Truman understood that a leadership decision must be carefully weighed, with all shadings and subtleties taken into account. But he also understood that, once the decision has been made, it has to be announced and explained with absolute clarity and vigor. The process of pondering a decision typically requires many *shoulds*. Executing the deci-sion, however, can admit only *musts*.

The Greek strategy worked well, and the Communist Party was defeated there. In the meantime, Kennan refined his "Long Telegram" (as the eight-thousand-word missive was called in State Department circles) into an article titled "The Sources of Soviet Conduct," which was published in *Foreign Affairs* in July 1947 under the pseudonym "X." The "X Article" became the further basis for the Truman Doctrine and for the whole of the Cold War. It was a strenuous policy of maintaining the "long-term, patient but firm and vigilant containment of Russian expan-sive tendencies." Kennan advised that "Soviet pressure against the free institutions of the Western world" had to be checked by the "adroit and vigilant application of counter-force at a series of constantly shifting geo-graphical and political points, corresponding to the shifts and maneuvers of Soviet policy." This policy, Kennan argued, would "promote tendencies which must eventually find their outlet in either the break-up or the gradual mellowing of Soviet power."

The "X Article" recommendations were highly controversial, but Truman was persuaded that they provided a way of fighting Communist aggression in a world that could not afford a new world war. This policy of supporting free nations against Communist insurgency and domination—without, however, igniting World War III—moved Truman and the Western allies of the United States to make a strong stand in Germany, which had been divided after World War II into an Eastern Sector, controlled by the Soviets, and a Western Sector, controlled by the United States, Britain, and France. Berlin, the traditional capital of Germany, was deep inside the Soviet sector, but it too was divided into separate zones of occupation, the Soviets controlling the east, the Western allies the west. From the beginning, this galled the Soviets, who, starting in March 1948, began the practice of detaining troop and supply trains bound for West Berlin.

In defiance of this effort at intimidation, on June 7, 1948, the Western allies announced their intention to create a separate, permanent democratic and capitalist state of West Germany, to include West Berlin. Two weeks later, the Soviets made *their* response: They set up a blockade of West Berlin, protesting that a *West* Germany could not include a city located in Soviet-controlled territory.

Under international law, a blockade is an act of war. Dangling the threat of a catastrophic new world war, the Soviets expected the West to back down.

Truman reasoned that backing down would make a hollow mockery of the Truman Doctrine. Certainly, it would throw open the door to more Soviet aggression and expansion. He decided, therefore, to defy the blockade by supplying West Berlin with food and fuel.

"The main question was," Truman later wrote, "how could we remain in Berlin without risking all-out war?"

He needed to find a course of action that was neither a retreat nor outright armed aggression. The idea of an airlift of supplies to the besieged city seemed to fill this bill. General Hoyt Vandenberg, chief of staff of the air force, objected, however, pointing out that the airlift would drain air force strength from other places in the dangerous postwar world, leaving the United States and its allies vulnerable.

Truman listened carefully. After a silence, he asked Vandenberg "if he would prefer to have us attempt to supply Berlin by ground convoy.

Then, if the Russians resisted that effort and plunged the world into war, would not the Air Force have to contribute its share to the defense of the nation?" In a memoir, Truman recalled, "I answered my own question: The airlift involved less risks than armed road convoys. Therefore, I directed the Air Force to furnish the fullest support possible to the problem of supplying Berlin."

Vandenberg was an imaginative and aggressive officer, who was among the principal architects of the modern air force, but, at least in this instance, he lacked the vision of Harry Truman. Vandenberg saw in the airlift a short-term threat to security, whereas Truman looked through and beyond the short term to identify a far greater threat in the alternative to the airlift: ground convoys that would very likely provoke all-out war. Effective decisions balance immediate needs with long-term results.

———

IN THE END, THE BERLIN AIRLIFT PROVED to be one of the great early triumphs of the Cold War. That Truman succeeded in winning Vandenberg to his own long-term point of view is suggested by the extraordinary achievement of the air force Vandenberg commanded. American Air transports flew round the clock from June 26, 1948, to September 30, 1949, making 189,963 flights over Soviet-held territory into West Berlin (British forces made 87,606 flights). The U.S. Air Force transported 1,783,572.7 tons of food, coal, and other cargo (the British, 541,936.9 tons) and carried 25,263 inbound passengers and 37,486 outbound (Britain, 34,815 in and 164,906 out).

On May 12, 1949, the Soviets lifted the blockade, and East and West Germany were formally created later in the month. The airlift not only saved West Berlin; it became the basis for the North Atlantic Treaty Organization (NATO), the West's principal military alliance against Soviet aggression.

Edmund Hillary and Everest (1953)

THE DECISION TO CONQUER

On June 2, 1953, BBC radio interrupted its coverage of the corona-tion of Queen Elizabeth II with the message, "We have great pleasure in announcing that the British Everest expedition has finally reached the summit of Mt. Everest." Two climbers, a New Zealand bee-keeper named Edmund Hillary and his Sherpa guide, Tenzing Norgay, had actually reached the summit on May 29. They were the first to conquer the 29,035-foot mountain, the highest on the planet. After the world had learned about the achievement, one question was uni-versal: *Why?*

George Mallory, Hillary's most famous predecessor in attempting Everest, met his death on the peak's North Face in June 1924. Asked before he left why he had decided to climb Everest, Mallory replied famously, "Because it's there."

It was an answer both highly unsatisfying and yet eminently apt and enigmatically heroic. Now that someone had climbed the mountain and lived to tell about it, there came a clamor for a fuller answer. How does someone decide to climb a mountain no one had ever successfully scaled before and about which Hillary himself had expressed much uncertainty? "We didn't know if it was humanly possible to reach the top of Mt. Everest," he remarked more than once.

Hillary repeatedly tried to oblige the curious with an answer, but he never quite pinned it down to a moment of decision.

"I never had a vision to climb Mt. Everest," Hillary explained to an interviewer in 1991. "As with everything else, it just more or less grew."

Born in 1919 in Auckland, New Zealand, Edmund Percival Hillary was a beekeeper and the son of a beekeeper. As a child, he was some-thing of a loner who daydreamed and read a lot of books about adventure. He loved to walk alone through the New Zealand countryside, all the while "slashing villains with swords and capturing beautiful maidens and doing all sorts of heroic things, just purely in my dreams." While walking, his "mind would be far away in all sorts of heroic efforts."

When it came time for high school, Hillary, who lived in the country, had to make the two-hour daily commute to Auckland, where he found it difficult to catch up to his city-schooled classmates. He felt himself inadequate and an outsider, and he turned more and more to reading. But then, when he was sixteen, he went on a trip with classmates to a national park some two hundred miles outside the city. It was midwinter, and the great volcanic mountains were covered in snow. For ten days he skied and wandered around the hills. He had, he realized, found himself at last. From that moment on, his childish dreams of heroic adventure began to merge with the physical reality of mountaineering. He joined several climbing parties in the Southern Alps of New Zealand. Driven by a combination of seemingly incurable restlessness and a growing love of climbing, Hillary transformed himself into a virtuoso climber.

Still, he had no specific ambition to become a *professional* mountain climber. He knew only that he wanted to "get involved in adventurous activity," and he also became increasingly aware that he enjoyed telling stories about his adventures to others.

Service in the air force during World War II interrupted this natural drift into mountaineering, but he picked it up again after the war. He also discovered, in his postwar climbing, that he had a certain talent for leadership. His role model in this regard was not some military or political figure, but Sir Ernest Henry Shackleton, the renowned British explorer who had attempted to reach the South Pole in 1902, 1907, and 1914. That Shackleton failed in three attempts to reach the Pole hardly mattered to Hillary. What he admired was his ability, as a leader, to inspire his men and lead them into and out of danger. Even more important for Hillary, he saw Shackleton as a great improviser, who believed in careful planning and preparation and who was well prepared to make a decision, but who was also willing to change his mind quickly when the situation warranted. "The main objective remained," Hillary observed about Shackleton's leadership style, "but there were always a multitude of alternatives of how you achieve these objectives." Hillary realized that he, too, enjoyed making careful plans, but also liked changing them. He relished leading others, but not telling them what to do. Instead, he endeavored to lead them to do the utmost of what they were capable— and that meant becoming a highly flexible leader within the focus of a particular goal.

Hillary did not feel that he was born to adventure or to lead others in adventure. He was, however, born into a kind of restlessness, and that drove him into situations and contacts that nurtured his hunger for adventure and developed his talent for leadership. Anyone, he thought, could develop these qualities. And that notion both excited and disappointed many people who spoke with Hillary. It excited them because it opened up new horizons of achievement to perfectly ordinary people. It disappointed them for precisely the same reason. Hillary insisted that he was an "ordinary person," really a "mediocre person," no great athlete (he insisted), who developed competent physical strength and skills simply by pursuing climbing, a thing he loved.

Yet there was one quality that, he admitted, set him apart from many others. He expressed it in a single word: *motivation.* Physical fitness and technical skill were certainly important in mountain climbing, he observed, but a "sort of basic motivation, the desire to succeed, to stretch yourself to the utmost is the most important factor." Yet, when he was asked who encouraged him, who fed his motivation, Hillary could think of no one. Neither friends, nor teachers, nor parents had encouraged him to climb. Pressed, he identified his source of motivation as an essential need to aim high. Aiming high provided the motivation. Was failure unthinkable? On the contrary, it was quite possible. But to aim high and fail was far better than to aim for the middle and succeed. In fact, the possibility of failure added an element of excitement that served to fuel motivation. If he felt certain of success, Hillary found a deficiency of motivation. Why do something you know will succeed? he asked. The prospect of failure was a necessary catalyst to achievement, especially combined with a determination to "carry things through to a conclusion" once he had started. The yin and yang of possible failure and the determination to succeed energized Edmund Hillary and drove his decision-making.

Driven in this way, everything necessary to heroic achievement came to him naturally—but not always easily. Hillary explained that he always had on his expeditions people who were "academically far cleverer" than he, but he kept ahead of them by, each night as he drifted into sleep, letting his mind dwell on the likely things that might happen the next day. As these potential circumstances occurred to him, one by one, he would carefully think out the decisions necessary to cope with them. Come the next day, therefore, he was almost always ready for whatever happened, while the academically cleverer members of the expedition simply had not spent time thinking about it.

Night and rest are the times for dwelling on the potential and the possible. During the climb itself, however, Hillary rigorously concentrated "on the job at hand." Every step required thought, and, at the higher altitudes of Everest, there was the necessity of continually doing mental arithmetic to determine the critical rate of oxygen usage. A lapse in concentration could mean a fatal fall or an equally fatal shortage of precious oxygen.

By the time the opportunity to climb Everest presented itself, Edmund Hillary had a profound awareness of his own abilities, his own character, and his own personality. He emphatically did not know that he (or anyone else) could actually climb Everest, but he did know that the fear and doubt produced by this uncertainty drove him to decide to make the attempt. Hillary's decision, then, was based not on a certainty that he would succeed, or even on a great confidence that he would *probably* succeed, but on his recognition that he very much wanted to make the attempt.

In 1951, he joined a New Zealand party to the central Himalayas. Their object was not to climb Everest, but to climb in and around the Indian Garhwal Himalayas. After climbing a half-dozen peaks of over twenty thousand feet, later in the year Hillary was invited to join a British reconnaissance expedition of the southern flank of Everest, which had just been made accessible when Nepal—for the first time in history—was opened to Western visitors. As Hillary explained years later, it was almost "like a football team. If you're pretty competent and if you don't make any grave errors, once you're in, you're in. You're sort of appointed next time." That "next time" came in 1953, when Hillary was seen as an obvious choice to join the team of mountaineers who planned to climb Everest via its South Face. Hillary, in turn, chose the Sherpa, Tenzing Norgay, as his primary guide and climbing companion.

THE ACHIEVEMENT BROUGHT Edmund Hillary great fame, a knighthood, substantial wealth, and other honors. For the first thirty-three years of his life, until he had climbed Everest, he described himself as "very restless and slightly unhappy." Having conquered the mountain, his greatest reward was a feeling, lifelong, of nothing more than "quiet satisfaction." More than the spectacular achievement itself, this peaceful sense of fulfillment was, to Hillary, a sign that he had made the right decision after all.

Richard M. Nixon and China (1972)
THE DECISION TO COEXIST

Before 1972, the same adjective could have applied to both Nixon and China: *implacable.*

Richard Milhous Nixon was born in 1913 in Yorba Linda, California, into the family of a grocer and filling-station operator. He graduated from Whittier College in Whittier, California, and from Duke University law school. After practicing law in Whittier, he served briefly in the Office of Price Administration in Washington, D.C., then, during World War II, joined the navy as an aviation ground officer. After the war, in 1946, he defeated five-term liberal Democratic Congressman Jerry Voorhis for a seat in the U.S. House of Representatives. His campaign relied heavily on innuendos branding his opponent as a Communist sympathizer. It was a nasty campaign that earned him charter credentials as a hard-line anti-Communist and a reputation as a down-and-dirty, take-no-prisoners political battler. Many people started to hate him as a result of that very first campaign, and even those who admired Richard M. Nixon didn't much like him. But when he ran for reelection in 1948, he entered—and won—both the Democratic and Republican primaries, thereby eliminating the need to compete in the general election.

He got noticed, and he was put on the powerful House Un-American Activities Committee (HUAC), where he took the lead in investigating Alger Hiss, a former State Department official from the FDR administration, who stood accused of spying for the Soviet Union. In public hearings, Representative Nixon was openly hostile to Hiss, a polarizing stance that garnered both more enemies and more admirers, and that certified Nixon as an implacable Cold Warrior.

In 1950, he was ready to make his move to the Senate, running against Democratic Representative Helen Gahagan Douglas. The campaign was even dirtier than the one against Voorhis. Innuendo became invective, as Nixon accused Douglas of being "pink right down to her underwear." He distributed "pink sheets," which quite unfairly, but effectively, compared her voting record to that of Vito Marcantonio, a notorious leftist representative from New York. During the campaign, the *Independent Review*, a California paper, called Nixon "Tricky Dick," an epithet he would never succeed in shedding.

In 1952, Senator Nixon was nominated as running mate to presidential candidate Dwight D. Eisenhower. He answered a potentially career-wrecking accusation that he had maintained a secret campaign "slush fund" by delivering, on September 23, 1952, his famous "Checkers" speech, admitting the existence of the fund but denying that it had been used improperly. He was hardly wealthy, he claimed, and, to prove it, recited his family's modest assets, including his wife's "respectable

Republican cloth coat" (in contrast to the furs allegedly worn by Demo-cratic wives) and the one political gift he had in fact accepted, a cocker spaniel puppy his six-year-old daughter Tricia had named Checkers. "Regardless of what they say about it, we are going to keep it," he said.

Maudlin in the extreme, especially coming from a red-baiting Cold Warrior, the Checkers speech saved Nixon's place on the ticket, and he and Ike easily defeated Democratic candidates Adlai E. Stevenson and John Sparkman. Nixon served two terms as vice president, then received his party's presidential nod in 1960, losing by a razor-thin margin to John F. Kennedy. He ran for California governor in 1962, but was defeated by the popular incumbent Edmund G. "Pat" Brown, a loss that prompted him to announce his retirement from politics with a special jab at the press, who, he felt, had always hated him. "You won't have Dick Nixon to kick around anymore," he bitterly declared.

Nixon began a lucrative law practice in New York City and modu-lated his image from that of vehement anti-Communist to moderate conservative. This made him more attractive to his party, and, in 1968, he again won the Republican nomination for president, going on to defeat Democrat Hubert H. Humphrey and third party candidate George Wallace largely by promising that he had a "secret plan" to end the Vietnam War. In fact, while Nixon reduced the number of U.S. ground forces in Vietnam, he stepped up bombing and expanded the war to neighboring Cambodia and Laos, even as his national security adviser Henry Kissinger conducted peace negotiations in Paris with North Viet-namese foreign minister Le Duc Tho. As Nixon groped after what he called "peace with honor" in Vietnam, wanting to withdraw but refusing to surrender to Communism, he began to think the unthinkable: normal-izing relations with the biggest and most implacable Communist nation in the world—the People's Republic of China.

That nation had been created in 1949 after a savage revolution, and its government, under Mao Zedong, vowed to disseminate Communism throughout the world. This, and China's military support of North Korea against U.S.-led United Nations forces in the Korean War of 1950–53,

made China and the United States unyielding foes. Diplomatic and economic relations were totally severed, and Americans decried "Red China"
as a "mad dog" among nations. The most populous country in the world,
China was also the most closed and mysterious. When it developed
nuclear weapons in the mid-1960s, the fear the United States and other
Western nations felt was immeasurably deepened. With the United
States, the Soviet Union, and China each in possession of a nuclear
arsenal, the world had become a most dangerous place.

Yet, as the 1960s progressed, relations between China and the
Soviet Union—which the United States had thought of as comprising a
monolithic Communist bloc—deteriorated. This offered an opportunity
for improvement in relations between China and the United States. It
was an opportunity to make the world a less dangerous place. What was
necessary was a leader who possessed the perception, the will, and the
proper political credentials to see and to seize that opportunity. To the
surprise of America, China, and the rest of the world, that leader turned
out to be Richard M. Nixon.

At 7:30 P.M. on July 15, 1971, President Nixon appeared on national
television for three and a half minutes to "announce a major development
in our efforts to build a lasting peace in the world." He told the nation
that he had accepted an invitation from Chou En-lai, premier of the
People's Republic of China, to meet in Beijing with Chinese leaders "to
seek the normalization of relations between the two countries and also to
exchange views on questions of concern to the two sides."

Nixon later explained that he had first discussed the importance
of relations between the United States and China in a 1967 article in
Foreign Affairs and he even alluded to it in his inaugural address, in
which he declared that he sought "an open world . . . a world in which
no people, great or small, will live in angry isolation." Two weeks after his
inauguration, he wrote a memorandum to Kissinger urging that "every
encouragement" be given to the "attitude that the administration was
exploring possibilities of rapprochement with the Chinese." Nixon
stressed that this should be done in private, and it was fully a year later

that the president took the first public step, raising the issue in his February 1970 Foreign Policy Report to Congress. In this report, he called the Chinese a "great and vital people who should not remain solated from the international community" and declared that "it is certainly in our interest, and in the interest of peace and stability in Asia and the world, that we take what steps we can toward improved practical relations with Peking."

As Nixon knew it would, the report to Congress was read by the Chinese leaders. Two days later, in a meeting with U.S. ambassador Walter Stoessel in Warsaw, Poland—in the absence of diplomatic relations, the place at which American and Chinese representatives irregularly met— the Chinese ambassador suggested that the meetings be moved to Beijing. He also hinted, indirectly, that the Chinese government would welcome there a high-ranking American official as head of the delegation. The signal was unmistakable, and, in March 1970, Nixon reciprocated with a signal of his own, instructing the Department of State to relax most official restrictions on travel to China. The following month, many trade controls were also eased.

When Nixon extended the Vietnam War into Cambodia, the idea of moving the Warsaw meetings to Beijing was suspended, but Nixon's original initiative had already acquired a momentum of its own. The decision to thaw relations even a little, to reach out ever so slightly, exposed to light what Nixon called an "underlying logic . . . based on clear-cut assessments of mutually advantageous interests." After a few months' silence, the Chinese sent a new signal, releasing from prison a Roman Catholic bishop, James Edward Walsh, who had been held since 1958.

If the Cold Warrior Nixon was moved by a perception of "mutually advantageous interests" in opening relations with the nation that represented Communist ideology at its most uncompromising and, to Nixon's right-wing supporters, its most threatening and offensive, he was also propelled by a very personal perception. Early in October 1970, he told a *Time* interviewer that "if there is anything I want to do before I die, it is to go to China. If I don't, I want my children to." The point was this:

As long as he, Richard M. Nixon, an American, could not freely travel to China, the world would be that much more dangerous. It would be a threat to him and to his own children. Old-time political beliefs and ideological posturing were not worth the lives of one's children.

Richard Nixon was a secretive man, often a devious man—these very qualities would bring down his presidency by 1974—and the lead-up to his meeting with Mao Zedong and Chou En-lai in Bejing was delicate and subtle—a "diplomatic minuet," as Nixon described it—yet his decision to go to China was straightforward, emotional, and personal.

Done clumsily, Nixon knew, the meeting could have profoundly embarrassing diplomatic consequences, which might impede rather than improve relations between the two countries. Even riskier were the potential personal political consequences. The hard-line Cold Warriors who had supported and stood by Nixon hated and condemned his overtures to the "Red Chinese." But Nixon was prepared for this and had already made two decisions concerning the hard-liners. First, he correctly believed that his own credentials as an anti-Communist and a Cold Warrior gave him unique license to approach China. If a known liberal, a Democrat, tried such an approach, he would be opposed and condemned by more than just a handful of hard-liners. No one, however, could seriously accuse Richard Nixon of harboring Communist sympathies. Second, he had come to believe that history, the evolution of events, made right-wing objections to normal relations with China simply irrelevant. Right now, China was still relatively isolated in the world—and Nixon had already spoken of the dangers of "angry isolation"—but that was changing. One by one, other nations were recognizing the People's Republic and, soon enough, the United States, in its ongoing refusal to recognize this Communist giant, would find itself in the minority. The United States would become isolated. For years, the United States had blocked China's admission to the United Nations, insisting that the international body recognize Taiwan, the remaining vestige of Nationalist China, as the official Chinese government. It was now becoming increasingly clear that the United States would soon lack the votes to continue to block admission. "Personally, I have never believed in bowing to the inevitable just because it is inevitable," Nixon wrote in his 1978 book *RN: The Memoirs of Richard Nixon*. "In this case, however, I felt that the national security interests of the United States lay in developing our relations with the [People's Republic of China]." Not only had recognition of China become grimly inevitable, Nixon concluded, it was now positively desirable.

Nixon sent Kissinger to China for secret talks, which led, perhaps somewhat incongruously, to an invitation for the U.S. table tennis team to compete in China against the Chinese team. This so-called "ping-pong diplomacy" was conducted through reciprocal visits by the teams of the two nations in 1971 and 1972, paving the way for the president's visit in February–March 1972.

The immediate dividends of Nixon's visit to China and the U.S.-Chinese rapprochement that developed from it included an opportunity to exploit the already substantial rift between China and the other great Communist power, the Soviet Union. This gave Nixon considerable leverage in his dealings with Moscow, which led to a number of formal agreements, including the SALT I nuclear-arms-limitation treaties. In the longer term, China was enabled to end its political and economic isolation and emerge as both an industrial giant and a major U.S. trading partner.

IN THE YEARS SINCE PRESIDENT NIXON'S FATEFUL VISIT to Beijing, the Soviet Union has crumbled, and while China remains officially a Communist country, it is also a powerful force in the world capitalist economy and a partner in international capitalist enterprise. This in itself poses new challenges for the United States and the rest of the West, yet it presents a prospect far brighter and far more productive than the specter of an ideological, political, and military foe, unwilling to talk, unwilling to reason, possessing a population of a billion, an army of millions, and an arsenal of nuclear weapons.

Boris Yeltsin and the Communist Coup (1991)

THE DECISION TO EMBRACE
A NEW WORLD ORDER

The Soviet Union and the Communist government into which Boris Nikolayevich Yeltsin was born in 1931 seemed eternal, both to Soviet citizens and to those on the outside, in the Western world. Yeltsin attended the Ural Polytechnic Institute and worked on construction projects in his native Sverdlovsk (now called Yekaterinburg) from 1955 to 1968, becoming in 1961—like any young Soviet citizen bent on professional success—a member of the Communist Party. In 1968, he made the transition from engineering to politics, becoming a full-time worker for the party. By 1976 he was first secretary of the Sverdlovsk party committee and was befriended by Mikhail Gorbachev, first secretary of the party committee in the city of Stavropol.

In contrast to Yeltsin, a rough-edged bear of a man, Gorbachev was suave and engaging, and he rose more quickly to national prominence. But he did not forget Boris Nikolayevich, and in 1985, when Gorbachev became general secretary of the Communist Party of the Soviet Union— de facto head of the Soviet state—he tapped Yeltsin to come to Moscow to reform the corrupt party organization of the capital. By 1986, Yeltsin was a nonvoting member of the Politburo and mayor of Moscow (first secretary of the Communist Party committee of Moscow).

Gorbachev won admiration in the West for his determination to reform the Soviet system, moving it toward what he called *glasnost* (openness and transparency) and *perestroika* (restructuring toward a free-market economy). His single boldest move was to repeal the so-called "Brezhnev Doctrine." Put into place by Gorbachev's hard-line Communist predecessor, Leonid Brezhnev, this was a declaration of the Soviet Union's right to intervene politically and militarily in the affairs of any Warsaw Pact (Soviet satellite) nation. Despite their scope, Gorbachev's reforms moved too slowly for Yeltsin, who grew increasingly estranged from his former patron. Yeltsin's dissidence forced his resignation from the Moscow party leadership in 1987 and from the Politburo the following year.

Yet the die was cast. Yeltsin had earned great popularity among Soviet citizens, and when Gorbachev introduced genuinely competitive elections to the USSR Congress of People's Deputies—the Soviet parliament—Yeltsin was elected to a seat by a landslide in March 1989. On May 29, 1990, the Congress in turn elected him president of the Russian republic, in defiance of Gorbachev's opposition.

As Russian president, Yeltsin demanded the right of the Soviet republics to more autonomy and also pushed for an outright embrace of the free-market economy and a multiparty political system. He quit the Communist Party in July 1990, then won a spectacular victory in the first direct popular elections for the presidency of the Russian republic in June 1991. This was widely interpreted as a mandate for sweeping economic and political reform. The quiet, more-or-less gradual revolution begun by Gorbachev's reforms had now overtaken Gorbachev, and Yeltsin outdistanced him, emerging at the head of the vanguard.

The Communist Party was ailing and failing, but Gorbachev was still its master. Caught midway in the process of reform, the nation was in economic and political limbo. Whereas Yeltsin's faith in the emerging forces of democracy was unshaken in this time of turmoil, Gorbachev wavered, perhaps somewhat stunned by what he himself had wrought. He issued decrees reminiscent of the old Soviet days, and he brought back into administrative roles a number of old-time Communists in an effort to slow changes he perceived as spinning out of control. Late in 1990, Gorbachev openly allied himself with Communist Party conservatives, and this proved to be a nearly fatal error.

In the wee hours of the morning of August 19, 1991, those conservatives, including hard-liners from the KGB (secret police) and the army, moved against Mikhail Gorbachev; army units placed him and his family under house arrest in their *dacha* (vacation home). Another military detachment arrived at the Yeltsin dacha in Arkhangelskoye at 4:00 A.M.

Their original orders had been to arrest Yeltsin—by force—but they hesitated because the coup plotters decided that Boris Yeltsin should not be arrested arbitrarily, but needed to be provoked into violation of the law.

Awakened by his daughter, shouting, "Papa, get up! There's a coup!" Yeltsin, half-asleep, responded rather absurdly: "That's illegal!" He immediately recognized the comedy of these words, but, during the course of the day, they also assumed great significance for him.

A successful coup d'état is swift and decisive. These qualities are, in fact, the very nature of such an action. Yeltsin looked out his window and saw soldiers and vehicles outside of his house. But the attack had not come. "People with real assault rifles were rushing around with worried expressions on their faces," he later recalled. Swift and decisive? What Yeltsin saw was faltering indecision. The AK-47s were intimidating, to be sure, but the people holding them were not. And Yeltsin knew that it was people, not weapons, who created power and authority. He was not intimidated.

While the soldiers moved against Gorbachev and Yeltsin, other troops, columns of tanks, and armored personnel carriers rumbled through the streets of Moscow. To many outsiders, it looked as if the democratic revolution Gorbachev had begun was about to die aborning, the Soviet Union's reforms going the way of China's after the Tiananmen Square massacre of 1989. French President François Mitterrand even appeared before television cameras, apparently eager to be the first Western leader to acknowledge one of the leading figures of the coup, Gennady Yanayev, as the "new leader" of the USSR. He cheerfully assured his countrymen that France could "do business" with the new hard-liners.

But France and the rest of the world did not know the Soviet mentality as Boris Yeltsin knew it. The hard-liners had the KGB and they had the army, but, Yeltsin soon understood, they wanted even more. They wanted it all to be somehow legal. Soviet *apparatchiks*—bureaucrats—could not function without rules, even when they were trying to pull off a counterrevolution. Just as Yeltsin had recognized the incongruity of a *hesitant* coup, so he came to recognize the absurdity of a *legal* coup. In neither case was the adjective compatible with the noun. The apparent balance of power, therefore, was deceptive, and Yeltsin's decision to stand up to the coup plotters—their tanks, soldiers, and assault rifles—was not bravado, foolhardiness, or even an abundance of patriotic passion. It was logical. He had good reason to believe they were bound to fail—*if* he and others did not surrender.

Surrounded by his family—his wife and two daughters—Yeltsin telephoned everyone he knew and "told them they would now be needed to work." They began by writing an appeal to the citizens of Russia. While Yeltsin's daughters typed the text, Yeltsin made more phone calls in an effort to get the appeal distributed as quickly and as widely as possible. It was one symptom of the halting quality of the coup that his telephones and fax machine had not been cut off, but Yeltsin knew they would not remain available forever. What he soon discovered was that in the short time that the Soviet Union had been open to business with the West, telephones and fax machines had burgeoned throughout the country. Within an hour of being typed, the appeal was being read in Moscow and other cities, and the Western wire services had picked it up and were disseminating it worldwide. Photocopiers, banned under old-time Communism, were now relatively abundant in the USSR, and they were working overtime. The appeal was not only broadcast on radio and television; it was being passed from hand to hand all over Moscow and elsewhere.

Yeltsin correctly understood that the middle-aged coup plotters, lockstepping products of the Soviet era, simply failed to grasp the "extent and volume of the information age." They were "faced with a country completely different from the one they had imagined. Instead of a quiet and inconspicuous coup executed party-style, they suddenly had a totally public fight on their hands." They could easily defeat Boris Yeltsin and those around him, but, even with AK-47s, they could not prevail against the people of Russia.

Yeltsin next gained insight into the military's role in the coup. Some time before the event, he had spoken to Pavel Grachev, a commander of elite paratroopers, and asked him "if our lawfully elected government in Russia were ever to be threatened . . . could the military be relied upon, could you be relied upon?" Grachev answered yes. However, when Yeltsin spoke to Grachev on August 19, it became clear that Grachev had been ordered to command the military side of the coup. Nevertheless, the general volunteered to dispatch a security detachment to protect Yeltsin—an action that persuaded Yeltsin that the military support for the coup was very soft, even among top commanders, and he believed that it would not stand.

In his 1994 memoir, *The Struggle for Russia*, Yeltsin wrote that, in the months after the events of August 19–21, he tried to "understand what saved us":

> I turned over various possibilities in my mind. As an athlete, I know very well how sometimes all of a sudden you get a push and feel as if the game were going well, and you can seize the initiative. I felt that kind of uplift on the morning of August 19 in Arkhangelskoye. It was almost 9:00 A.M., the telephone was working and there were no visible troop movements near the dacha. It was time. I set off for the White House [the Russian parliament building in Moscow].

Boris Yeltsin had decided not to hole up in the dacha, nor to run away and set up a government in exile, but to march into the very teeth of the coup d'état. "By the abstract logic of security precautions," he wrote, "it was foolish to leave the compound," but he did. Yeltsin's wife stopped him.

"Where are you going? There are tanks out there. They won't let you through."

"We have a little Russian flag on our car," Yeltsin replied. "They won't stop us when they see that."

And, at some deep level, he actually believed what he said. "[A] little Russian flag. It was so tiny. . . . The familiar ground was crumbling under our feet, but this little flag was something real and meaningful."

I think the people around us had the same feeling. We had something to fight for. We had that symbol of hope. This wasn't a political game, which later the Congress and the opposition press
would viciously accuse us of playing, but just the opposite. It was
a wish once and for all to shake off this filth, this chain of
betrayal and slippery schemes, to leave it all and defend this little
Russian flag, symbolizing our faith in the future of our great
country, a decent and benevolent future.

Although he was aware that he could be ambushed at any time as he
made his way to Moscow and the White House, Boris Yeltsin did not
believe the coup plotters would commit such a public act, especially
because they wanted the coup to have the color of legality. He took a
gamble, and he won. He reached the White House, went to his office
inside, and set about monitoring the activity around the building. He
believed that the White House, symbol of the new parliamentary and
democratic Russia, would be ground zero for the coup, the place at
which the coup would either succeed or be defeated. What he saw hour
by hour was that people were unafraid of the soldiers and the tanks. The
sight of this gave him a "jolt inside," and Yeltsin suddenly decided to venture out of the White House to stand with the people. He exited the
building, "clambered onto a tank, and straightened myself up tall. . . .
Next I greeted the commander of the tank upon which I was standing
and talked with the soldiers. From their faces, from the expression in
their eyes, I could see they would not shoot us."

Yeltsin addressed the crowd, then returned to his office in the
White House. "By that time, however, I was already a completely
different person. . . . I felt a surge of energy and an enormous sense of
relief inside."

By the evening of the nineteenth, barricades hastily erected by ordinary Muscovites had been reinforced with disabled trucks and heavy
pipes, which sympathetic construction workers had transported to the
site by crane. Thousands of Soviet citizens now formed a circle around

the White House, a human chain, several layers deep. If the soldiers and their tanks attacked the building, they would have to go through or over the bodies of their countrymen and countrywomen.

The standoff lasted through the night of August 19 and all through the next day. There was some bloodshed in the streets, but no general crackdown. Many soldiers—entire units—openly sided with the people surrounding the White House, and even those troops who apparently remained loyal to the coup plotters were clearly unwilling to obey any order to attack.

At about 2:30 a.m. on August 21, shooting broke out. Yeltsin's aides bundled him into a bulletproof vest and told him that they were going to take him out of the White House and to the residence of the American Embassy, where U.S. officials had offered safe haven.

"From the perspective of security," Yeltsin later remarked, "the plan to go to the U.S. Embassy was 100 percent correct. But from the point of view of politics, it was 100 percent failure." Yeltsin refused to leave the White House. Despite the shooting, despite warnings that the building was about to be stormed, "I had the feeling that some sort of miraculous force was helping us. . . . There is a simpler explanation for everything, of course. On one hand was an impersonal machine that seemed invincible by virtue of its incredible might and the resources invested in it. On the other hand, in the end everything depends on people. . . . On our side there was no machine—just the opposite—but whether by instinct or inspiration, the right people were at the right place at the right time." Yeltsin would not abandon the people.

The White House was never stormed. Later in the morning of August 21, the order was given to withdraw the soldiers from Moscow. Late that night, Mikhail Gorbachev and his wife, Raisa, released from house arrest, stepped off a plane in Moscow. The coup had collapsed and, soon after, the Communist Party itself dissolved, elevating Boris Yeltsin into a position of prestige and power as Gorbachev's authority continued to erode. Russia and most of the other republics formed the Commonwealth of Independent States to replace the Union of Soviet Socialist Republics, leaving Premier Gorbachev with neither a party nor a nation. He resigned on December 25, 1991, the same day that the USSR officially ceased to exist. Under Yeltsin's leadership, the government of the Russian republic became dominant within the new Commonwealth.

YELTSIN SAW VICTORY OVER THE COUP as even more significant than the end of the Soviet Union and the beginning of a democratic Commonwealth. "I believe," he said, "that history will record the twentieth century essentially ended August 19 through 21, 1991. . . . The twentieth century was largely a century of fear. Humankind had never before known such nightmares as totalitarianism, fascism, communism, concentration camps, genocide, or the atomic plague. Yet during these three days, this century ended and another began. Perhaps people will find this claim too optimistic, but I am convinced it's true because during those days in August, the last empire collapsed. The imperial way of thinking and the policies of empire in the early part of the century were what played such an evil trick on humankind and eventually served themselves as a catalyst for all modern revolutions."

PART FIVE

The Decision to Hope

Chief Joseph and the End of Battle (1877)

THE DECISION FOR PEACE

On January 16, 1493, Columbus set sail from the Caribbean island he named Hispaniola to return to Spain from his first voyage to the New World. He left behind a garrison of thirty-nine men. No sooner did Columbus depart than the garrison began raping the women of the native people Columbus miscalled "Indians" and stealing their food and other goods. The Indians retaliated by killing the entire garrison, most of them while they slept.

That was the first war in four hundred years of combat between whites and Indians in the New World. Among the last of the wars was the one fought in 1877, between a part of the Nez Perce tribe of the Northwest and soldiers of the United States Army.

The Nez Perce lived in and about the Wallowa Valley of the present state of Oregon. In 1863, a gold rush prompted the U.S. government to revise an existing treaty with the tribe to exclude the gold fields from the Nez Perce reservation. Those Indians whose homes remained within the revised boundaries signed the new document and agreed to sell the excluded lands to the government. But those who were dispossessed by the revision refused to sign. Most prominent among this group, which the government called the "nontreaty Indians," was the old and much-respected Chief Joseph. Having refused to sign, he led his people—others who would be dispossessed by the new treaty—in defiantly remaining within the Wallowa Valley.

For several years, nothing happened, as prospectors mined elsewhere. Indeed, in 1873, two years after Old Chief Joseph died, President Ulysses S. Grant even issued a proclamation setting aside part of the Wallowa Valley as a legitimate reservation. Yet soon afterward, as Washington and Oregon became increasingly thick with settlers, local interests pressed the Grant administration to reopen the Wallowa tract to white settlement. Accordingly, the Nez Perce were again ordered to leave the valley. Young Joseph—who had become Chief Joseph after the death of his father—refused, as his father had before him, to leave the disputed land. In May 1877, the military commander responsible for the Northwest, Oliver O. Howard—a gallant general who had lost his right arm in the Civil War and who (after the war) had dedicated years to promoting the welfare of former slaves, even helping to found Howard University for African Americans—warned Joseph and the others that they had just one month to move to the reservation or they would be driven off by force.

Although proud and defiant, Joseph was not a war chief, and he knew that an armed struggle against the forces of the United States would ultimately be fruitless. Reluctantly, Chief Joseph led his people out of the Wallowa Valley and toward the reservation. As they marched, however, a band of young, angry, impulsive warriors killed four whites who had become notorious for their mistreatment of Indians. Joseph and his brother Ollikot were horrified, but they tried to persuade their followers that the best thing to do was to appeal to the white authorities and explain to them that the killings had not been sanctioned by tribal council. However, a group of die-hard non-treaty Indians broke out and fled south, toward the Salmon River, where they killed fifteen more settlers.

Howard sent a force of one hundred cavalry troopers under Captain David Perry to intercept the rogue Nez Perce before they reached the mountains beyond the Salmon River. At dawn on June 17, Perry's command, exhausted from a forced march, arrived at White Bird Canyon. Under a flag of truce, Joseph sent a delegation to the canyon, intending even now to talk peace. By this time, a handful of civilian volunteers had joined Perry's troopers, and it was these undisciplined men who first encountered the truce party. Ignoring the white flag, they opened fire on the Indians. The truce party responded in kind. The Nez Perce were skilled hunters and superb marksmen. They fired against Perry's front and both flanks, routing his command, killing thirty-three enlisted men and one officer.

The Nez Perce War was on.

On June 22, Howard led about four hundred men to seal off White Bird Canyon. Locals persuaded Howard that Looking Glass, a Nez Perce chief whose village was near the forks of the Clearwater, planned to ally his people with Chief Joseph's group. Accordingly, Howard dispatched Captain Stephen G. Whipple with two troops of cavalry and a pair of Gatling guns, together with a band of local civilian volunteers, to surprise Looking Glass, but Whipple soon learned that Looking Glass actually wanted no part of the war. Whipple therefore decided to open up talks with the chief. Yet again, however, the volunteers provoked a fight. A deadly exchange on July 1 propelled Looking Glass into the camp of the militants. He and his followers held a force of volunteers under siege during July 9–10 at a place the whites dubbed Mount Misery. Then, on July 11, the two-day Battle of Clearwater began. Howard's men drove the Indians from the field, but, bloodied and exhausted, they did not give chase.

It was not until August 9 that the army again made contact with the Nez Perce, at Big Hole River, Montana. Although taken by surprise, Looking Glass quickly rallied his warriors, who killed two cavalry officers, twenty-two enlisted troopers, and six civilians. They wounded many more and sent the army limping away. The Nez Perce rode swiftly through the countryside, killing ten settlers, seizing 250 horses, raiding a wagon train, then entering the newly established Yellowstone National Park, where they created great panic among the tourists. Howard, along with the 7th Cavalry under Colonel Samuel D. Sturgis, gave chase, but to no avail.

There was a skirmish on August 19, and a bigger battle on September 13, which prompted the Nez Perce to seek refuge among the Crow Indians, only to discover that Crow scouts had been fighting on Howard's side. The one rational hope remaining, as both Looking Glass and Joseph saw it, was to flee across the border to Canada, where they could join Sitting Bull and his followers, who had exiled themselves there.

About forty miles south of the Canadian border, on the northern edge of the Bear Paw Mountains in Montana, the followers of Looking Glass and Chief Joseph, now joined together in a group of about eight hundred men, women, and children, paused to rest, having fought and run for some three months and over 1,700 miles of the most difficult terrain on the North American continent.

It was here, on September 30, that Colonel Nelson A. Miles, with about four hundred men, located them and attacked. The Battle of Bear Paw Mountain would be fought during six days of snow storms whipped by frigid winds. When the attack first came, the Nez Perce were dazed. They dug in as best they could, some taking shelter in frozen coulees—steep-walled gulches—others taking flight to the north. Under fire, the Indians' ponies stampeded, but Joseph managed to catch one and sent his daughter riding off with some companions. He was now cut off from the rest of his family: "I thought of my wife and children, who were now surrounded by soldiers, and I resolved to go to them or die."

> With a prayer in my mouth to the Great Spirit Chief who rules above, I dashed unarmed through the line of soldiers. It seemed to me that there were guns on every side, before and behind me. My clothes were cut to pieces and my horse was wounded, but I was not hurt. As I reached the door of my lodge, my wife handed me my rifle, saying: "Here's your gun. Fight!"

The Indians and the soldiers fought at close range, "not more than twenty steps apart," and Joseph and the others managed to drive the troopers back upon their main line, "leaving their dead in our hands. We secured their arms and ammunition. We lost, the first day and night, eighteen men and three women."

Over the next few days, the fighting was hard on the soldiers, but catastrophic for the Nez Perce. Joseph's brother Ollikot was killed, as were the prominent war chiefs Pile of Clouds, Toohoolhoolzote, and Hahtalekin. Almost as bad was the loss of most of the Indians' pony herd, without which they could not complete the flight to Canada.

The only hope for the Nez Perce now was that Sitting Bull's Sioux, to whom they had sent runners, would heed their plea and cross the Canadian border to aid them. For a few days, it was this hope that kept the fight alive, and the soldiers as well as the Indians suffered mightily. But there was one great difference: Frontline troops could pull back from time to time and rest comfortably in the well-supplied shelter of their camp. The Nez Perce, as one Indian woman recalled, could do nothing more than dig "trenches with camas hooks [implements for digging camas roots, a Nez Perce staple crop] and butcher knives. With pans we threw out the dirt. . . . I was three days without food. Children cried with hunger and cold. Old people suffering in silence. Misery everywhere. Cold and dampness all around." As the widow of Ollikot recounted, "We slept only by naps; sitting in our pits; leaning forward or back against the dirt wall."

Each day ushered in renewed battle. The warrior Yellow Wolf recalled the morning of the third day, which brought "Bullets from every-where! A big gun throwing bursting shells. . . . Wild and stormy, the cold wind was thick with snow. Air filled with smoke of powder. Flash of guns through it all. As the hidden sun traveled upward, the war did not weaken. . . . A young warrior, wounded, lay on a buffalo robe dying without complaint. Children crying with cold. No fire. There could be no light. Everywhere the crying, the death wail. . . . All night we remained in those pits. The cold grew stronger. The wind was filled with snow. . . . I felt the coming end. All for which we had suffered lost!"

On the fourth day, October 3, came a moment of hope as some thought they saw Indians—Could they be Sitting Bull's warriors?—coming to their aid. Chief Looking Glass rose above the hated pits and coulees to take a look. He was instantly struck dead, shot in the forehead. This was a sudden and terrific blow. Looking Glass was the fifth Nez Perce chief killed in fighting with the army. Chief by chief, the tradition, the heritage, the leadership of the tribe was dying. And now it also became apparent that the Sioux were not riding to rescue. What to wishful eyes had looked like mounted warriors proved to be nothing more than a passing herd of snow-covered bison.

The situation, miserable and deadly, was also hopeless. Looking Glass had believed that white men could not be trusted, so his counsel had been never to surrender. White Bird—with Joseph, now the only surviving chief—agreed and continued to agree. He would never surrender, he said.

Nez Perce tribal government did not make the decision of any one chief binding on all members of the tribe. White Bird could go his way, Chief Joseph decided, and he would go his. Joseph saw himself not as a war chief, but as the guardian of his people, and he now wanted to find for them some honorable way of surrender. "We could have escaped from the Bear Paw Mountains," he later said, "if we had left our wounded, old women, and children behind." But that was unthinkable to him, the guardian. "We never heard of a wounded Indian recovering in the hands of white men." On October 4, Joseph and White Bird formally agreed: each would act as he saw fit. "What Joseph does is all right," White Bird pronounced. "I have nothing to say."

On October 5, General Howard, who had arrived at Colonel Miles's camp, sent two Nez Perce scouts who were in the employ of the army, Captain John and Old George, under a flag of truce to Joseph and White Bird.

"All my brothers," Captain John called out, "I am glad to see you alive this sun! . . . We are glad to hear you want no more war, do not want to fight. We are all glad."

It was the wrong thing to say, implying, as it did, that the gallant non-treaty faction had lost its will to fight.

Fortunately, Old George next spoke up: "We have come far from home. You now see many soldiers lying down side by side. We see Indians, too, lying dead. I am glad today to be shaking hands. We are all not mad. We all think of Chief Joseph and these other brothers. We see your sons and relations lying dead, but we are glad to shake hands with you today." This was the proper, respectful greeting to warriors, and Joseph and White Bird admitted the two scouts into their camp.

Captain John and Old George promised that General Howard would treat the chiefs and the other Nez Perce well, would spare their lives, return to them their horses and their rifles, and send them to a pleasant reservation. That sounded inviting. Joseph considered it their only hope. Others, however, believed it was all a trick and that they would be hanged or shot if they surrendered.

The two scouts left so that the deliberations could continue. After a time, they returned, warning that the generals were becoming impatient. Joseph stood his ground: "We will council over this. We will decide what to do!" he snapped.

At this, the two scouts took a different tack: "Those generals said tell you, 'We will have no more war!'"

As Joseph saw it, this message provided just the opening he needed. *They*, the generals, would have no more war. Here was an opportunity to end the fighting without appearing to give up.

"You see," Joseph said, turning to White Bird and the other warriors, "it is true, I did not say, 'Let's quit.' You see, it is true enough! I did not say, 'Let's quit!'"

Yellow Wolf later explained that this persuaded the others to stop fighting. They all said, "Yes, we believe you now. We were not captured," said Yellow Wolf. "It was a draw battle."

White Bird continued to resist. He would not surrender. Later that night—with Yellow Wolf, who had had a change of heart and chose not to surrender—he managed to slip through the line of soldiers and escape to Canada, where he joined the camp of Sitting Bull. As for Joseph, he felt himself responsible for the survival of the starving women and children as well as the wounded warriors. "It is for them I am going to surrender," he said.

He understood that surrender would end the existence of the Nez Perce as an independent nation, and he told this to his followers, explaining as well that the reservation they had been promised was pleasant. In any case, the alternative was to starve, freeze, and die. It was time, he decided, to end the war.

Joseph appeared before Howard and Miles. He dismounted from his horse, took his rifle from its place across the pommel of his saddle, and offered it to Howard, who indicated that Colonel Miles would receive it. This done, Joseph spoke:

> Tell General Howard I know his heart. What he told me before I have in my heart. I am tired of fighting. Our chiefs are killed. Looking Glass is dead. Toohoolhoolzote is dead. The old men are all killed. It is the young men who say yes or no. He who led the young men [Ollikot] is dead. It is cold and we have no blankets. The little children are freezing to death. My people, some of them, have run away to the hills and have no blankets, no food; no one knows where they are, perhaps freezing to death. I want time to look for my children and see how many of them I can find. Maybe I shall find them among the dead. Hear me, my chiefs, I am tired; my heart is sick and sad. From where the sun now stands, I will fight no more forever.

General Howard knew much about courage and much about loss. He was clearly moved: "You have your life," he said. "I am living. I have lost my brothers. Many of you have lost brothers, maybe more than on our side. I do not know. Do not worry more." Colonel Miles added: "No more battles and blood. From this sun, we will have a good time on both sides, your band and mine."

JOSEPH HAD MADE THE HEARTBREAKING DECISION to end a hopeless war. He and many of his people survived into old age, although, despite his petitions as well as earnest support from both Howard and Miles, Joseph and his people were transported not to a Wallowa reservation, but to eastern Kansas and then to a reservation in Indian Territory (present-day Oklahoma). In these alien places and climates, some sickened and died. Thanks to Howard and Miles, Joseph secured an audience with President Rutherford B. Hayes in 1879, but it was not until 1885 that he and his surviving followers were finally returned to the Pacific Northwest. Half the survivors, including Joseph, were taken to the non–Nez Perce Colville Reservation in northern Washington, while the others were settled in Idaho and in the Wallowa Valley. Joseph died in Colville in 1904.

Andrew Carnegie
and the Gospel of Wealth (1889)
THE DECISION TO GIVE ALL YOU HAVE

No figure in the history of American enterprise is more remarkable than Andrew Carnegie. He was born in Scotland in 1835, not into a realm of privilege but a world of want. His father, a hand-loom weaver, possessed a valued skill, but when Andrew was still a child, the arrival of the power loom in his native Dunfermline combined with a general economic depression to throw his father out of work. Desperate for a living, the Carnegies immigrated to the United States in 1848 and settled in a Scottish colony in Allegheny, Pennsylvania (today part of Pittsburgh). That Andrew went to work at age twelve, as a bobbin boy in a cotton factory, was not unusual during this era, but what was extraordinary was his unquenchable enthusiasm, which drove a vision of the potential of life beyond the mill. After working a twelve-hour day, he gave himself an education through reading and night-school classes.

After a year in the mill, Carnegie saw a brighter future in the realm of a more advanced technology and became a messenger boy in a telegraph office. He made it his business to be the best messenger in the office, performing with sufficient brilliance to attract the attention of Thomas Scott, a Pennsylvania Railroad superintendent, who promoted the young man in 1853 to the position of private secretary and personal telegrapher. These were still humble jobs, but they put Carnegie very near the center of power and authority, ultimately positioning him in 1859 to succeed Scott as superintendent of the PRR's Pittsburgh division.

Earning a good salary, Carnegie was not content to become rich. His ambition was to build wealth. Accordingly, he continued to live modestly, investing his surplus funds in the Woodruff Sleeping Car Company, holder (at the time) of the Pullman patents. Having invested in the company, he used his post as a PRR superintendent to introduce the first practical—and successful—sleeping car on an American railroad. It was a sensation, which was quickly adopted not only throughout the Pennsylvania system, but by many other railroads as well. Carnegie's investment grew, and he parlayed his earnings into other firms whose businesses were related to his. Because he had a leadership position in a major railroad, he was able to influence the fortunes of such companies as the Superior Rail Mill and Blast Furnaces, Union Iron Mills, and Pittsburgh Locomotive Works, all of which he invested in. These and other ventures earned him an annual income of more than $50,000 by the time he was thirty—this in an era before income taxes and when the average American workingman made perhaps a dollar a day.

During investment-related trips to Britain, Carnegie became familiar with the steel industry. He believed that steel and iron would increasingly become the materials from which the rest of the nineteenth century would be built, and he decided to invest in what he deemed the very fabric of future civilization. In a bold move, he resigned from the Pennsylvania Railroad in 1865 and took over management of the Keystone Bridge Company, of which he owned a large share. This allowed him to make the transition to steel, beginning in the early 1870s, when he founded the J. Edgar Thomson Steel Works (the firm that would become the Carnegie Steel Company) near Pittsburgh.

Carnegie saw himself as creating the material from which the future was being built; therefore, he decided to ensure that his steel plants used the most advanced methods of making steel. He imported from Britain the Bessemer process, a relatively new process for the mass-production of steel from molten pig iron. He also applied a host of innovative business practices, including accounting systems that enabled him to monitor and control costs, creating the greatest possible efficiency. Carnegie refused to become wedded to any technology, and when the revolutionary open-hearth furnace proved itself, Carnegie introduced it during the 1890s. He also sought a greater degree of vertical integration by obtaining ownership of coke fields and iron-ore deposits so that he could control the raw materials of steelmaking. He obtained controlling shares of shipping and rail companies to handle the transportation of the raw materials to his mills. By 1890, thanks mainly to Carnegie, the output of the American steel industry overtook that of Britain.

Carnegie's father had been a labor activist, and Andrew Carnegie professed lifelong support for the rights of labor and labor unions. Yet Carnegie supported local management of the Homestead Steel Works in 1892 when it employed Pinkerton thugs to assault strikers in an attempt to break the Amalgamated Association of Iron, Steel, and Tin Workers. Carnegie could be as ruthless as any of the other great captains of ndustry during the period of American business expansion, which many have called the Gilded Age or the era of the robber barons. Yet, even at the height of his power and wealth, something set Andrew Carnegie apart.

In 1889, the very year he consolidated his extensive holdings into the Carnegie Steel Company, which dominated the American steel industry, Carnegie published in the June issue of the *North American Review* a remarkable article that detailed an extraordinary decision he had made. It was titled, simply, "Wealth."

"The problem of our age," the article began, "is the proper adminis-tration of wealth, so that the ties of brotherhood may still bind together the rich and poor in harmonious relationship." This opening sentence announced the decision on which Carnegie would increasingly base the conduct of the rest of his life. It was a decision not merely to accumu-late wealth, which is a choice to be selfish, but a decision to administer wealth with the objective of improving society by enhancing the "ties of brotherhood." This was a choice to be selfless.

Carnegie explained his observation that the progress of civilization had entailed an increasing separation between the poor and the wealthy:

> In former days there was little difference between the swelling, dress, food, and environment of the chief and those of his retainers. The Indians are to-day where civilized man then was. When visiting the Sioux, I was led to the wigwam of the chief. It was just like the others in external appearance, and even within the difference was trifling between it and those of the poorest of his braves. The contrast between the palace of the millionaire and the cottage of the laborer with us to-day measures the change which has come with civilization.

Unlike Marx or Engels, Carnegie did not deplore this historical change, but "welcomed [it] as highly beneficial. It is well, nay, essential for the progress of the race, that the houses of some should be homes for all that is highest and best in literature and the arts, and for all the refinements of civilization, rather than that none should be so. Much better this great irregularity than universal squalor." Carnegie believed that "the 'good old times' were not good old times," that "neither master nor servant was as well situated then as to-day. A relapse to old conditions would be disas-trous to both—not the least so to him who serves—and would sweep away civilization with it." He did not argue with those who might say that all of this was merely a way to rationalize social injustice. Instead, Carnegie continued: "But whether the change be for good or ill, it is upon us, beyond our power to alter, and therefore to be accepted and made the best of." What was entailed in making the "best of" social disparity? Carnegie wrote that a person of wealth has a decision to make—to wit, how to dispose of his wealth. He concluded that there were but three choices: wealth can be left to the families of the wealthy after they die; or wealth "can be bequeathed for public purposes," again, after death; "or, finally, it can be administered during their lives by its possessors. Regarding the first alternative—bequeathing wealth to one's heirs—Carnegie asked "Why should men leave great fortunes to their children?"

> If this is done from affection, is it not misguided affection? Observation teaches that, generally speaking, it is not well for the children that they should be so burdened. Neither is it well for the state. Beyond providing for the wife and daughters moderate sources of income, and very moderate allowances indeed, if any, for the sons, men may well hesitate, for it is no longer question-able that great sums bequeathed oftener work more for the injury than for the good of the recipients. Wise men will soon conclude that, for the best interests of the members of their families and of the state, such bequests are an improper use of their means.

Indeed, Carnegie approved of inheritance taxes as an appropriate means by which the state might recoup some of an individual's wealth, after death, for the benefit of the greater good. As to the second alternative, posthumously endowing some public charity, Carnegie concluded simply that "this is only a means for the disposal of wealth, provided a man is content to wait until he is dead before it becomes of much good in the world." Furthermore, a powerful man dead is no longer powerful. The fortune he has bequeathed is out of his control and subject to the will of others.

That left Carnegie with the third choice: the voluntary distribution of one's wealth for the public good, which is, Carnegie wrote, "the true antidote for the temporary unequal distribution of wealth, the reconcili-ation of the rich and the poor—a reign of harmony." The decision to redistribute wealth in this way "is founded upon the present most intense individualism. . . . Under its sway we shall have an ideal state, in which the surplus wealth of the few will become, in the best sense, the property of the many, because administered for the common good, and this wealth, passing through the hands of the few, can be made a much more potent force for the elevation of our race than if it had been distributed in small sums to·the people themselves." For Carnegie did not advocate charity. Instead, he called on the wealthy to decide to "help those who will help themselves . . . to give those who desire to rise the aids by which they may rise." Carnegie pointed to the example set by some other wealthy benefactors:

> The rich man is thus almost restricted to following the examples of Peter Cooper, Enoch Pratt of Baltimore . . . and others, who know that the best means of benefiting the community is to place within its reach the ladders upon which the aspiring can rise— parks, and means of recreation, by which men are helped in body and minds; works of art, certain to give pleasure and improve the public taste, and public institutions of various kinds, which will improve the general condition of the people;—in this manner returning their surplus wealth to the mass of their fellows in the forms best calculated to do them lasting good.

Certainly, Carnegie followed these examples. During his lifetime, he distributed some $350,000,000, creating and funding such major foundations as the Carnegie Trust for the Universities of Scotland; the Carnegie Dunfermline Trust, to aid the educational institutions of his native town; the Carnegie United Kingdom Trust, which built libraries, theaters, child-welfare centers, and other facilities; the Carnegie Institute of Pittsburgh, for the improvement of Pittsburgh's cultural and educational institutions; the Carnegie Institution of Washington, to fund scientific research; and the Carnegie Corporation of New York, his crowning achievement, for "the advancement and diffusion of knowledge and understanding among the people of the United States" and, later, Canada and the British colonies as well.

These endowments represented most of Carnegie's accumulated fortune. He believed he had no other worthwhile choice, and failure to make this decision, he wrote, carried the most dire consequences:

> Poor and restricted are our opportunities in this life; narrow our horizon; our best work most imperfect; but rich men should be thankful for one inestimable boon. They have it in their power during their lives to busy themselves in organizing benefactions from which the masses of their fellows will derive lasting advantage, and thus dignify their own lives. . . . The man who dies leaving behind him millions of available wealth, which was his to administer during life, will pass away 'unwept, unhonored, and unsung,' no matter to what uses he leaves the dross which he cannot take with him. Of such as these the public verdict will then be: 'The man who dies thus rich dies disgraced.'

THUS ANDREW CARNEGIE EXPLAINED HIS DECISION to devote a large part of his life to giving away all of his money, in accordance with what he called "the true Gospel concerning Wealth, obedience to which is destined some day to solve the problem of the Rich and the Poor, and to bring 'Peace on earth, among men Good-Will.'"

Dwight Eisenhower and D-Day (1944)
THE DECISION TO GIVE THE ORDER

On December 24, 1943, under the authority of Winston Churchill and Franklin D. Roosevelt, U.S. Army chief of staff George C. Marshall named Dwight David Eisenhower supreme commander of Allied Expeditionary Force, Europe, and put him in absolute command of Operation Overlord, the assault on Nazi-held Europe via the English Channel.

The following month, Eisenhower arrived in London to finalize plans for what history would call D-Day, the biggest, most ambitious, most consequential, and perhaps most dangerous invasion in the history of warfare.

Planning and executing the invasion of mainland Europe required thousands of decisions made over weeks and months, but, in the end, everything turned on just one, a decision that had to be made on the eve of D-Day itself: the decision to give the final order to go.

Like all of the other decisions related to the invasion, that one rested first and last with Eisenhower. On it depended, most immediately, the lives of more than 156,000 troops committed to the initial assault (many more would follow). Beyond these immediate stakes, great as they were, were stakes even greater: victory or defeat in a war that pitted democratic civilization against the death-dealing totalitarianism of Adolf Hitler and his followers. Eisenhower's single decision would determine the liberation or continued enslavement of much of the world.

On June 3, 1944, General Eisenhower drew up a memorandum listing the five factors bearing on the probable success or failure of the invasion. The most vexing of these was the weather. Everything depended on it. Not only did the troopships have to cross the treacherous English Channel, then deploy landing craft along the dangerous shore of Normandy, but conditions had to be right for air operations, including the airlift and deployment of thousands of paratroops.

The weather was not only the universally pervasive factor on which the success or failure of the landings depended, it was also the one factor that neither Eisenhower nor anyone else could influence or change. To make matters infinitely more difficult, Eisenhower actually faced not one, but three problems where the weather was concerned. First, English Channel weather was notoriously unpredictable. Second, the weather required for the invasion had to be good enough to allow the perfectly coordinated conduct of operations not just in the water, but in the air and on the ground as well. What might be acceptable in one of these environments could be catastrophic in another. Finally, good weather had to coincide with the right tidal conditions and an acceptable degree of moonlight. Eisenhower and the other planners were grimly aware that the Germans, under their legendary commander Erwin Rommel, had sown the Norman coast with all manner of treacherous obstacles— including explosive mines—with the intention of destroying landing craft and killing men. At high tide, these hazards would be invisible, and any attempt to land would be suicidal. Low tide, however, would reveal most of the traps and also expose them sufficiently so that specially trained engineers could deal with them. Moreover, sufficient moonlight would be required for the safe and effective deployment of paratroops behind the German lines in preparation for the main amphibious assault in the morning.

The D-Day planners had carefully plotted the few days and hours on which just the right combination of tidal and lunar conditions would occur. This yielded a small cluster of narrow windows during which the cross-Channel voyage and the landings could be made. Miss a window, and the invasion would have to be delayed by a matter of weeks. Delay the invasion that long, and it was virtually certain that the Germans would discover the presence of the invasion forces on the English coast. The vital element of surprise—on which the success or failure of the invasion might well hinge—would be lost. Perhaps even worse, the men of the invasion force, keyed up and primed to launch, would be forced to idle for weeks. The psychological toll could be devastating. And yet a stormy Channel, with high seas, low visibility, and bad flying weather, would doom the operation just as surely as an effective German defense.

Eisenhower knew he faced a situation freighted with imponderables, yet he insisted on pondering them. Admitting that the Channel weather was "practically unpredictable," he nevertheless met with weather experts almost hourly in the days leading up to the scheduled invasion. At least once, sometimes twice daily, he convened commander-in-chief meetings to discuss and analyze the weather reports and predictions, however uncertain and tentative they were. Faced with an all but totally unmanageable situation, Eisenhower was determined to manage whatever he could.

As June 5, the day scheduled for the launch of the invasion, approached, the weather looked increasingly dangerous. Yet Eisenhower decided that "the uncertainty of the weather is such that we could never anticipate really perfect weather coincident with proper tidal conditions." Based on this conclusion, he was able to make the preliminary decision that would govern his final go/no-go decision: "we must . . . go unless there is a real and very serious deterioration in the weather." That is, even if the weather was far from perfect when the tides were right, if it still allowed any reasonable chance for success, the invasion must be launched. To go in poor or even marginal weather involved significant risk, but to wait invited more certain failure—especially in view of the fact that the weather at the next available opportunity might be just as bad or even worse.

Primed though he was to give the order, Eisenhower refused to relinquish freedom of judgment even to his own rule. Therefore, when June 5 promised nothing but violent and unrelenting storms, he decided to delay the launch one more day, his chief weather advisor, Royal Air Force captain J. M. Stagg, having predicted for June 6 an interval of acceptable weather between massive storms.

It was the thinnest of slivers in which this most momentous of undertakings would have to succeed or fail. It offered precious little hope and absolutely no margin for error. But aware that if the invasion did not take place on June 6, it would have to wait for three weeks, Eisenhower seized it. His chief of staff, Walter Bedell Smith, later wrote of the moment of decision: "Finally he looked up, and the tension was gone from his face."

Eisenhower turned to his subordinate commanders. "The question is, just how long can you hang this operation on the end of a limb and let it hang there?" No one offered an answer. So it was the supreme commander himself who broke the silence. "I am quite positive we must give the order. I don't like it but there it is. . . . I don't see how we can do anything else."

The time was 21:45 (9:45) on Sunday night, June 4, 1944. Sometime during the next day, Eisenhower scribbled a note. Its first sentence was "Our landings in the Cherbourg-Havre area have failed to gain a satisfactory foothold and I have withdrawn the troops." Then he continued, "This particular operation," but crossed it out. In place of these impersonal words, he began the next sentence with a pronoun, both personal and possessive:

> My decision to attack at this time and place was based upon the best information available. The troops, the air and the Navy did all that Bravery and devotion to duty could do. If any blame or fault attaches to the attempt it is mine alone.

He folded what he had written and tucked it into his wallet.

On July 11, 1944, five days after the June 6 landings had succeeded even better than anyone had dared hope, Eisenhower fished the piece of paper out of his wallet. He showed it to his naval aide, Commander Harry C. Butcher, remarking that he had written a similar note before every amphibious operation of the war. The earlier notes, however, he had torn up once he was certain of success. This one he had apparently forgotten about. When Butcher asked to have it for his own war diary, Eisenhower handed it over.

——

WITHIN HOURS OF MAKING a decision with the highest stakes imaginable, a decision to take a course with a reasonable chance for success but also a significant chance for catastrophic failure, Eisenhower wrote out his ownership deed to that decision—but only if the worst should happen. He meant to ensure that no one but he would have to accept the blame. As for the credit in the event of success, Ike left that open for all to own.

Menachem Begin and Anwar el-Sadat (1978)

THE DECISION FOR MUTUAL SURVIVAL

On September 17, 1978, at Camp David, Maryland, Israeli prime minister Menachem Begin and Egyptian president Anwar el-Sadat, after thirteen days of talks mediated by U.S. president Jimmy Carter, signed the Camp David Accords, paving the way for a formal

peace treaty between Israel and Egypt. The magnitude of the achievement was captured in paragraph two of the preamble to the Accords:
"After four wars during thirty years, despite intensive human efforts, the
Middle East, which is the cradle of civilization and the birthplace of
three great religions, does not enjoy the blessings of peace. The people
of the Middle East yearn for peace so that the vast human and natural
resources of the region can be turned to the pursuits of peace and so
that this area can become a model for coexistence and cooperation
among nations."

Even in a twentieth century marked by incredible and continuous
change in many spheres of human endeavor, the existence of an
implacable enmity between Israel and Egypt, rooted in Old Testament
times, seemed eternal, and eternally unalterable. The Camp David
Accords shattered that perception, and, remarkable as that fact was, even
more astounding were the two leaders who decided to shatter it. They
were not, by nature and past history, men of peace, and they were both
patriots and intense nationalists, for whom compromise had long seemed
the equivalent of betrayal and therefore out of the question.

Anwar el-Sadat was born on Christmas day, 1918, in the small Nile
Delta village of Mit Abul Kom, and moved with his family to Cairo in
1925. There young Sadat grew to manhood amid the oppressive presence
of British imperialism, which he learned to hate. His ambition became to
free Egypt from British domination and to preserve and protect the land
of his country.

He graduated from the Royal Military Academy of Cairo in 1938
and, during World War II, plotted with the Germans to force the British
from Egypt. British authorities arrested and imprisoned him in 1942, but
he subsequently escaped. After the war, in 1950, Sadat joined Gamal
Abdel Nasser's Free Officers group, which, in 1952, staged a
successful military coup against the Egyptian monarchy. Sadat supported
Nasser's election to the presidency in 1956, and was elevated by Nasser
to a number of government posts, culminating in the vice presidency
during 1964–66 and 1969–70.

In the public eye, Sadat was very much overshadowed by Nasser. Yet his vision was both bolder and narrower than that of Egypt's second president. Whereas Nasser was willing to accept a significant degree of Soviet domination in order to develop Egypt's economy and military, Sadat wanted genuine independence. Whereas Nasser saw Egypt as part of the greater Arab world, Sadat saw it more narrowly as a nation first and an Arab nation second. If the choice were between realizing Egypt's role in a pan-Arab destiny or realizing a greater national identity exclusively for Egypt, Sadat would willingly sacrifice the first to achieve the second. Although he remained more or less behind the scenes in the Nasser government, his goals were to free Egypt from Soviet domination and to restore Sinai to Egyptian sovereignty. One thing that he firmly agreed with Nasser about was that Israel was the absolute enemy of Egypt and an illegitimate nation that had no right to exist.

On Nasser's death, September 28, 1970, Sadat became acting president of Egypt and was confirmed as president by a plebiscite two weeks later. This came as no surprise to him, since he had what has been described as a mystical, even prophetic feeling that the average Egyptian wholly supported him. He saw himself not merely as the political leader of his nation, but as the father of his country. This led him to act boldly in diversifying Egypt's economy and relaxing the nation's rigid political structure. It also prompted him in 1972 to expel thousands of Soviet technicians and advisers from Egypt.

He offered as his reason for the expulsion the Soviet Union's failure to give adequate support in Egypt's ongoing warfare with Israel, but, in truth, he wanted to avoid foreign domination of the country. He did not want merely to exchange British hegemony for Soviet control. The break with the USSR was a sharp departure from the policies of the Nasser era, but his invasion of Israel, launched in October 1973 with Syrian cooperation, was very much in keeping with the values of the old order—or so it seemed. In contrast to its dismal performance in the 1967 war with Israel, the Egyptian army achieved tactical surprise in its attack on the Sinai Peninsula, which dazed and staggered Israel. That nation managed to rally its forces and stage a successful counterattack, but Sadat emerged from the war a hero to his people and to others in the Arab world. Although he had not taken Israeli Sinai, he did acquire some territory—and was the first Arab leader to succeed in doing so. This, however, did not lead him into a renewed campaign against Israel, but, in a stunning turn of events, set him on a long road to negotiating a lasting peace with Israel.

In retrospect, his decision to go to war in October 1973 came to seem not so much as a new attempt to destroy Israel, but as a move to negotiate with Israel from a position of strength, as a military and political equal.

And not just with Israel. His break with the Soviet Union *before* his attack on Israel put Sadat in a strong position to appeal to the United States for diplomatic and economic aid. He offered, in effect, to realign Egypt with America and did so in part by indicating a willingness to hammer out peace with America's ally Israel. In many ways, alignment with the United States—whose aid he wanted, but whose domination (in contrast to that of the Soviet Union) he did not fear—was more important to Sadat than a peace treaty with Israel. Such a treaty was, as he saw the situation at the end of 1973, a step toward a positive relationship with the United States, on whose friendship Israel would no longer enjoy an exclusive claim. For Sadat, the decision to seek peace with Israel, therefore, was really a decision to create a strong alliance with the world's greatest superpower, the United States.

That is where the situation stood at the end of 1973. Anwar el-Sadat had not suddenly become a friend of Israel. As always, his motive was the advancement of Egypt. What he now realized was that remaining Israel's unalterable enemy actually threatened the advancement of Egypt.

In many ways Sadat's Israeli counterpart, Menachem Begin, was similar to the Egyptian president. Both were fierce nationalists who took pride in having contributed to the very establishment of their respective nations' independence. Both had fought against British domination. Both had risen patiently through the ranks of their national governments. Both feared and loathed the Soviet Union. Both sought national legitimation from the international community. Both sought the alliance of the United States and approval from Washington. Both had an almost messianic passion where national destiny was concerned.

Yet their very similarities set them poles apart. Begin's nationalism, like that of Sadat, represented the right wing of Middle Eastern politics. "Compromise" was not a familiar word for either man. Begin was the product of the Holocaust generation. All of his closest relatives had been killed by the Nazis—made vulnerable because the Jews had no homeland. As he had been determined to create a Jewish homeland in Israel, so he was now determined to see to its perpetual survival and prosperity. This prompted his fierce opposition to the claims of the Palestinians for a homeland at the expense of Israel, and when extremists from the Palestine Liberation Organization attacked Israelis, Begin's first recourse was always to compare them to the Nazis. As Sadat's first and last concern was the fate of Egypt, Begin's first and last question about any issue was "Is it good or bad for the Jewish people?"

On the face of it, Sadat and Begin, leaders of their nations, were also the very embodiment of the seemingly eternal opposition of their nations. Both wanted to survive, and, over the years, the survival of one nation seemed to exclude the survival of the other. But both Sadat and Begin increasingly saw the survival and prosperity of their two nations as dependent on strong positive relations with the United States. When President Richard Nixon's secretary of state, Henry Kissinger, and, subsequently, President Jimmy Carter, made it increasingly clear that the United States would not choose between Egypt and Israel, both Sadat and Begin took the message to heart. Both were persuaded that strong, positive relations with America had become the common ground on which they could—indeed, must—meet. They were not willing to create—perhaps not even capable of creating—peace with each other directly, but, for the sake of relations with the United States, they almost simultaneously decided to talk to each other.

By 1977, the two men were poised to face down opposition within their own nations, to sacrifice old ideas of nationalism and patriotism, to give up old ideas of an absolute political order, and reach out to one another. People who knew both men well were of the opinion that they shared an actor's talent for spectacular theatrical gestures. As Israeli prime minister Golda Meir remarked when it was learned that Sadat and Begin were to share a Nobel Peace Prize, "I do not know if they should get the Nobel. But they certainly deserve an Oscar."

Sadat strode onto the stage first. On November 9, 1977, he suddenly departed from the written text of a speech to the Egyptian parliament and announced his decision to "go to the ends of the earth" to reach an accommodation with Israel. By that he meant nothing less than traveling to Jerusalem to present his proposal for a peace settlement to the Knesset, the Israeli parliament. His own parliament was shocked, and, at first, no one in Israel believed him.

He would not go to Israel hat in hand, but called for an Israeli invitation, to be sent through American channels. Opposition in Egypt was simply too great for him to accept an invitation directly from Begin, and when Begin issued an oral invitation through the media on November 11 and, again, on November 14, Sadat responded that he needed a written invitation. That was sufficient for the Knesset to take him seriously. A written invitation was drawn up and conveyed to Sadat via a U.S. state department diplomat, Hermann Eilts, and, early on the evening of November 19, 1977, Anwar el-Sadat's plane landed at Ben Gurion Airport outside of Tel Aviv.

The visit to Israel was in itself a great historic—and histrionic— moment, but Sadat's address to the Knesset was positively epoch- making. It simultaneously created great uncertainty and great hope, hope that faded as initial talks reached an apparent deadlock. But that is when Sadat and Begin accepted President Jimmy Carter's invitation to a U.S.- Israeli-Egyptian summit at Camp David, and there, in the Maryland woods, two world-changing agreements were concluded: a broad frame- work for achieving peace in the Middle East, and a more specific blue- print for a peace treaty between Egypt and Israel. The first document called for Israel to gradually grant self-government to the Palestinians in the Israeli-occupied West Bank and Gaza Strip and to partially withdraw its forces from these areas as a prelude to negotiations on their final status. It was a spectacular concession from Israel.

The second document called for a phased withdrawal of Israeli forces from the Sinai and specified the return of that region to Egypt within three years of the signing of a peace treaty. In addition to guaranteeing the right of passage for Israeli ships through the Egyptian-controlled Suez Canal, the Camp David Accords included a concession both Nasser and Sadat swore Egypt would never make. The documents affirmed the right of the state of Israel to exist.

———

SINCE THE CONCLUSION OF THE ACCORDS and the subsequent Egyptian-Israeli treaty, the Middle East has remained a violent place. Sadat himself became a victim of the region's violence when, on October 6, 1981, while reviewing a military parade commemorating the Arab-Israeli war of October 1973, he was assassinated by Egyptian Muslim extremists. Yet Egypt and Israel, the two most elemental enemies in the region—to all appearances, *natural* enemies—have continued to coexist peacefully.

And today, as the Middle Eastern convulsions continue, the region and the world repeatedly look to the decisions made by Anwar el-Sadat and Menachem Begin for the hope that even the most committed of foes can find common ground on which to make peace.

Todd Beamer and Flight 93 (2001)
THE DECISION AGAINST TERROR

It was not the morning of a holiday or a special day. It was an ordinary morning of an ordinary day. Or, if you were living in the Northeast, maybe you thought the morning was not ordinary at all, but exceptional—exceptional in the way that some mornings on the cusp of autumn can be: sharp and lucid with a bright blue light like an acetylene flame. A rare morning, really. A morning when it felt good to be alive. Certainly a good morning to fly. The clear skies promised minimum delay and a smooth flight. That was gratifying to the thirty-seven passengers of the undersold United Airlines Flight 93 bound for San Francisco out of Newark International. Scheduled for an 8:00 A.M. departure, the Boeing 757 pushed back from Gate A-17 at 8:01. But then the crush of Newark ground and air traffic backed up all departures, and Flight 93 alternately sat and crawled on the tarmac for the next forty minutes.

There was a vacationer or two among the passengers and a few students returning to classes in the Bay area, but most aboard were businesspeople, ordinary people doing what they needed to do to provide a living for themselves and their families.

Of course, as with the exceptionally beautiful morning, the ordinariness of the passengers of Flight 93 was really a matter of perception. The wives, husbands, parents, children, friends, and even business associates of the passengers did not think of them as ordinary. And there were some impressive-looking passengers with backgrounds interesting enough to make for very good seat-to-seat conversation. Jeremy Glick, for example, was a former NCAA judo champion with a passion for waterskiing and for his new baby. Tom Burnett, a health-care company executive, was a big, imposing figure who had been quarterback of his high school football team. Another big man, six-foot-five Mark Bingham had played rugby with a national championship team. His family told stories about how he had run with the bulls in Pamplona and, in San Francisco, had once faced down an armed mugger. In contrast to Glick, Burnett, and Bingham, Lou Nacke stood just five-foot-nine, but weighed two-hundred pounds. He worked for a toy retailer, lifted weights, and was not just a Superman fan—he had a tattoo of the Man of Steel on his shoulder—but was celebrated by friends and relatives for having tried, as a child, to run through a glass window while wearing his Superman cape.

There was also Rich Guadagno, who worked as an enforcement officer with the California Department of Fish and Wildlife, a tough outdoorsman who had a cop's training in personal combat. And Bill

Cashman. Age sixty but tough as nails, he had been a paratrooper with the Screaming Eagles, the 101st Airborne. A former member of another storied organization, Alan Beaven had been a Scotland Yard detective and now spent a lot of his free time rock climbing.

As for the women on board, lawyer Linda Gronlund was a karate brown belt, and flight attendant CeeCee Ross-Lyles had been a street cop. Two passengers, Don Greene and Andrew Garcia, knew their way around aircraft. Greene was a highly experienced private pilot who was an executive with an aircraft instrument firm, and Garcia was an Air National Guard air traffic controller. All interesting people, all exceptionally capable of taking care of themselves.

In contrast, Todd Beamer seemed a bit more ordinary. Like these others, he was athletic, but he had an ordinary background and an ordinary job as an account manager at the Oracle Corporation, a database software firm. He was thirty-two, living in Cranbury, New Jersey, with a wife and two children. Another child was on the way. He was a very good businessman, a real team player whom Oracle coworkers called the "go-to guy." Like the other business passengers on Flight 93, he made productive use of the forty-minute ground delay, working on his laptop and squeezing in several business calls on his cell phone.

There were four other passengers no one would ever call ordinary. Certainly, they thought of themselves as very special—indeed, as the chosen of God. Unlike the other thirty-three passengers that morning, who believed they were going to San Francisco, these four were certain they were on their way to paradise. Ziad Samir Jarrah, a twenty-six-year-old Lebanese, was seated in 1B near the cockpit door. A licensed pilot, he had been living in Florida, where he had enrolled in self-defense classes. Before moving to Florida, he lived in Hamburg, Germany, as part of an al-Qaeda terrorist cell. The other three, also seated up in first class, were Saeed al-Ghamdi, a young man from rural Saudi Arabia, who had made a farewell video recorded by al-Qaeda; twenty-year-old Ahmed al-Haznawi, another native of an undeveloped Saudi region, who also made a farewell video; and twenty-three-year-old Ahmed al-Nami, a college-educated Saudi who had trained as an al-Qaeda terrorist in Afghanistan. The three Saudis shared the same tribal affiliation, and all four men were committed to martyrdom in the name of Allah and in the cause of *jihad*—religious war—against the United States. At least one carried handwritten instructions from Mohamed Atta, an Egyptian who had dispatched them and three other groups of young Muslim men, all passengers on three other doomed aircraft. In addition to such pragmatic reminders as to bring "knives, your will, your IDs, your passport, all your papers," Atta's instructions closed with: "You will be entering paradise. You will be entering the happiest life, everlasting life."

Soon, each of the passengers on Flight 93 would have decisions to make. These four men had already made theirs.

At 8:42 A.M., the delay of Flight 93 came to an end as the 757 rose off the Newark runway and began its climb above the coast. Four minutes and forty seconds later, American Airlines Flight 11, out of Boston, exploded into the North Tower of the World Trade Center in lower Manhattan. One of the pilots in the cockpit of Flight 93 noticed a smoke plume in the otherwise clear sky. "Is everything okay on the ground?" he called to air traffic control. "Everything is fine," the controller replied.

At 9:03, as television cameras were already focused on the catastrophe of the North Tower, United Airlines Flight 175 crashed into the South Tower.

By the time Flight 93 was over Harrisburg, Pennsylvania, United Airlines quickly transmitted a warning message to the cockpit computer screens in all of its aircraft: "Beware cockpit intrusion."

"Confirmed," came the response from Flight 93.

When the crew made a routine check-in with the Cleveland air-traffic control center at 9:25, as the airliner made its way west, one of the pilots, apparently having heard that something was wrong back in New York, asked Cleveland for information. At this moment, Cleveland air-traffic control was receiving bomb threats, but could give no further information. Then, at 9:28, the Cleveland controllers heard more than threats. Screams came over the open microphone in Flight 93's cockpit. The controllers called the plane. There was no answer. After about forty seconds of silence, they heard more cries—these muffled—then a voice:

"Get out of here! Get out of here!" Who was talking? To whom was he talking? Moments later, a jumble of voices crackled over the Cleveland controllers' headphones, followed by a single voice, breathless, speaking in a heavy Middle Eastern accent: "Ladies and gentlemen, it's the captain. Please sit down. Keep remaining sitting. We have a bomb aboard."

Clearly, the hijackers did not realize that they had left the mike open. After several seconds, the voice resumed: "This is the captain. Remain sitting. There is a bomb aboard. We are going back to the airport to have our demands. Remain quiet." At that point, the hijackers must have realized their mistake and shut off the microphone. The Cleveland controllers heard no more from Flight 93. But others did.

Tom Burnett, the former high school quarterback, used his cell phone to call his wife, Deena. "Are you okay?" "No. I am on the airplane, United Flight 93, and it has been hijacked. They've knifed a guy and there's a bomb on board. Please call the authorities, Deena."

It was the first of several calls from the airliner.

The second came from Todd Beamer, who used the GTE Airfone mounted on the seat back in front of him to call the operator. She immediately signaled to her supervisor, Lisa Jefferson, for help, telling her that she had a hijacking in progress. Jefferson took over the call, simultaneously alerting the FBI. Introducing herself as Mrs. Jefferson, she spoke to Todd Beamer: "I understand this plane is being hijacked. Can you please give me detailed information as to what is going on?" Beamer, Jefferson later remarked, was "very calm and soft-spoken" as he responded to each of her questions, giving her very specific information about what was going on: That three people had taken over the plane, two with knives and one with a bomb strapped around his waist "with a red belt." The men with the knives had locked themselves in the cockpit and had ordered everyone to sit down. Because one of the hijackers had pulled the curtain separating first class from coach, Beamer did not know what was going on up front, except that he had seen two people on the floor. He did not know if they were dead or alive, but a flight attendant, who was sitting next to him, was pretty certain that the two were the pilot and copilot. ("They already slit two people's throats," a passenger named Marion Britton said in a separate phone call to a friend.)

In the midst of this terrifying crisis, Todd Beamer made careful, thoughtful decisions. Noting how quietly he spoke, Jefferson thought he was trying to whisper to keep from being heard. She told him that if he thought his life was in danger due to staying on the line, he should put the phone down but keep the line open, so she could still hear what was going on. Jefferson later remarked that he replied he was fine. He did say that maybe he should call his wife, but then instantly thought the better of it: "No, I just want to let someone know this is happening." Later, when Lisa Jefferson spoke with Lisa Beamer, she told her that "he didn't want to call you and give you bad news if he didn't have to. I offered to try and connect him with you. He went back and forth on it several times before he decided against it."

Lisa Beamer was glad that he had chosen not to call her. There was nothing she could have done to help him. She believed that his decision was meant to protect her: "I have tremendous respect for those family members and friends who received calls from hijacked flights that day and were able to maintain their composure," she wrote in her 2002 memoir *Let's Roll!* "But I honestly don't think I would have responded so well. And Todd knew that. . . . In the only way he could, Todd was still looking out for me." Perhaps he also thought it was more important to keep in continuous contact with someone who was linked to the authorities. It was a cool, clear decision.

At 9:36, Flight 93 turned sharply south and then east. At this point, the hijackers turned off the aircraft's transponder, which sends signals to air-traffic controllers. At about this time, Burnett made a second call to his wife. Some passengers, making cell phone calls, had by now heard about the catastrophe at the World Trade Center. Burnett asked his wife if the planes that hit the World Trade Center were commercial airliners. She did not know. "We're turning back to New York," he told her. Then: "No, we're heading south." With that, he said he had to go, and he hung up.

At 9:37, American Airlines Flight 77 plowed into the Pentagon outside of Washington, D.C.

While Bennett spoke with his wife, Jeremy Glick talked with his.

"Three Iranian-looking guys wearing red headbands, one with a red box strapped to his waist, say they have a bomb and have taken control of the plane." They spoke for some twenty minutes, then Glick said: "Lyz, I need to know something. One of the other passengers talked to his wife and said that planes had crashed into the World Trade Center. Is that true?"

"Please be strong, but yes, they are doing that."

"Is that where we're going, too?" Glick asked his wife. She replied that there was nothing left of the World Trade Center. By that time, the South Tower—its structure compromised by the impact and fire—had fallen, and the North Tower was burning and near collapse.

Bennett called his wife a third time. Now she told him: "Tom, they just hit the Pentagon. They seem to be taking planes and driving them into landmarks all over the East Coast." It was during this third call that Bennett told his wife that the passengers didn't believe the hijackers really had a bomb. "I think they're bluffing. We're going to do something. I've got to go." Almost simultaneously, Glick told his wife that some of the passengers were talking about rushing the hijackers. By this time, too, Beamer was mentioning Jeremy Glick to Lisa Jefferson, the GTE Airfone supervisor. Apparently, the two were talking about a plan to retake control of the airplane.

It is, of course, impossible to know just what was going on. However, from these conversations and others, we do know that many passengers were now aware of the other hijackings and suicide attacks. It is also clear that Todd Beamer, Jeremy Glick, and Tom Bennett, along with some other passengers and flight attendants (who were in the galley boiling coffee pots full of water to throw in the faces of the hijackers) were planning an attempt to take back the airplane.

Under the circumstances, it would have been a desperate plan. Yet, when we look beyond the superficial ordinariness of the passengers of Flight 93 and recognize the strength and training they possessed among them, it could have been a plan with at least a hope of success. Was their decision to fight based on some hastily gathered knowledge of just who each of them was—a collection of athletes, former cops, experienced pilots, a former paratrooper, a karate expert, a guy who wanted to be Superman? We don't know.

Jeremy Glick told his wife that the passengers were discussing what to do and were going to take a vote. "What do you think we should do?" he asked her. "Go for it," Lyz Glick answered. She had been watching television. She knew they really had no other choice.

Tom Bennett's wife, a former flight attendant, had a different response when her husband told her, "We're going to do something."

"Tom, sit down. Please! Be still. Be quiet. Don't draw attention to yourself. Wait for the authorities." "We can't wait, Deena," he said, "If they are going to run this plane into the ground, we're going to do something."

Throughout these conversations, Todd Beamer had left the line open to Lisa Jefferson. "In case I don't make it through this," he said to her, "would you please call my family and let them know how much I love them?" He told her: "We're going to do something. . . . I don't think we're going to get out of this thing. I'm going to have to go out on faith." Jefferson reported later that Beamer said they were talking about jumping the hijacker with the bomb. "Are you sure that's what you want to do, Todd?" Jefferson asked. "It's what we have to do." And he asked her to recite the Lord's Prayer with him, after which he recited the Twenty-third Psalm, with its hope-filled walk through the valley of the shadow of death. Jefferson believed that some of the other men joined in.

After that, Jefferson recalled "a sigh in [Beamer's] voice." She heard him take a deep breath. She could tell that he was still holding the phone, but that he had turned away from it to talk to someone else.

"Are you ready?" she heard. "Okay. Let's roll!"

That was the moment.

Jeremy Glick said to his wife, "Hang on the line. I'll be back. They're doing it!" Flight attendant Sandy Bradshaw said to her husband: "I have to go. We're running to first class now." Passenger Elizabeth Wainio told her stepmother: "I have to go. They're breaking into the cockpit. I love you. Good-bye." CeeCee Ross-Lyles, the ex-cop flight attendant, shouted to her husband: "They're doing it! They're doing it!" The rest—for Lisa

Jefferson, and the husbands, wives, friends, and mothers with telephone receivers to their ears—was silence.

At approximately 10:03, Flight 93 augured into a field near Shanksville in Stonycreek Township, Somerset County, Pennsylvania, not far from Pittsburgh, disintegrating on impact. The flight voice recorder was later recovered from the wreckage. Where the phone calls stopped, the recorder continued—with sounds of dishes shattering. Apparently, the passengers were using a heavy service cart as a battering ram against the cockpit door. Objects were hurled. The hijackers shouted and screamed in Arabic to *hold the cockpit door.* "Let's get them!" is heard, in English. Pounding is heard, pounding against the cockpit door. Shouting. Screaming. The aircraft dives steeply. "Allahu akbar!" is distinctly heard. *God is great!*

There are the sounds of the hijackers fighting, apparently among themselves, for the controls. "Give it to me!" says one in Arabic. They are the last words the machine recorded.

LISA BEAMER RECOGNIZED "LET'S ROLL!" as typical Todd Beamer. It was the phrase he often used with their boys. It was, she said, something that meant "Let's get ready for the next thing we're going to do. . . .It showed he felt he could still do something positive in the midst of a crisis." They were Beamer's last words and nearly the last words heard from Flight 93. They spoke of an extraordinary decision made by an "ordinary" person in concert with other "ordinary" people. We cannot know the details of the decision, except that it was a decision not to give up, a decision to "get ready for the next thing we're going to do," and a decision to do it. Although the actions—whatever they were, exactly— that followed this phrase didn't save the passengers of Flight 93, subsequent analysis of evidence showed that the hijackers intended to fly the fuel-laden Boeing 757 into the U.S. Capitol, the very heart of the American democracy. Todd Beamer and the others did not let that happen on the uncommonly clear but otherwise ordinary morning of September 11, 2001.

Further Reading

The following selection, which includes the books used as sources for *Profiles in Audacity*, are suggestions for reading further about history's great decision makers.

CLEOPATRA AND THE ROMANS

Chauveau, Michel. *Egypt in the Age of Cleopatra: History and Society under the Ptolemies*. Ithacca, NY: Cornell University Press, 2000.

Grant, Michael. Cleopatra: A Biography. London: Book Sales, 2004.

Kleiner, Diana E. E. *Cleopatra and Rome*. Cambridge, MA: Belknap Press, 2005.

Walker, Susan, and Peter Higgs, eds. *Cleopatra of Egypt: From History to Myth*. Princeton, NJ: Princeton University Press, 2001.

QUEEN BOUDICCA AND THE INVADERS

Fraser, Antonia. *The Warrior Queens: The Legends and the Lives of the Women Who Have Led Their Nations in War*. New York: Vintage, 1990.

Hunt, Richard. *Queen Boudicca's Battle of Britain*. London: Spellmount Publishers, 2003.

Trow, M. J. *Boudicca: The Warrior Queen*. London: Sutton Publishing, 2004.

Webster, Graham. *Boudica: The British Revolt Against Rome, AD 60*. New York and London: Routledge, 2000.

ELIZABETH I AND THE SPANISH ARMADA

Black, John B. *The Reign of Elizabeth, 1558–1603*. 2d ed. Oxford, U.K.: Clarendon Press, 1959.

Erickson, Carolly. *The First Elizabeth*. New York: St. Martin's Griffin, 1983.

Ridley, Jasper. *Elizabeth I: The Shrewdness of Virtue*. New York: Fromm Internat'l, 1989.

Thomas, Jane Resh. *Behind the Mask: The Life of Queen Elizabeth I*. New York: Clarion Books, 1998.

Weir, Alison. *The Life of Elizabeth I*. New York: Ballantine, 1999.

BEETHOVEN AND DEAFNESS

Beethoven, Ludwig van. *Beethoven's Letters*. New York: Dover Publications, 1972.

Davies, Peter J. *Beethoven in Person: His Deafness, Illnesses, and Death*. Westport, CT: Greenwood Press, 2001.

Kerst, Friedrich, and H. Krehbiel, eds. *Beethoven, the Man and the Artist, as Revealed in His Own Words*. New York: Dover Publications, 1964.

Lockwood, Lewis. *Beethoven: The Music and the Life*. New York: W. W. Norton, 2005.

Morris, Edmund. *Beethoven: The Universal Composer*. New York: HarperCollins, 2005.

Solomon, Maynard. *Beethoven*. New York: Schirmer, 2001.

TECUMSEH AND AN INDIAN NATION

Eckert, Allan W. *A Sorrow in Our Heart: The Life of Tecumseh*. New York: Bantam, 1992.

Edmunds, R. David. *The Shawnee Prophet*. Lincoln: University of Nebraska Press, 1985.

_____. *Tecumseh and the Quest for Indian Leadership*. New York: Longman, 1997.

Sugden, John. *Tecumseh: A Life*. New York: Owl Books, 1999.

TRUMAN AND THE A-BOMB

Ferrell, Robert H., ed. *Off the Record: The Private Papers of Harry S. Truman*. 1980; reprint ed., Columbia: University of Missouri Press, 1997.

McCullough, David. *Truman*. New York: Simon and Schuster, 1992.

Truman, Harry S. *Memoirs, Volume 1: Year of Decisions*. Garden City, NY: Doubleday, 1955.

_____. *Memoirs, Volume 2: Years of Trial and Hope*. Garden City, NY: Doubleday, 1956.

_____. *Truman Speaks*. New York: Columbia University Press, 1960.

JOHN F. KENNEDY AND THE CUBAN MISSILE CRISIS

Frankel, Max. *High Noon in the Cold War: Kennedy, Khrushchev, and the Cuban Missile Crisis*. Novato, CA: Presidio Press, 2004.

Kennedy, Robert F. *Thirteen Days: A Memoir of the Cuban Missile Crisis*. New York: W. W. Norton, 1999.

May, Ernest R., and Philip D. Zelikow, eds. *The Kennedy Tapes: Inside the White House during the Cuban Missile Crisis.* New York: W. W. Norton, 2002.

Stern, Sheldon M. *The Week the World Stood Still: Inside the Secret Cuban Missile Crisis.* Palo Alto, CA: Stanford University Press, 2005.

COLUMBUS AND THE NEW WORLD

Columbus, Christopher. *The Four Voyages: Being His Own Log-Book, Letters and Dispatches with Connecting Narratives.* New York: Penguin Classics, 1992.

Least Heat-Moon, William. *Columbus in the Americas.* New York: Wiley, 2002.

Morison, Samuel Eliot. *Admiral of the Ocean Sea: A Life of Christopher Columbus.* Boston: Little, Brown; Reissue edition, 1991.

GALILEO AND THE UNIVERSE

Biagioli, Mario. *Galileo, Courtier.* Chicago: University of Chicago Press, 1993.

De Santillana, Giorgio. *The Crime of Galileo.* Chicago: University of Chicago Press, 1955.

Shea, William R., and Marioano Artigas. *Galileo in Rome: The Rise and Fall of a Troublesome Genius.* New York: Oxford University Press, 2003.

Sobel, Dava. *Galileo's Daughter: A Historical Memoir of Science, Faith, and Love.* New York: Penguin, 2000.

LEWIS, JEFFERSON, AND THE AMERICAN WILDERNESS

Ambrose, Stephen. *Undaunted Courage: Meriwether Lewis, Thomas Jefferson and the Opening of the American West.* New York: Simon & Schuster, 1997.

Bedini, Silvio A. *Jefferson and Science.* Charlottesville, VA: Thomas Jefferson Foundation, 2002.

Kaplan, Lawrence S. *Thomas Jefferson: Westward the Course of Empire.* Lanham, MD: SR Books, 1998.

Tubbs, Stephanie Ambrose, and Clay Jenkinson. *The Lewis and Clark Companion: An Encyclopedic Guide to the Voyage of Discovery.* New York: Owl, 2003.

CHARLIE GOODNIGHT AND THE FIRST CATTLE DRIVE

Abbott, E. C. *We Pointed Them North.* Norman: University of Oklahoma Press, 1955.

Haley, J. Evetts. *Charles Goodnight, Cowman and Plainsman.* Norman: University of Oklahoma Press, 1981.

Hunter, J. Marvin. *The Trail Drivers of Texas: Interesting Sketches of Early Cowboys.* Austin: University of Texas Press, 1992.

Rollins, Philip Ashton. *The Cowboy: An Unconventional History of Civilization on the Old-Time Cattle Range.* Norman: University of Oklahoma Press, 1997.

EDISON AND THE ELECTRIC LIGHT

Baldwin, Neil. *Edison: Inventing the Century.* Chicago: University of Chicago Press, 2001.

Friedel, Robert Douglas, Paul Israel, and Bernard S. Finn. *Edison's Electric Light: Biography of an Invention.* New Brunswick, NJ: Rutgers University Press, 1986.

Israel, Paul. *Edison: A Life of Invention.* New York: Wiley, 1998.

THEODORE ROOSEVELT AND THE PANAMA CANAL

Espino, Ovidio Diaz. *How Wall Street Created a Nation: J. P. Morgan, Teddy Roosevelt, and the Panama Canal.* New York: Four Walls Eight Windows, 2001.

Hunt, John Gabriel, ed. *The Essential Theodore Roosevelt.* New York: Gramercy, 1994.

McCullough, David. *Path Between the Seas: The Creation of the Panama Canal, 1870–1914.* New York: Simon & Schuster, 1978.

Roosevelt, Theodore. *An Autobiography.* New York: Scribner's, 1913.

THE WRIGHT BROTHERS AND THE AIRPLANE

Crouch, Tom. *The Bishop's Boys: A Life of Wilbur and Orville Wright.* New York: Norton, 1989.

Howard, Fred. *Wilbur and Orville: A Biography of the Wright Brothers.* New York: Knopf, 1987.

Walsh, John Evangelist. *One Day at Kitty Hawk: The Untold Story of the Wright Brothers and the Airplane.* New York: Crowell, 1975.

SIGMUND FREUD AND SEX

Foucault, Michel. *The History of Sexuality: An Introduction.* New York: Vintage, 1990.

Freud, Sigmund. *Three Essays on the Theory of Sexuality.* New York: Basic Books, 2000.

Gay, Peter. *Freud: A Life for Our Time.* New York: Norton, 1998.

FRANK X. MCNAMARA AND DINERS CLUB

Calder, Lendol. *Financing the American Dream: A Cultural History of Consumer Credit*. Princeton, NJ: Princeton University Press, 2001.

Evans, David S., and Richard Schmalensee. *Paying with Plastic: The Digital Revolution in Buying and Borrowing*. Cambridge, MA: The MIT Press, 2005.

Mandell, Lewis. *Credit Card Industry: A History*. New York: Twayne, 1990.

Manning, Robert D. *Credit Card Nation: The Consequences of America's Addiction to Credit*. New York: Basic Books, 2001.

JOHN F. KENNEDY AND THE MOON

Breuer, William B. *Race to the Moon: America's Duel with the Soviets*. New York: Praeger, 1993.

Scott, David, and Alexei Leonov. *Two Sides of the Moon: Our Story of the Cold War Space Race*. New York: St. Martin's Griffin, 2006.

Shepard, Alan, and Deke Slayton. *Moon Shot: The Inside Story of America's Race to the Moon*. Atlanta: Turner, 1994.

TED TURNER AND CNN

Auletta, Ken. *Media Man: Ted Turner's Improbable Empire*. New York: Norton, 2004.

Bibb, Porter. *Ted Turner: It Ain't as Easy as It Looks—The Amazing Story of CNN*. London: Virgin Books, 1996.

Whittemore, Hank. *CNN, The Inside Story: How a Band of Mavericks Changed the Face of Television News*. Boston: Little, Brown, 1990.

BILL GATES AND MS-DOS

Manes, Stephen, and Paul Andrews. *Gates: How Microsoft's Mogul Reinvented an Industry—and Made Himself the Richest Man in America*. New York: Touchstone, 1994.

Wallace, James, and Jim Erickson. *Hard Drive: Bill Gates and the Making of the Microsoft Empire*. New York: HarperCollins, 1993.

JOAN OF ARC AND THE DAUPHIN

Brooks, Polly Schoyer. *Beyond the Myth: The Story of Joan of Arc*. Boston: Houghton Mifflin, 1999.

Pernoud, Regine, and Marie-Veronique Clin. *Joan of Arc: Her Story*. New York: Palgrave Macmillan, 1999.

Twain, Mark. *Personal Recollections of Joan of Arc*. New York: Dover, 2002.

LINCOLN AND EMANCIPATION

Foner, Eric. *Forever Free: The Story of Emancipation and Reconstruction*. New York: Knopf, 2005.

Franklin, John Hope. *The Emancipation Proclamation*. Wheeling, IL: Harlan Davidson, 1995.

Guelzo, Allen C. *Lincoln's Emancipation Proclamation: The End of Slavery in America*. New York: Simon & Schuster, 2004.

CLARA BARTON AND THE SOLDIERS

Freemon, Frank R. *Gangrene and Glory: Medical Care during the American Civil War*. Urbana and Chicago: University of Illinois Press, 2001.

Oates, Stephen B. *A Woman of Valor: Clara Barton and the Civil War*. New York: The Free Press, 1994.

Pryor, Elizabeth Brown. *Clara Barton: Professional Angel*. Philadelphia: University of Pennsylvania Press, 1988.

GANDHI AND NONVIOLENT REVOLUTION

Fischer, Louis, ed. *The Essential Gandhi: An Anthology of His Writings on His Life, Work, and Ideas*. New York: Vintage, 1983.

Gandhi, Mohandas K. *An Autobiography: The Story of My Experiments with Truth*. Boston: Beacon, 1993.

W. E. B. DU BOIS AND THE NAACP

Du Bois, W. E. B. *Autobiography of W .E .B. Du Bois: A Soliloquy on Viewing My Life from the Last Decade of Its First Century*. New York: Penguin, 1986.

Lewis, David Levering. *W. E. B. Du Bois: Biography of a Race, 1868–1919*. New York: Owl, 1994.

Lewis, David Levering, ed. *W. E. B. Du Bois: A Reader*. New York: Owl, 1995.

MARSHALL AND THE MARSHALL PLAN

Cray, Ed. *General of the Army: George C. Marshall, Soldier and Statesman*. New York: Norton, 1990.

Hogan, Michael J. *The Marshall Plan: America, Britain and the Reconstruction of Western Europe, 1947–1952*. New York: Cambridge University Press, 1989.

Stoler, Mark A. *George C. Marshall: Soldier-Statesman of the American Century*. New York: Twayne, 1989.

BRANCH RICKEY AND JACKIE ROBINSON

Chalberg, John C. *Rickey and Robinson: The Preacher, the Player, and America's Game.* Wheeling, IL: Harlan Davidson, 2000.

Polner, Murray. *Branch Rickey: A Biography.* New York: Atheneum, 1982.

Rampersad, Arnold. *Jackie Robinson: A Biography.* New York: Ballantine Books, 1998.

Robinson, Jackie. *I Never Had It Made: An Autobiography of Jackie Robinson.* New York: Harper Perennial, 2003.

Tygiel, Jules. *Baseball's Great Experiment: Jackie Robinson and His Legacy.* New York: Oxford University Press, 1997.

ROSA PARKS AND THE RIGHT TO SIT

Brinkley, Douglas. *Rosa Parks.* New York: Penguin, 2000.

Parks, Rosa. *Rosa Parks: My Story.* New York: Dial, 1992.

Robinson, Joann. *Montgomery Bus Boycott and the Women Who Started It.* Knoxville: University of Tennessee Press, 1987.

BETTY FRIEDAN AND A WOMAN'S PLACE

Friedan, Betty. *The Feminine Mystique* New York: Norton, 2001.

Horowitz, Daniel. *Betty Friedan and the Making of "The Feminine Mystique": The American Left, the Cold War, and Modern Feminism.* Amherst: University of Massachusetts Press, 2000.

LYNDON JOHNSON AND THE CIVIL RIGHTS ACT

Smolla, Rodney A., and Chester James Antieau. *Federal Civil Rights Acts,* 3d ed. New York: Clark Boardman Callaghan, 1994.

Unger, Irwin, and Debi Unger. *LBJ: A Life.* New York: Wiley, 1999.

Williams, Juan. *Eyes on the Prize: America's Civil Rights Years, 1954–1965.* New York: Penguin Books, 1988.

DANIEL ELLSBERG AND THE PENTAGON PAPERS

Ellsberg, Daniel. *Secrets: A Memoir of Vietnam and the Pentagon Papers.* New York: Viking, 2002.

Rudenstine, David. *The Day the Presses Stopped: A History of the Pentagon Papers Case.* Berkeley: University of California Press, 1998.

U.S. Department of Defense. *The Pentagon Papers: The Defense Department History of United States Decision Making on Vietnam.* Boston: Beacon Press, 1971.

JAMES BURKE AND THE TYLENOL MURDERS

Flynn, James, Paul Slovic, and Howard Kunreuther, eds. *Risk, Media, and Stigma: Understanding Public Challenges to Modern Science and Technology.* London and Sterling, VA: Earthscan, 2001.

Hartley, Robert F. *Management Mistakes and Successes,* 7th ed. New York: Wiley, 2003.

Staffs of the Food and Drug Letter, Washington Drug Letter, and Product Safety Letter. *Product Survival: Lessons of the Tylenol Terrorism.* Washington, D.C.: Washington Business Information, 1982.

WILLIAM THE CONQUEROR AND THE NORMAN CONQUEST

Bates, David. *William the Conqueror.* Stroud, UK: Tempus, 1989.

Douglas, David C. *William the Conqueror: The Norman Impact upon England.* Berkeley: University of California Press, 1964.

Howarth, David. *1066: The Year of the Conquest.* New York: Penguin, 1981.

WASHINGTON AND THE DELAWARE CROSSING

Ellis, Joseph J. *His Excellency: George Washington.* New York: Knopf, 2004.

Fischer, David Hackett. *Washington's Crossing.* New York: Oxford University Press, 2004.

Lengel, Edward G. *General George Washington: A Military Life.* New York: Random House, 2005.

WOODROW WILSON AND WORLD WAR I

Farwell, Byron. *Over There: The United States in the Great War, 1917–1918.* New York: Norton, 1999.

Ferrell, Robert. *Woodrow Wilson and World War I, 1917–1921.* New York: Harper & Row, 1985.

Knock, Thomas J. *To End All Wars: Woodrow Wilson and the Quest for a New World Order.* New York: Oxford University Press, 1992.

JIMMY DOOLITTLE AND THE TOKYO RAID

Doolittle, James, with Carroll V. Glines. *I Could Never Be So Lucky Again: An Autobiography*. New York: Bantam, 2001.

Glines, Carroll V. *The Doolittle Raid*. Atglen, PA: Schiffer, 2000.

Lawson, Ted W. *Thirty Seconds over Tokyo*. Dulles, VA: Potomac Books, 2003.

TRUMAN AND THE BERLIN AIRLIFT

Ferrell, Robert H., ed. *Harry S. Truman: A Life*. Columbia: University of Missouri Press, 1994.

McCullough, David. *Truman*. New York: Simon and Schuster, 1992.

Miller, Roger G. *To Save a City: The Berlin Airlift, 1948–1949*. College Station: Texas A&M University Press, 2000.

Tusa, Ann, and John Tusa. *The Berlin Airlift*. New York: Sarpedon Publishers, 1998.

EDMUND HILLARY AND MOUNT EVEREST

Hillary, Sir Edmund. *View from the Summit*. New York: Pocket, 1999.

Johnston, Alexa. *Reaching the Summit: Edmund Hillary's Life of Adventure*. New York: DK, 2005.

RICHARD M. NIXON AND CHINA

Mann, James. *About Face: A History of America's Curious Relationship with China, from Nixon to Clinton*. New York: Knopf, 1998.

Nixon, Richard M. *RN: The Memoirs of Richard Nixon*. New York: Simon and Schuster, 1990.

BORIS YELTSIN AND THE COMMUNIST COUP

Yeltsin, Boris. *Against the Grain: An Autobiography*. New York: Summit, 1990.

_____. *Putsch—The Diary: Three Days That Collapsed the Empire, August 19–21, 1991*. New York: Mosaic Press, 1992.

_____. *The Struggle for Russia*. New York: Times Books, 1995.

CHIEF JOSEPH AND THE END OF BATTLE

Beal, Merrill D. *"I Will Fight No More Forever": Chief Joseph and the Nez Perce War*. Seattle and London: University of Washington Press, 1963.

Moulton, Candy. *Chief Joseph: Guardian of the People*. New York: Forge Books, 2005.

Nerburn, Ken. *Chief Joseph and the Flight of the Nez Perce: The Untold Story of an American Tragedy*. San Francisco: HarperSanFrancisco, 2005.

ANDREW CARNEGIE AND THE GOSPEL OF WEALTH

Carnegie, Andrew. *The Autobiography of Andrew Carnegie*. Boston: Northeastern University Press, 1986.

_____. *The Gospel of Wealth*. Bedford, MA: Applewood Books, 1998.

Wall, Joseph Frazier. *Andrew Carnegie*. Pittsburgh: University of Pittsburgh Press, 1989.

DWIGHT EISENHOWER AND D-DAY

Ambrose, Stephen E. *D-Day, June 6, 1944: The Climactic Battle of World War II*. New York: Simon and Schuster, 1994.

D'Este, Carlo. *Eisenhower: A Soldier's Life*. New York: Owl, 2002.

Eisenhower, Dwight D. *Crusade in Europe*. Garden City, NY: Doubleday, 1948.

Eisenhower, John S. D. *General Ike: A Personal Reminiscence*. New York: Free Press, 2003.

MENACHEM BEGIN AND ANWAR EL-SADAT

Finklestone, J. *Anwar Sadat: Visionary Who Dared*. London: Frank Cass, 1996.

Stein, Kenneth W. *Heroic Diplomacy: Sadat, Kissinger, Carter, Begin, and the Quest for Arab-Israeli Peace*. New York and London: Routledge, 1999.

Temko, Ted. *To Win or to Die: A Personal Portrait of Menachem Begin*. New York: William Morrow, 1987.

TODD BEAMER AND FLIGHT 93

Beamer, Lisa, with Ken Abraham. *Let's Roll!: Ordinary People, Extraordinary Courage*. Carol Stream, IL: Tyndale House Publishers (August 2002)

National Commission on Terrorist Attacks. *The 9/11 Commission Report: The Final Report of the National Commission on Terrorist Attacks upon the United States*. New York: Norton, 2004.

Index

About the Author

ALAN AXELROD is the author of many popular history, business, and management books, including the *BusinessWeek* bestsellers *Patton on Leadership* and *Elizabeth I, CEO*. He has served as a leadership consultant to various businesses, government, and cultural institutions and has been a creative consultant (and on-camera personality) for *The Wild West* television documentary series, *Civil War Journal*, and the Discovery Channel. He has appeared on MSNBC, CNN, CNNfn, CNBC, and his work has been featured in *BusinessWeek, Fortune, Men's Health, Cosmopolitan, Inc., Atlanta Business Chronicle*, the *Atlanta Journal-Constitution* and *USA Today*.

A former college professor and publishing executive, Axelrod founded the Ian Samuel Group, Inc., in 1997, a research, publishing, and creative services firm. He lives with his wife and son in Atlanta.